React Programming

THE BIG NERD RANCH GUIDE

Loren Klingman & Ashley Parker

Big Nerd Ranch

React Programming: The Big Nerd Ranch Guide

by Loren Klingman and Ashley Parker

Big Nerd Ranch
750 Glenwood Ave SE, Suite 200
Atlanta, GA 30316
(770) 817-6373
https://www.bignerdranch.com
book-comments@bignerdranch.com

The 10-gallon hat is a trademark of Big Nerd Ranch.

Exclusive worldwide distribution of the English edition of this book by

Pearson Technology Group
800 East 96th Street
Indianapolis, IN 46240 USA
http://www.informit.com

ISBN-10 0137901763
ISBN-13 978-0137901760

First edition, first printing, March 2023

Acknowledgments

While our names appear on the cover, many people helped make this book a reality. We would like to take this chance to thank them.

- Chris Aquino and Todd Gandee, the authors of *Front-End Web Development: The Big Nerd Ranch Guide*, which morphed into this book.

- Jake Sower, for contributing to previous React sections of the book.

- Eric Wilson, for guiding the process and handling the logistics of finding the required time and reviewers.

- Dave Severns, for helping with challenges in Ottergram and proofreading.

- Cameron Tharp, for helping to proofread Code Café and Performance Penguins.

- Angie Terrell, Big Nerd Ranch's UX practice director, for designing the Code Café icons and items.

- Our proofreaders, technical reviewers, and guinea pigs: Josh Justice, Liv Vitale, John Harrison, Taylor Martin, Jeremy Sherman, Sean Farahdel, Megan Mason, and Adam Friedman. Thank you for volunteering as tribute.

- Liz Holaday, our faithful editor, for many rounds of suggestions and revisions.

- Samantha Eng, our copyeditor, who made the text clearer and more concise.

- Ellie Volckhausen, for designing the cover.

- Yellowstone National Park and the U.S. Fish and Wildlife Service, for the public domain otter images.

- Giovanna Roda, for the public domain penguin image.

- Our families, for their support and encouragement in all things.

Lastly, thank you to the countless students who have taken Big Nerd Ranch's React training. Without your curiosity and your questions, none of this would matter. This work is a reflection of the insight and inspiration you have given us over the span of those many weeks. We hope the coffee made the training a little lighter.

Table of Contents

Introduction

Learning Web Development

Front-end development requires a shift in perspective if you have never built anything for the browser. Here are a few things to keep in mind as you get started.

The browser is the ubiquitous platform.

Perhaps you have done native development for iOS or Android; written server-side code in Go, Ruby, or PHP; or built desktop applications for macOS or Windows. Development of those kinds targets platforms that might have large reaches but are not universal.

As a front-end developer, you will write code that targets the browser – the only platform available on nearly every mobile phone, tablet, and personal computer in the world.

Front-end development requires visual and programmatic thinking.

At one end of the spectrum is the look and feel of a web page: rounded corners, shadows, colors, fonts, whitespace, and so on. At the other end of the spectrum is the logic that governs the intricate behaviors of that web page: swapping images in an interactive photo gallery, adding items to a cart, validating data entered into a form, and so on. You will need to gain proficiency in several core technologies and understand how they work together to build great web applications.

Web technologies are open.

No single company controls the standards for web browsers. This means that front-end developers do not get a yearly SDK release that contains all the changes they will need to deal with for the next 12 months.

Native platforms are a frozen pond on which you can comfortably skate. The web is a river; it curves, moves quickly, and is rocky in some places – and that is part of its appeal. The web is the most rapidly evolving platform available. Adapting to change is a way of life for a front-end developer.

Learning React

We designed this book to teach you how to write React programs for the browser. Though we touch on other front-end technologies, such as HTML and CSS, our focus is React. Because experience is the best teacher, you will build two React applications as you work through the book.

Prerequisites

This book is not an introduction to programming. It assumes you have experience with the fundamentals of writing code. It expects you to be familiar with HTML, CSS, and JavaScript. If you have not worked on front-end development before, you would benefit from starting with materials to learn HTML and CSS.

How This Book Is Organized

This book walks you through writing two web applications:

- *Ottergram* – A photo-sharing site for some of the most charming marine animals, Ottergram introduces you to React applications and components.

- *Code Café* – Code Café takes you through a number of React techniques for managing state, setting up routing, and communicating with a server.

Working through these applications will introduce you to a number of tools, including

- the Visual Studio Code editor
- Node.js and npm (the Node package manager)
- documentation resources such as the Mozilla Developer Network
- Google Chrome's Developer Tools
- React hooks
- ESLint
- React Router
- Websockets
- the React Testing Library
- Cypress

How to Use This Book

This is not a reference book. Its goal is to get you started with React development so you can get the most out of the reference and recipe books available. It is based on our class at Big Nerd Ranch and, as such, is meant for you to work through in succession.

That is how students in our classes work through these materials. But they also benefit from having the right environment, which includes a group of motivated peers and an instructor to answer questions.

As a reader, you want your environment to be similar. Try these ideas:

- Start a reading group with your friends or coworkers.

- Arrange blocks of focused time to work on chapters.

- Participate in the forum for this book at forums.bignerdranch.com, where you can discuss the book and find errata and solutions.

- Find someone who knows React to help you out.

Typographical conventions

To make this book easier to read, certain items appear in certain fonts. Variables, constants, and types appear in a fixed-width font. Function and method names appear in a bold fixed-width font.

All code listings are in a fixed-width font. Code that you need to type in is always bold. Code that should be deleted is struck through. For example, in the following change, you are deleting the title React App and adding the title Ottergram.

```
<head>
  ...
  <title>React App</title>
  <title>Ottergram</title>
</head>
```

For the More Curious

Many chapters in this book end with one or more "For the More Curious" sections. These sections offer deeper explanations or additional information about topics presented in the chapter. Though the information in these sections is not absolutely essential to understanding or completing the projects this book, we hope you will find it interesting and useful.

Challenges

Challenges are opportunities to review what you have learned and take your work in the chapter a step further. We recommend that you tackle as many of them as you can to cement your knowledge and gain a deeper understanding of the concepts discussed.

Challenges come in three levels of difficulty:

- Bronze challenges typically ask you to do something very similar to what you did in the chapter. These challenges reinforce what you learned in the chapter and force you to type in similar code without having it laid out in front of you. Practice makes perfect.

- Silver challenges require you to do more digging and more thinking. Sometimes you will need to use functions, events, markup, and styles that you have not seen before. However, the tasks are still similar to what you did in the chapter.

- Gold challenges are difficult and can take hours to complete. They require you to understand the concepts from the chapter and then do some quality thinking and problem solving on your own. Tackling these challenges will prepare you for the real-world work of React development.

Before beginning a challenge, make a copy of your project and attack the challenge in that copy. Many chapters build on previous chapters, and working on challenges in a copy of the project ensures that you will be able to progress through the book.

The Create React App tool you will use to create your projects makes a Git repository of your projects automatically. If you are familiar with Git, you can use branches to create separate workspaces for challenges. You can also copy and paste the files in your file explorer to create a copy.

The Necessary Tools

To get started with this book, you will need three basic tools: a browser, a text editor, and a way to run a JavaScript application.

There are countless tools and resources you can use for React development, with more being built all the time. For the purposes of this book, we recommend that you use the same software we use, so you can get the most benefit from the directions and screenshots.

This chapter walks you through installing and configuring the Google Chrome browser, the Visual Studio Code text editor, and Node.js. You will also learn about good documentation options and get a crash course in using the command line on Mac and Windows. In the next chapter, you will put all these resources to use as you begin your first project.

Installing Google Chrome

Google Chrome is a great tool for React development because of its built-in Developer Tools. If you do not already have the latest version of Chrome, get it from www.google.com/chrome (Figure 1).

Figure 1 Downloading Google Chrome

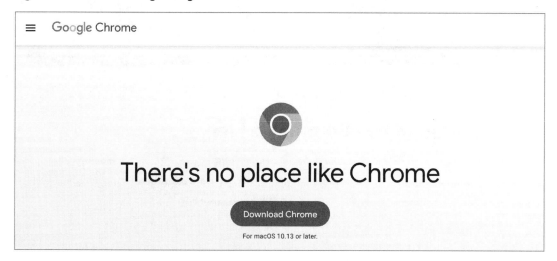

Installing Visual Studio Code

Of the many text editor programs out there, one of the best for React development is the Visual Studio Code editor by Microsoft. It is highly configurable, has many extensions to help with writing code, and is free to download and use.

Download Visual Studio Code for Mac or Windows from code.visualstudio.com (Figure 2).

Figure 2 Downloading Visual Studio Code

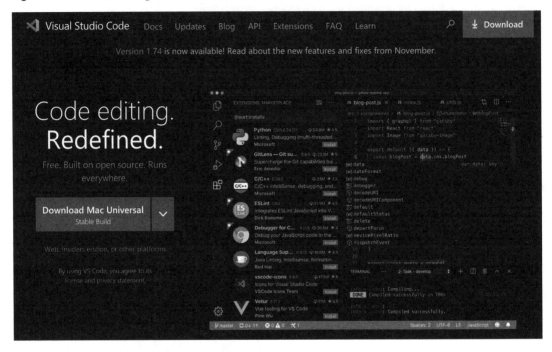

Follow the installation instructions for your platform.

Crash Course in the Command Line

Throughout this book, you will use the *command line* or *terminal*.

To access the command line on a Mac, press Command-Space to open Spotlight. Then type "terminal" in the search bar. Press Return when the Terminal application is selected (Figure 3).

Figure 3 Finding the Terminal app on a Mac

You should see a window that looks like Figure 4.

Figure 4 Mac command line

To access the command line on Windows, go to the Start menu and search for "PowerShell." Find and open the program named Windows PowerShell (Figure 5).

Figure 5 Finding the PowerShell on Windows

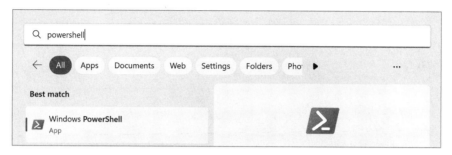

Click it to run the standard Windows command-line interface, which looks like Figure 6.

Figure 6 Windows command line

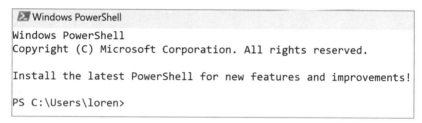

From now on, we will refer to "the terminal" or "the command line" to mean both the Mac Terminal and the Windows PowerShell.

If you are unfamiliar with using the command line, here is a short walk-through of some common tasks. If you already use the command line, you can skip ahead to the section called "Installing Node.js" later in this chapter.

Finding the current directory

You enter all terminal commands by typing at the prompt and pressing the Return key.

The command line is location based. This means that at any given time, it is "in" a particular directory within the file structure, and any commands you enter will apply within that directory. The command-line prompt shows an abbreviated version of the path of the directory it is in.

To see the whole path, enter the command pwd (which stands for "print working directory"), as shown in Figure 7 and Figure 8.

Figure 7 Showing the current path using pwd on a Mac

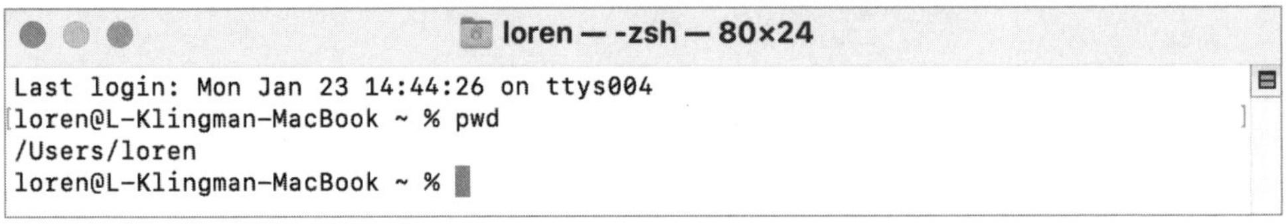

```
● ● ●                    🔲 loren — -zsh — 80×24

Last login: Mon Jan 23 14:44:26 on ttys004
[loren@L-Klingman-MacBook ~ % pwd                                              ]
/Users/loren
loren@L-Klingman-MacBook ~ % █
```

Figure 8 Showing the current path using pwd on Windows

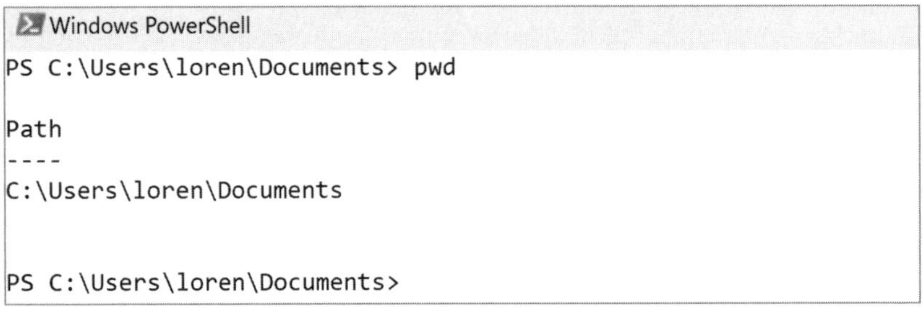

```
🔷 Windows PowerShell
PS C:\Users\loren\Documents> pwd

Path
----
C:\Users\loren\Documents


PS C:\Users\loren\Documents>
```

Changing directories

To move around the file structure, you use the command cd, or "change directory," followed by the path of the directory you want to move into.

You do not always need to enter a complete directory path in your cd command. For example, to move down into a subdirectory of the current directory, simply use the name of the subdirectory. So when you are in your home directory (/Users/YourName or C:\Users\YourName\), the path to the Documents directory is just Documents.

Now move into the Documents directory:

    cd Documents

To move up to the parent directory, use the command cd .. (that is, cd followed by a space and two periods). The pair of periods represents the path of the parent directory. Move into the parent directory:

    cd ..

Now navigate to the directory where you would like to create the projects in this book. This might be Documents or Desktop or Projects or Sites, depending on how you like to organize things on your machine. For example, you might move back into Documents:

    cd Documents

Creating a directory

The directory structure of front-end projects is important. Your projects can grow quickly, and it is best to keep them organized from the beginning. You will create new directories regularly during your development. You do this using the mkdir or "make directory" command followed by the name of the new directory.

To see this command in action, set up a directory for the projects you will build as you work through this book. Enter this command:

```
mkdir react-book
```

Next, create a new directory to house needed resources, which you will add later in this chapter. Make it a subdirectory of react-book. You can do this from your home directory by prefixing the new directory name with the name of the projects directory and, on a Mac, a slash:

```
mkdir react-book/resources
```

On Windows, you use the backslash instead:

```
mkdir react-book\resources
```

Remember that you can check your current directory by using the pwd command. Figure 9 and Figure 10 show examples of creating directories, moving between them, and checking the current directory.

Figure 9 Changing and checking directories on a Mac

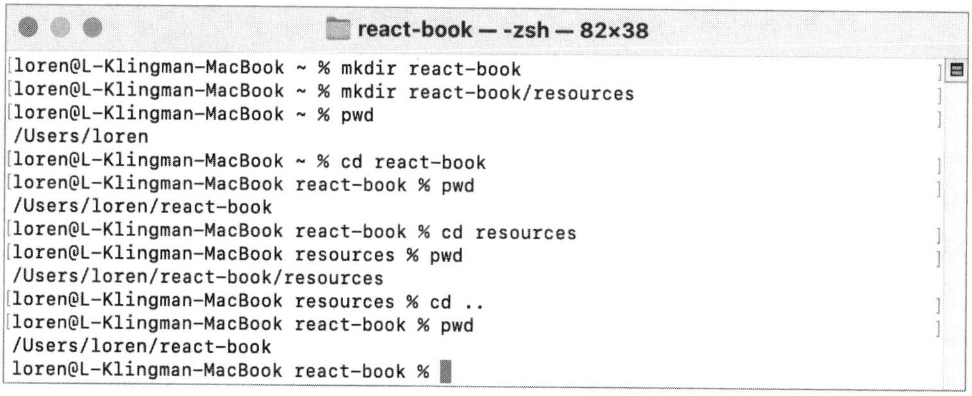

```
● ● ●                     📁 react-book — -zsh — 82×38
[loren@L-Klingman-MacBook ~ % mkdir react-book
[loren@L-Klingman-MacBook ~ % mkdir react-book/resources
[loren@L-Klingman-MacBook ~ % pwd
/Users/loren
[loren@L-Klingman-MacBook ~ % cd react-book
[loren@L-Klingman-MacBook react-book % pwd
/Users/loren/react-book
[loren@L-Klingman-MacBook react-book % cd resources
[loren@L-Klingman-MacBook resources % pwd
/Users/loren/react-book/resources
[loren@L-Klingman-MacBook resources % cd ..
[loren@L-Klingman-MacBook react-book % pwd
/Users/loren/react-book
loren@L-Klingman-MacBook react-book % ▊
```

Figure 10 Changing and checking directories on Windows

```
Windows PowerShell
PS C:\Users\loren> cd Documents
PS C:\Users\loren\Documents> mkdir react-book


    Directory: C:\Users\loren\Documents


Mode                 LastWriteTime         Length Name
----                 -------------         ------ ----
d-----         1/23/2023     5:10 PM              react-book


PS C:\Users\loren\Documents> mkdir react-book\resources


    Directory: C:\Users\loren\Documents\react-book


Mode                 LastWriteTime         Length Name
----                 -------------         ------ ----
d-----         1/23/2023     5:10 PM              resources


PS C:\Users\loren\Documents> cd react-book
PS C:\Users\loren\Documents\react-book> cd resources
PS C:\Users\loren\Documents\react-book\resources> cd ..
PS C:\Users\loren\Documents\react-book> pwd

Path
----
C:\Users\loren\Documents\react-book


PS C:\Users\loren\Documents\react-book>
```

Listing files

You might need to see a list of files in your current directory. You can do this using the `ls` command. If you want to list the files in another directory, you can supply a path:

```
ls
ls react-book
```

Figure 11 and Figure 12 show this in action:

Figure 11 Using ls to list files in a directory on a Mac

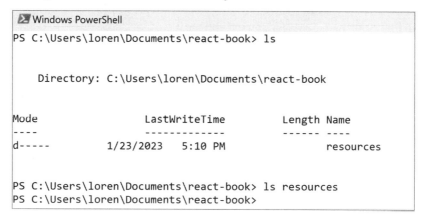

Figure 12 Using ls to list files in a directory on Windows

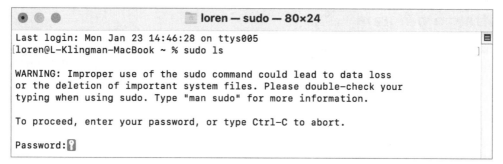

By default, ls will not print anything if a directory is empty.

Getting administrator privileges

On some versions of macOS and Windows, you need superuser or administrator privileges to run some commands, such as commands that install software or make changes to protected files.

On a Mac, you can give yourself privileges by prefixing a command with sudo. The first time you use sudo on a Mac, it will give you a stern warning (Figure 13).

Figure 13 sudo warning

```
● ● ●                        loren — sudo — 80×24
Last login: Mon Jan 23 14:46:28 on ttys005
[loren@L-Klingman-MacBook ~ % sudo ls

WARNING: Improper use of the sudo command could lead to data loss
or the deletion of important system files. Please double-check your
typing when using sudo. Type "man sudo" for more information.

To proceed, enter your password, or type Ctrl-C to abort.

Password:
```

sudo will prompt you for your password before it runs the command as the superuser. As you type, the terminal will not echo your keystrokes back, so type carefully.

On Windows, if you need to give yourself privileges, you do so when opening the PowerShell. Find the PowerShell application in the Start menu. Then, from the pane on the right, select Run as Administrator (Figure 14). When you run any commands in this command prompt, you will run them as the superuser, so be careful.

Figure 14 Opening PowerShell as an administrator

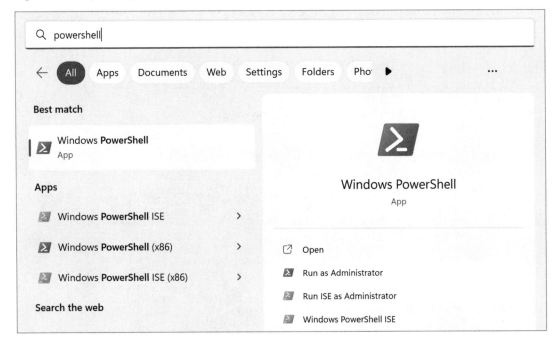

Windows users might need to change their script execution policy. If you get a warning about not being able to run one of the scripts for this book, you can change the policy as follows:

1. Start Windows PowerShell as an administrator.
2. Run Set-ExecutionPolicy -ExecutionPolicy RemoteSigned.
3. Confirm with Y and press Enter.
4. Close PowerShell and reopen it normally, without administrator privileges.

Quitting a program

As you proceed through the book, you will run many apps from the command line. Although some of them will do their job and quit automatically, others will run until you stop them. To quit a command-line program, press Control-C (on both Mac and Windows).

Installing Node.js

Node.js lets you use JavaScript programs from the command line. Most front-end development tools, including React, are written for use with Node.js.

You can check whether you have Node.js installed on your computer by entering the following command in your terminal:

```
node --version
```

If Node.js is installed, a version number will print out.

The version of Node.js that this book uses is 18.12.0. Using an older version of Node.js could result in errors as you work through the book. If you do not have Node.js installed or if you need to update the version, follow the steps below.

(If you already have Node.js installed and want to change versions, you must uninstall your existing version first. A new install will not overwrite an existing install.)

Install Node.js by downloading the installer from nodejs.org (Figure 15).

Figure 15 Downloading Node.js

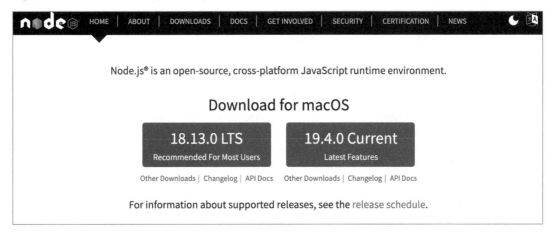

We recommend downloading the LTS (or "long term support") version. You will likely see a newer version available for download than the one this book uses. That is OK; download the most recent LTS version.

Double-click the installer and follow the prompts.

When you install Node.js, it provides two command-line programs: node and npm. The node program does the work of running programs written in JavaScript. The npm command-line tool can perform a variety of tasks, such as installing third-party code that you can incorporate into your project and managing your project's workflow and external dependencies.

You will use both programs in this book.

After installation is complete, check your version of node by running the following command in your terminal:

```
node --version
```

Resources

Download the resources for the book from www.bignerdranch.com/solutions/react-resources.zip. This file contains images, files, and other assets you will use throughout this book. Unzip the file and save its contents in the `react-book/resources` directory you created earlier. Any mentions in later chapters of the resources file or its contents will refer to the files in this directory.

Finding Documentation and Help

Before you begin, it is important to know where to access documentation if you run into any issues as you work through this book or in your future development endeavors. The web is bursting with information, both official and unofficial. Here are a few sources that might be helpful:

The React documentation is at reactjs.org/docs/getting-started.html. It is a great resource for learning more about the concepts we introduce in this book.

The Mozilla Developer Network (MDN) is the best reference for anything to do with HTML, CSS, and JavaScript. You can access it at developer.mozilla.org.

DevDocs is also a good resource. DevDocs pulls documentation from MDN for core front-end technologies, including React – and it works offline, so you can check it even when you do not have an internet connection. You can access it at devdocs.io.

Finally, there is Stack Overflow: stackoverflow.com. This is not a source of documentation; it is a place where developers can ask each other about code. Though the answers vary in quality, they are often very thorough and quite helpful. So it is a useful resource – as long as you bear in mind that the answers are not definitive, due to their crowdsourced nature.

1

Create React App

In this chapter, you will start building and customizing a React application. By the end of the chapter, you will have the beginnings of your first application running on your computer and be able to observe it in the browser. In the next three chapters, you will build on this foundation as you learn about new ideas and concepts.

There is a lot of information in this chapter. It is OK if you do not understand everything the first time. You will have opportunities to practice what you learn as you move through this book.

The application you will build is Ottergram: a photo-sharing site for sea otters, some of the most charming marine animals. Visitors to the site will be able to scroll through the image feed and select a post for more information.

Figure 1.1 shows what the completed application will look like when a post from the feed is selected:

Figure 1.1 Preview of the completed Ottergram app

Create React App

You will scaffold your Ottergram application using *Create React App*.

Create React App is a command-line interface (CLI) tool that allows you to quickly set up a React project with the latest configuration features. It is one of several toolchains available for getting a React project up and running. We like it because it is particularly simple to use.

Create React App uses Babel and webpack behind the scenes to build and run your app. Though you can configure these tools yourself, that is outside the scope of this book. When you use Create React App, these tools are preconfigured and hidden, so you can focus on developing in React.

With that in mind, let's get this project started.

In your terminal, navigate to your `react-book` projects folder.

The `create-react-app` command takes one argument, the name of your project. Create a new React application called `ottergram` with this command:

```
npx create-react-app ottergram
```

If you see a prompt asking you to confirm that you want to install `create-react-app`, press Y to continue.

Creating a new React application can take a few minutes. When Create React App has finished, the terminal output will show a list of dependencies that have been installed and the available commands you can run in your new application (Figure 1.2).

Figure 1.2 Creating a new React app

```
Success! Created ottergram at /Users/ashleyparker/react-book/ottergram
Inside that directory, you can run several commands:

  npm start
    Starts the development server.

  npm run build
    Bundles the app into static files for production.

  npm test
    Starts the test runner.

  npm run eject
    Removes this tool and copies build dependencies, configuration files
    and scripts into the app directory. If you do this, you can't go back!

We suggest that you begin by typing:

  cd ottergram
  npm start

Happy hacking!
→  react-book
```

One note before moving forward: Create React App always installs the latest versions of the included dependencies, so your code from this point on might look different from what you see in the book. If the differences are confusing, copy the solution code for this chapter from your downloaded resources file (`solutions/01-create-react-app`) and use that code when proceeding to the next chapter.

Running the Development Server

Create React App set up your React application in a subdirectory named `ottergram`. Change to this subdirectory in the terminal:

    cd ottergram

Create React App ships with its own development server to build and serve the application for you. The development server runs locally with Node.js, which you installed in The Necessary Tools.

Although you have not added any content to Ottergram, it is useful to start the development server right away to verify that the initial setup is working as expected. To start the server, run this command:

    npm start

This command will build your app and start a server so you can access it locally. It will also open a new browser window and navigate to http://localhost:3000. (If you see a prompt asking you to allow the terminal to open a browser window, click OK.)

Your React application should be running in your browser, as shown in Figure 1.3.

Figure 1.3 Viewing the React app in the browser

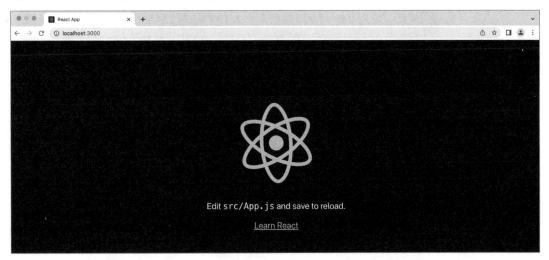

If you do not see the React logo and placeholder content, you might have the wrong version of Node.js. Check your version using the directions in The Necessary Tools. If that is not the problem, check your terminal for any error messages from the `npx create-react-app` command you ran earlier.

As an added convenience, Create React App includes a preconfigured script that watches your files for changes. If you change a file while your application is running, the page will automatically reload and reflect any saved changes. This makes development much faster than if you had to restart the server every time you wanted to make a change.

You will typically want to leave the development server running while you make changes to your application. To stop the server when you are finished working, press Control-C (Ctrl-C) in the terminal window where the development server is running.

Navigating Your App

Open Visual Studio Code and take a look at the files Create React App generated.

Open your project by selecting File → Open Folder… in the menu bar (Figure 1.4).

Figure 1.4 Opening a folder in Visual Studio Code

When the file explorer opens, navigate to your react-book projects directory. Select the new ottergram folder and click Open (Figure 1.5).

Figure 1.5 Opening Ottergram in Visual Studio Code

If you see a prompt asking you to confirm that you trust the authors of the files in this folder (Figure 1.6), click Yes, I trust the authors to give Visual Studio Code access to the ottergram directory.

Figure 1.6 Prompt to trust the authors

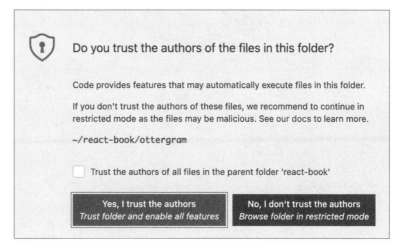

Take a look at the icons on the left side of the Visual Studio Code window. The top icon toggles the explorer pane: It shows (or hides) the files in your project (Figure 1.7).

Figure 1.7 Initial files and folders generated by Create React App

If you do not see a list of files in the left pane, click the explorer icon so you can inspect the files that Create React App generated for you.

Project metadata and dependencies

Click the `package.json` file you see in your top-level `ottergram` directory.

This will open the file in your code editor:

```json
{
  "name": "ottergram",
  "version": "0.1.0",
  "private": true,
  "dependencies": {
    "@testing-library/jest-dom": "^5.16.5",
    "@testing-library/react": "^13.4.0",
    "@testing-library/user-event": "^13.5.0",
    "react": "^18.2.0",
    "react-dom": "^18.2.0",
    "react-scripts": "5.0.1",
    "web-vitals": "^2.1.4"
  },
  "scripts": {
    "start": "react-scripts start",
    "build": "react-scripts build",
    "test": "react-scripts test",
    "eject": "react-scripts eject"
  },
  "eslintConfig": {
    "extends": [
      "react-app",
      "react-app/jest"
    ]
  },
  "browserslist": {
    "production": [
      ">0.2%",
      "not dead",
      "not op_mini all"
    ],
    "development": [
      "last 1 chrome version",
      "last 1 firefox version",
      "last 1 safari version"
    ]
  }
}
```

`package.json` acts as your Node.js project's manifest. It contains metadata about your project, such as the name, version number, and description. It also stores important configuration details, including linting instructions and a list of browsers that are targeted for support.

In addition, `package.json` houses the needed dependencies for your application. The package manager, npm, installs these dependencies. At this point, npm has installed several dependencies, including `react`, `react-dom`, and `react-scripts`, plus others needed for running tests.

Close package.json and click package-lock.json to open it:

```
{
  "name": "ottergram",
  "version": "0.1.0",
  "lockfileVersion": 2,
  "requires": true,
  "packages": {
    "": {
      "name": "ottergram",
      "version": "0.1.0",
      "dependencies": {
        "@testing-library/jest-dom": "^5.16.4",
        "@testing-library/react": "^13.2.0",
        "@testing-library/user-event": "^13.5.0",
        "react": "^18.1.0",
        "react-dom": "^18.1.0",
        "react-scripts": "5.0.1",
        "web-vitals": "^2.1.4"
      }
    },
    ...
  },
  "dependencies": {
    "": {
      "version": "2.2.0",
      "resolved": "https://registry.npmjs.org/[...]",
      "integrity": "sha512-[...]",
      "requires": {
        ...
      }
    },
    ...
  }
}
```

The package-lock.json file contains the specific version numbers of every dependency that npm installed.

In package.json, you can specify a range of acceptable versions; package-lock.json contains the exact version installed. This is important for testing and continuous delivery. package-lock.json ensures that remote deployments, such as to a server, install the same version that was used for testing.

Note that if you use version control, you should always commit package-lock.json along with package.json.

In Visual Studio Code's left sidebar, click the > icon next to the node_modules directory to expose its contents. This directory contains a cache of all installed dependencies. If you compare it to the specifications in package-lock.json, you will find that they match exactly.

The node_modules directory is already large and will grow each time you add a package. Because of this, developers usually choose not to commit it into version control. You can rebuild it by running the command npm install, which uses package.json and package-lock.json to install the exact package versions needed.

Go ahead and close the node_modules directory; you will not be working with its contents.

public directory

Now, click the > icon next to the public directory to expose its contents. public is the root folder of the React application and contains static files that are served to the browser (Figure 1.8).

Figure 1.8 public directory explorer

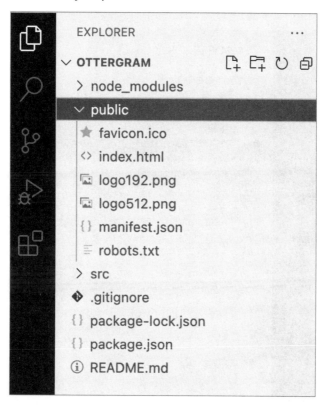

For now, focus on index.html, which is the only HTML file your app contains. Click this file to open it in your code editor.

The markup includes the node <div id='root'></div> in the body. React will look for this HTML node and render all the React code in it.

Also, this file does not contain any script tags, which means it does not load any external JavaScript files. We mentioned earlier that package.json contains a dependency called react-scripts. This dependency includes all scripts and configuration needed to get your React application up and running.

src directory

The src directory contains the example React app and is where you will spend most of your time in development. Most of the files in this folder are sample files to get you started. Expose the contents of the directory and take a look (Figure 1.9).

Figure 1.9 src directory explorer

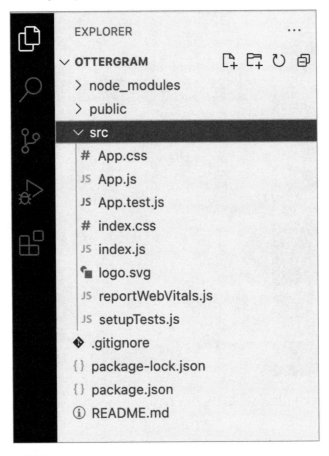

Click the src/index.js file to open it in your code editor. This file is the main JavaScript entry point – the first file that will be executed and, therefore, the starting point for the code in your app.

In `index.js`, a React root element is created from the `root` node identified in `public/index.html`:

```
const root = ReactDOM.createRoot(document.getElementById('root'));
```

Then, the React code is rendered directly to the root:

```
root.render(
  <React.StrictMode>
    <App />
  </React.StrictMode>
);
```

Create React App automatically renders the app using `React.StrictMode`, a developer tool that checks your code for potential problems and provides warnings when issues are detected.

Customizing Your App

Now that you have seen some of the initial app setup, you are ready to start modifying Ottergram and making it your own.

Find and open the `src/App.js` file. It defines a function called **App**. Take a look at the function's return statement:

```
return (
  <div className="App">
    <header className="App-header">
      <img src={logo} className="App-logo" alt="logo" />
      <p>
        Edit <code>src/App.js</code> and save to reload.
      </p>
      <a
        className="App-link"
        href="https://reactjs.org"
        target="_blank"
        rel="noopener noreferrer"
      >
        Learn React
      </a>
    </header>
  </div>
);
```

Although this looks a lot like a normal HTML file, it is actually a slightly different language called JSX. You will learn more about JSX in Chapter 2. For now, you can think of it as being like HTML.

Begin your work on Ottergram by replacing the placeholder content with your app's name. To do this, delete the sample code in the `return` statement (as well as one of the `import` statements) and add a simple header.

Listing 1.1 Adding a header (`App.js`)

```
import logo from './logo.svg';
import './App.css';

function App() {
  return (
    <div className="App">
    <div>
      <header className="App-header">
      <header>
        <img src={logo} className="App-logo" alt="logo" />
        <p>
          Edit <code>src/App.js</code> and save to reload.
        </p>
        <a
          className="App-link"
          href="https://reactjs.org"
          target="_blank"
          rel="noopener noreferrer"
        >
          Learn React
        </a>
        <h1>Ottergram</h1>
      </header>
...
```

Save the file with File → Save or Command-S (Ctrl-S). Switch to your browser.

Your app should still be running at http://localhost:3000. If it is not, run the command `npm start` from your `ottergram` directory in the terminal.

Now, instead of the default React logo and text, you should see your header (Figure 1.10). Although it is plain, now your users will know that they have located the otter social media application they were looking for.

Figure 1.10 Viewing the header in the browser

Title

Although the page text says "Ottergram," the title on the browser tab still says "React App." The title displayed on the tab plays a key role in search engine optimization and getting users to your site. Let's make sure the title accurately reflects the application.

Go back to `public/index.html` in Visual Studio Code. Locate the `<title>` tag in the `<head>` section of the HTML. Change the text from `React App` to `Ottergram` and save the file.

Listing 1.2 Changing the app title (`index.html`)

```
<!DOCTYPE html>
<html lang="en">
  <head>
    ...
    <title>React App</title>
    <title>Ottergram</title>
  </head>
...
```

Now the tab's title matches your header (Figure 1.11). (If it does not, manually refresh the page in your browser. Sometimes changes to files in the `public` directory do not propagate automatically.)

Figure 1.11 Viewing the new title in the browser

Favicon

Though the Ottergram title is an improvement, the tab still shows the React logo. A better fit for your app's branding would be a logo or image of an otter. Like the title, the favicon – the image shown in the tab – represents your site across the web. It is a visual identifier that helps users recognize your application.

In your downloaded resources file from The Necessary Tools, the `ottergram-resources` directory has favicon images as well as other images you will need for the app.

In your file explorer, copy the `favicon.ico`, `logo192.png`, and `logo512.png` files from `ottergram-resources` and use them to replace the files with the same names in your project's `public` directory.

Return to the browser and reload the page. Yay! Now you have an otter (Figure 1.12).

Figure 1.12 New favicon in the browser tab

How does the browser know to use the favicon files?

Create React App set up references to two of the favicon files in public/index.html. Back in Visual Studio Code, open public/index.html to find the links with the relationships of icon and apple-touch-icon.

```
...
<link rel="icon" href="%PUBLIC_URL%/favicon.ico" />
<meta name="viewport" content="width=device-width, initial-scale=1" />
<meta name="theme-color" content="#000000" />
<meta
  name="description"
  content="Web site created using create-react-app"
/>
<link rel="apple-touch-icon" href="%PUBLIC_URL%/logo192.png" />
...
```

Most browsers on web and mobile will use the standard icon link to display the favicon. Apple's iOS is unique and uses the apple-touch-icon link to select the favicon on mobile devices.

There are also references to the favicon files in `public/manifest.json`, which is used by some browsers. Open `public/manifest.json` to take a look:

```
...
"icons": [
  {
    "src": "favicon.ico",
    "sizes": "64x64 32x32 24x24 16x16",
    "type": "image/x-icon"
  },
  {
    "src": "logo192.png",
    "type": "image/png",
    "sizes": "192x192"
  },
  {
    "src": "logo512.png",
    "type": "image/png",
    "sizes": "512x512"
  }
],
...
```

Adding Elements

You are ready to add some otter posts to the home page so that users can start building their followings. You will begin by adding the provided images to your app.

You added the favicon images to the `public` directory. This allows other files in the same directory to use the favicon. But files in the `public` directory are not part of the webpack build process. So while your otter images are static files that *could* live outside the build process, if you put them in the `public` directory, you will miss out on some optimization that webpack takes care of for you.

Instead, you will add the files in `src`, in a new subdirectory called `otters`.

In your file explorer, copy the entire `otters` folder from your downloaded resources file to `src/otters`.

There are five otter images. Each post on Ottergram will consist of an image and the otter's name, so there will be five posts.

Add the posts to the home page in App.js. Put them in an unordered list, and make each list item a button, because the posts will eventually be clickable.

Listing 1.3 Adding posts (App.js)

```
import './App.css';
import Barry from './otters/otter1.jpg';
import Robin from './otters/otter2.jpg';
import Maurice from './otters/otter3.jpg';
import Lesley from './otters/otter4.jpg';
import Barbara from './otters/otter5.jpg';

function App() {
  return (
    <div>
      <header>
        <h1>Ottergram</h1>
      </header>
      <ul>
        <li>
          <button>
            <img src={Barry} alt='Barry'/>
            <p>Barry</p>
          </button>
        </li>
        <li>
          <button>
            <img src={Robin} alt='Robin'/>
            <p>Robin</p>
          </button>
        </li>
        <li>
          <button>
            <img src={Maurice} alt='Maurice'/>
            <p>Maurice</p>
          </button>
        </li>
        <li>
          <button>
            <img src={Lesley} alt='Lesley'/>
            <p>Lesley</p>
          </button>
        </li>
        <li>
          <button>
            <img src={Barbara} alt='Barbara'/>
            <p>Barbara</p>
          </button>
        </li>
      </ul>
    </div>
...
```

Here again, the function in App.js returns basic HTML tags. But there is a difference between a simple HTML file and the code above.

You import the image files at the top of your JavaScript file, then you pass each image file to an `<img>` tag as a variable. Importing files this way means they will automatically be bundled into the React build output. React will take care of getting the file path correct when the app is built, so you do not have to worry about where the image will live after deployment.

React appends extra characters to the image name to prevent browsers from caching old images. You can also tell React to use Base64 encoding to embed the images in the HTML and avoid an extra trip to the server.

One important caveat is that you can only import files this way in JavaScript files. That is why you did not import the favicon in `index.html`.

Save your file and return to the browser to see the otters' posts (Figure 1.13).

Figure 1.13 A list of otters

Styles

While those otters are cute, the Ottergram app is pretty plain. Next, you will add styles to make your app as stylish as an otter.

Stylesheets are imported just like images and other files. Go back to App.js. The file already has an import for App.css at the top:

```
import './App.css';
```

Open src/App.css. It contains default style rules that Create React App added. You do not need these rules anymore, since you removed the default code that they applied to.

For simplicity, instead of editing App.css directly, you will replace it with a stylesheet provided in your downloaded resources file. In your file explorer, replace src/App.css with the ottergram-resources/App.css file from your downloaded resources file.

After replacing App.css, switch back to the browser. Most of the new styles are not being applied, even if you reload the page. (The background color is an exception.)

Why not?

Take a look at your new App.css file:

```
body {
    background-color: #95c2d7;
    font-family: Arial, sans-serif;
}

.header-component h1 {
    ...
}

.post-list {
    ...
}

.post-component {
    ...
}
...
```

CSS *type* selectors, such as body, find all matching HTML elements in your application and apply the specified style rules to those elements. So the background-color style is being applied to the <body> in your code, resulting in a lovely ocean-blue background.

On the other hand, CSS *class* selectors, such as the .header-component and .post-list selectors in App.css, are not automatically associated with any elements. You need to add these selectors to the tags in App.js.

In HTML, you associate CSS class selectors with elements by using the keyword `class` as an attribute. JSX supports attributes as well – you used them earlier when you added `src` attributes to the image tags. But because `class` is a reserved word in JavaScript, React uses the attribute `className` to apply classes to elements.

Add `className`s to the elements in `App.js` to match the CSS selectors in the stylesheet:

Listing 1.4 Adding `className` attributes (`App.js`)

```
...
function App() {
  return (
    <div>
      <header>
      <header className='header-component'>
        <h1>Ottergram</h1>
      </header>
      <ul>
      <ul className='post-list'>
        <li>
        <li className='post-component'>
          ...
        </li>
        <li>
        <li className='post-component'>
          ...
        </li>
        <li>
        <li className='post-component'>
          ...
        </li>
        <li>
        <li className='post-component'>
          ...
        </li>
        <li>
        <li className='post-component'>
          <button>
...
```

Save your changes and take a look at the browser.

That is much better – now Ottergram has some nice colors reminiscent of sea otters' ocean homes (Figure 1.14).

Figure 1.14 Ottergram, with style

The Chrome Developer Tools

Chrome has built-in Developer Tools, commonly known as DevTools, that are among the best available for testing styles, layouts, and more on the fly. Using the DevTools is much more efficient than trying things out in code. The DevTools are very powerful and will be your constant companion as you do front-end development, including React development.

To open the Chrome DevTools, click the triple-dot icon to the right of the address bar in Chrome. Next, click More Tools → Developer Tools (Figure 1.15).

Figure 1.15 Opening the Chrome Developer Tools

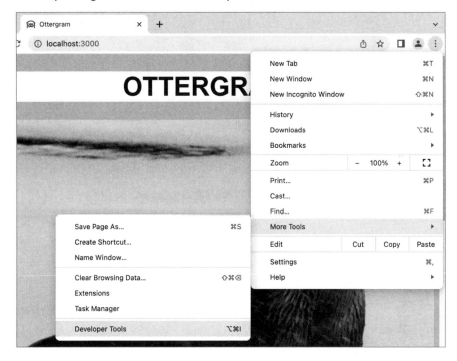

By default, Chrome displays the DevTools on the right. Your screen will look something like Figure 1.16:

Figure 1.16 Viewing the Chrome DevTools

In Figure 1.16, you can see the DevTools next to the web page, showing the Elements tab. The Elements tab displays all the HTML elements rendered as part of your application. Selecting an element shows you additional information about the element, including any applied styles.

Click the Inspect Element button at the left end of the DevTools menu bar (Figure 1.17):

Figure 1.17 Inspect Element button

Now, move your cursor over the word OTTERGRAM on the web page. As you hover over the word, the DevTools surround the header with a blue- and peach-colored rectangle (Figure 1.18):

Figure 1.18 Inspecting the header

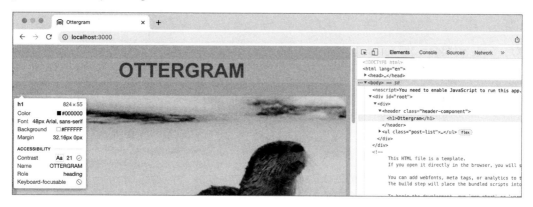

Now click the word "OTTERGRAM." The DevTools select the <h1> element in the Elements tab, displaying information about its styles in the lower pane (Figure 1.19):

Figure 1.19 <h1> information in the Elements tab

You can see the `class` attribute applied to the `<header>` element in the DevTools. Only the JavaScript file uses the `className` keyword – it is not included in the rendered page.

Conclusion

Good work! You used Create React App to generate a skeleton app and customized the default info to ensure users know what site they are on. You added a header, images, and text to the page so that it displays a feed of trendy otters. You also added styles using the React keyword `className`.

In the next chapter, you will build on the work you did here by taking advantage of a powerful React tool called components.

Are You More Curious?

Many chapters in this book end with one or more "For the More Curious" sections. These sections offer more details on topics from the chapter. You do not need to make any changes to your projects based on the code shown in these sections.

For the More Curious: npx

npx is a tool for executing npm package binaries. It starts with binaries within the local project and $PATH. If it does not find the package there, it will download a temporary copy of the latest version and execute the binary from that download.

Without npx, you would have needed several commands to create Ottergram using Create React App:

```
npm install --global create-react-app
create-react-app ottergram
npm uninstall --global create-react-app
```

With npx, you needed only one line:

```
npx create-react-app ottergram
```

Use npx with care. When you use it, you are executing code that has been downloaded from the internet on your local machine. Take care to vet the packages that you run – or read the source code yourself.

For more info, check out www.npmjs.com/package/npx.

For the More Curious: %PUBLIC_URL%

Because webpack does not process files in the `public` folder, it is necessary to include an absolute path to those files when they are copied to the `build` folder. Create React App provides `%PUBLIC_URL%` to solve this problem and prevent missing files or incorrect path errors.

When you build your app, `%PUBLIC_URL%` will resolve to the correct absolute path. It does not matter if your app is located at the URL root level (`localhost:3000/`) or not (for example, `localhost:3000/react/ottergram/`). This also works for client-side routing.

Challenges

Challenges are opportunities to review what you have learned and take your work in the chapter a step further. We recommend that you tackle as many of them as you can to cement your knowledge and gain a deeper understanding of the concepts discussed.

Challenges come in three levels of difficulty:

- Bronze challenges typically ask you to do something very similar to what you did in the chapter. These challenges reinforce what you learned in the chapter and force you to type in similar code without having it laid out in front of you. Practice makes perfect.

- Silver challenges require you to do more digging and more thinking. Sometimes you will need to use functions, events, markup, and styles that you have not seen before. However, the tasks are still similar to what you did in the chapter.

- Gold challenges are difficult and can take hours to complete. They require you to understand the concepts from the chapter and then do some quality thinking and problem solving on your own. Tackling these challenges will prepare you for the real-world work of React development.

Before beginning a challenge, make a copy of your project and attack the challenge in that copy. Many chapters build on previous chapters, and working on challenges in a copy of the project ensures that you will be able to progress through the book.

Create React App makes a Git repository of your projects automatically. If you are familiar with Git, you can use branches to create separate workspaces for challenges. You can also copy and paste the files in your file explorer to create a copy.

Bronze Challenge: Subtitle

Make Ottergram's header a little more descriptive to let users know what the app is all about. Below the <h1> tag, add a subtitle that matches the style of your main header. But make it a bit smaller, use an *italic* font style, and make it all lowercase.

Hint: You will need to add new CSS in App.css and apply that class to your new subheader.

Silver Challenge: Canarygram

Word about Ottergram has gotten out. The animal kingdom is clamoring for photo-sharing applications! And no creature is more eager than the lovable canary. Canaries have a reputation for being first for a lot of things, and they are a little bummed that the otters beat them to the punch. Fear not, canaries! From the makers of Ottergram comes the brand-new Canarygram.

Use create-react-app to spin up a new project called canarygram. Repeat the steps in this chapter, but see if you can add a bit of a canary theme to this application – maybe replacing the ocean-blue color scheme with canary yellow.

2

Components

Ottergram is looking good! But imagine trying to maintain it as it becomes popular and the user count skyrockets.

At the moment, each element is hardcoded into `App.js`. Although this works, and the elements render to the screen just fine, it does lead to a lot of repeated code.

If Ottergram were an enterprise application, it could have hundreds or thousands of users who all want to share their photos. You would need to add each post individually to the JSX (which, recall, is what your code that looks like HTML really is). This would quickly become unsustainable.

Thankfully, there is a better way.

In this chapter, you will learn about creating and working with *components*. By the end of the chapter, you will have moved the JSX markup from `App.js` into separate component files. Using components will help you organize your code, keep your code cleaner, and create dynamic, reusable functions. All of this will make Ottergram easier to develop and maintain.

At the end of this chapter, your application will have one visual change: The names of the otters will stand out more (Figure 2.1).

Figure 2.1 Ottergram with stand-out names

App Organization

As the name suggests, components are pieces of a larger whole.

When you look at, say, an airplane, it can be hard to wrap your mind around all the different pieces it is made of. But an airplane does not start out as a single unit. It is made from lots of individual parts, such as the wings, engine, tail, and so on – each with its own purpose and functionality. As the airplane is built and new parts are added, the pieces come together to form a new and different whole.

Similarly, a large web application might be difficult to wrap your mind around. But when the app is broken into its pieces, it becomes much easier to reason about. Like an airplane part, each piece of an app has its own functionality and manages its own logic, and it fits together with other pieces to form the whole application.

In React, these pieces are called *components*, and they are a powerful tool. Components are JavaScript functions that return React elements.

Header Component

Look at a wireframe of the Ottergram app at this point (Figure 2.2).

Figure 2.2 Ottergram wireframe

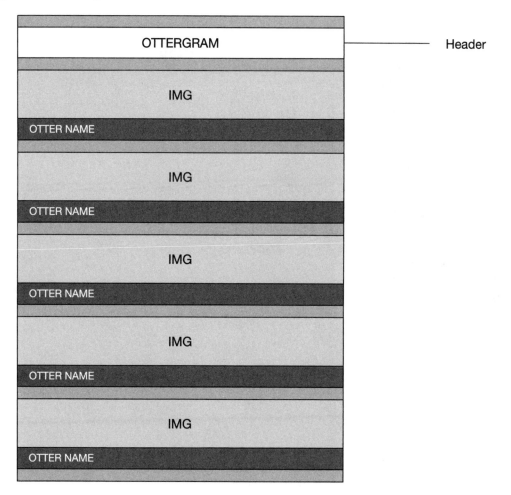

At the top of the page is a header that contains the title, Ottergram. The first component you build will encapsulate this header.

In Visual Studio Code, create a new folder in the src directory called components. To do this, select the src directory, then click the ⊟ icon at the top of the explorer (Figure 2.3).

Figure 2.3 Adding a new folder

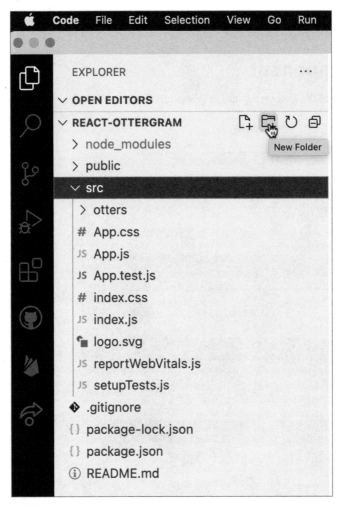

Type the name of the folder, components (Figure 2.4). Then press Return.

Figure 2.4 Naming the new folder

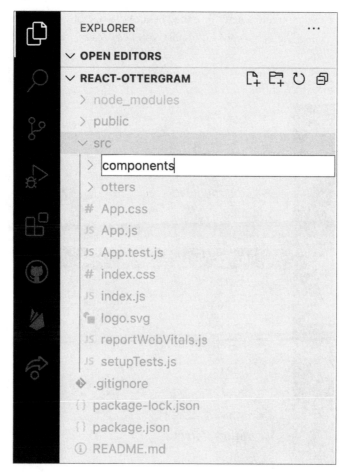

You will put all the components you create in this folder.

By convention, a file usually contains only one component and shares the name of the component it contains. Since you are creating a **Header** component, you will name the file that contains it Header.js.

Inside the components folder, create a new file called Header.js. Creating a new file is similar to creating a new folder: Select the components directory you just created, then click the ⊡ icon at the top of the explorer (Figure 2.5).

Figure 2.5 Adding a new file

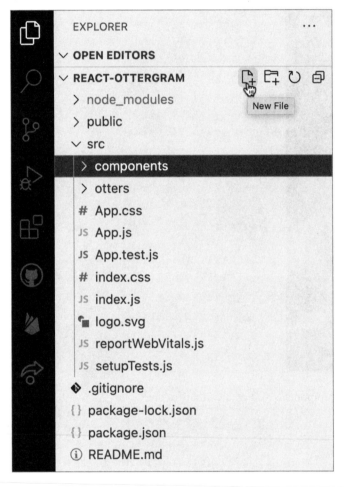

Type the name, Header.js (Figure 2.6). Then press Return.

Figure 2.6 Naming the new file

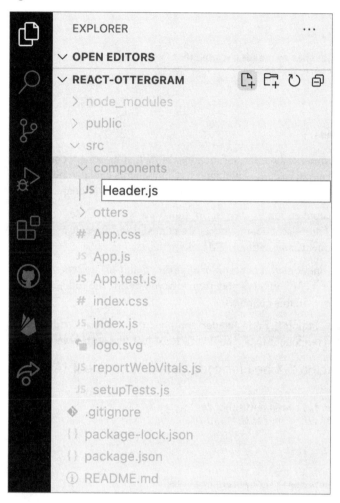

In the new `Header.js` file, create a function called **Header** that returns all the header code from `App.js`.

Listing 2.1 Creating a header component (`Header.js`)

```
function Header() {
    return (
        <header className='header-component'>
            <h1>Ottergram</h1>
        </header>
    )
}

export default Header;
```

Header looks similar to other JavaScript functions. In fact, at its core, a component like **Header** is a JavaScript function that returns a React element. (Components can also be classes. Though you will not build any class-based components, we will discuss them in later chapters.)

Although the naming convention for JavaScript functions is camelCase, your function name, **Header**, begins with a capital letter. React components are named using PascalCase to help you distinguish between React components and native HTML elements.

After you define the function, you export it using `export default`. Exporting the function allows other files to import and use it. (If you are wondering why you define the function and export it separately, we will explain that later in this chapter.)

Save `Header.js`. Now import the new **Header** component into `App.js` and replace the existing header markup. You use the component inside angle brackets, just like an HTML tag.

Listing 2.2 Replacing JSX header code with a component (`App.js`)

```
import './App.css';
import Header from './components/Header';
import Barry from './otters/otter1.jpg';
...
function App() {
  return (
    <div>
      <header className='header-component'>
        <h1>Ottergram</h1>
      </header>
      <Header />
      <ul className='post-list'>
...
```

Save `App.js` and check out the browser. Though the app looks the same, you are now looking at your first component. (If the page does not look the same, you might not have saved one of the files.)

Even though you did not import the stylesheet directly into the new `Header.js` file, your styles are still being applied. This is because all CSS becomes global, so any CSS you create is available to your entire application. You will often see separate stylesheets for each component. Although this helps with organization and maintainability, it does not isolate the CSS to the component.

CSS selectors should be unique throughout the components of your application. As long as you do not have components with duplicate names, using the component's name as the class prefix usually works well. Because this is a simple application, you will keep all the styles in `src/App.css`.

JSX

Although it looks like HTML, what the **Header** component returns is JSX. We have mentioned JSX before – it is a syntax extension that allows you to write declarative code in React, much like how you would write HTML. Compilers, such as Babel, compile the JSX to JavaScript, which then executes in the browser.

What would your code look like without JSX? The **Header** component would look like this:

```
import React from 'react';

const Header = () => React.createElement(
  'header',
  null,
  React.createElement(
    'h1',
    {className: "title"},
    'Ottergram'
  )
);

export default Header;
```

Instead of having easy-to-read tags, this version of the **Header** function calls the React API's **createElement** function directly.

Both versions are valid code that returns a React element. But imagine creating a component with more than a simple header, such as the **App** component. Your code could quickly become messy and difficult to read.

JSX allows you to write code that is easy to read and understand.

Post Component

Take another look at Ottergram's wireframe (Figure 2.7). Below the header, repeating elements display each otter's image and name.

Figure 2.7 Wireframe highlighting repeated elements

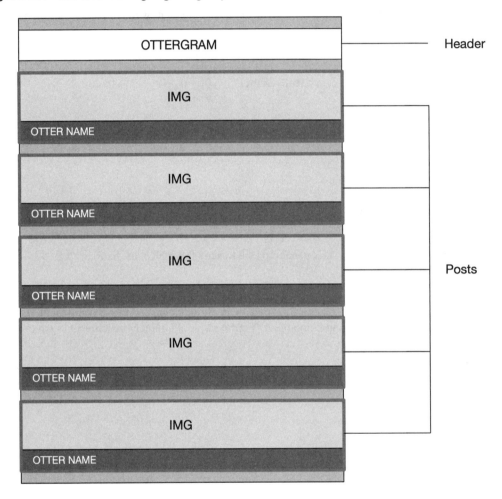

Each of these elements shares the same visual structure onscreen and in the wireframe. In code, these elements share the same structure as well: Each is a list item containing a button that displays the image and name.

To add another element, you have to add a new list item with its own button, image, and text. This means you cannot reuse the code from previous items, because you must specify the image and name of each item individually.

But because the underlying structure of each item is the same, you can extract the structure into a single, reusable component. We will call this component a "post," since it will contain a single post on the website.

Create a new file in the components directory using the **New File** icon. Name the file Post.js (Figure 2.8).

Figure 2.8 Creating Post.js

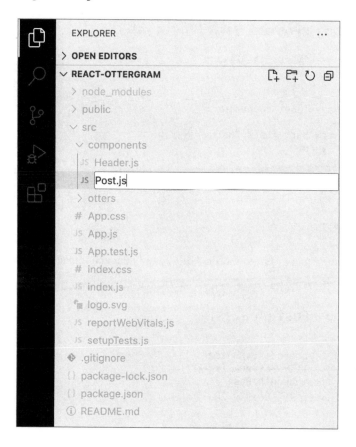

Back in App.js, copy the code for the first list item, from `<li className='post-component'>` to `</li>`.

In Post.js, define a **Post** function and paste the list item code into the return statement. Import the Barry image file. (If you copy the import statement from App.js, you will need to add a `.` to the file path, because Post.js is nested in the `components` directory.) Finally, add an export statement.

Listing 2.3 Creating a **Post** for Barry (Post.js)

```
import Barry from '../otters/otter1.jpg';

function Post() {
    return (
        <li className='post-component'>
          <button>
            <img src={Barry} alt='Barry'/>
            <p>Barry</p>
          </button>
        </li>
    )
}

export default Post;
```

Save Post.js and return to App.js. Import the **Post** component and replace the Barry list item with a **Post**:

Listing 2.4 Adding a **Post** (App.js)

```
import './App.css';
import Header from './components/Header';
import Barry from './otters/otter1.jpg';
import Post from './components/Post';
import Robin from './otters/otter2.jpg';
...
function App() {
  return (
    <div>
      <Header />
      <ul className='post-list'>
        <li className='post-component'>
          <button>
            <img src={Barry} alt='Barry'/>
            <p>Barry</p>
          </button>
        </li>
        <Post />
        <li className='post-component'>
...
```

Save App.js and check out the browser. Although everything should look the same, your app now includes two React components. Later in this chapter, you will see how to reuse the **Post** component to simplify your code base. But first, let's take a moment to inspect your components using the React Developer Tools.

React Developer Tools

The React Developer Tools, a Chrome browser extension, integrate with the Chrome Developer Tools to show you additional useful information about your components in the browser.

Install the extension to take a look. Visit the Chrome Web Store at chrome.google.com/webstore/category/extensions. Search for "React Developer Tools" (Figure 2.9). On the extension's page, the Additional Information section should show that it is offered by Meta.

Figure 2.9 Chrome Web Store

Click Add to Chrome. Follow the prompts to install the extension.

In your Ottergram browser tab, make sure the Chrome DevTools are open. (If they are not, click the triple-dot icon to the right of the address bar, then click More Tools → Developer Tools.)

Because you have added the React DevTools, you will see two additional tabs: Components and Profiler (Figure 2.10). (You might need to click the >> icon in the tab bar to see them.) If you do not see them, try restarting Chrome and checking again.

Figure 2.10 Opening the React DevTools

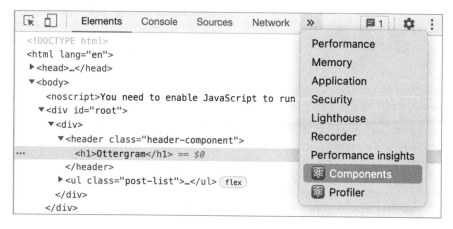

Select the Components tab. The React DevTools show your new **Header** and **Post** components as part of the app structure (Figure 2.11).

Figure 2.11 Viewing components in the React DevTools

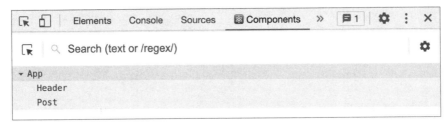

Click the **Post** component to learn more about it (Figure 2.12).

Figure 2.12 **Post** component in the DevTools

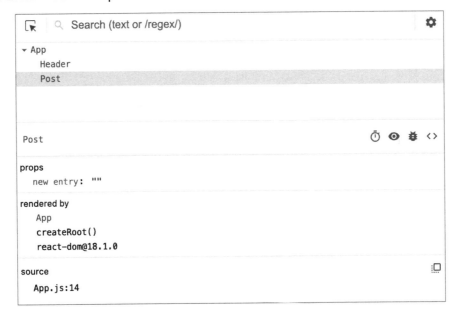

In the next section, you will learn more about component *props*. Though **Post** does not currently have any props, the props section is where those would be listed.

The React DevTools also provide information about how your component is being used in the application. The **Post** component, for example, is rendered by the **App** component. **App** is considered the parent component of **Post**, because it lives directly above it in the component tree. And the source section shows the filename and line where your component is referenced.

Why name components?

If you are already familiar with JavaScript, you might be wondering why we had you create and export your component in separate steps. For **Header**, for example, an arrow function like this would have saved several lines of code:

```
export default () => (
 <header>
   <h1>Header</h1>
 </header>
);
```

If you defined **Header** like this, it would still render. But the React DevTools would not be able to identify it by name, because the DevTools learn the component name from the function name (Figure 2.13).

Figure 2.13 Anonymous component name

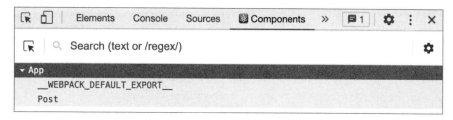

Being able to see the component names in the DevTools is very helpful for debugging, so we recommend creating and exporting your components in separate steps. You will be glad you took the time to write those extra lines later.

Props

Although your **Post** component is great, it is not doing much work yet. All five list items in App.js have the same structure and should be able to use the same component. But so far, you are using the **Post** component for only one otter post, because the component's image and text are specific to that one otter.

How can you reuse the **Post** component for all five list items? The answer is another React feature: *props*.

Because React components are JavaScript functions, they can take in arguments just like any other function. In React, you use props to pass data to components.

Props can be any type of data: JavaScript strings, numbers, objects, arrays, functions, and so on. In JSX, you send props to components using attributes, similar to HTML attributes. You group these attributes into the props object, which you pass as the first parameter when calling the component function.

Post needs to know the image and name of the otter to display. These will be the props that **App** passes down.

In App.js, use attributes to pass values for these two props to the **Post** component. You will also need to import Barry's image again.

Listing 2.5 Passing props using attributes (App.js)

```
import './App.css';
import Header from './components/Header';
import Post from './components/Post';
import Barry from './otters/otter1.jpg';
import Robin from './otters/otter2.jpg';
...
function App() {
  return (
    <div>
      <Header />
      <ul className='post-list'>
        <Post />
        <Post image={Barry} name='Barry' />
        <li className='post-component'>
...
```

Now you are ready to receive the props in Post.js. React uses the image and name attributes specified above as keys on the props object, allowing you to access their values.

In Post.js, add props as the first parameter of the function. (It is standard practice to name this parameter props.) Then, use dynamic values to replace the hardcoded values in the component.

Listing 2.6 Using prop values in a component (Post.js)

```
import Barry from '../otters/otter1.jpg';

function Post() {
function Post(props) {
    return (
        <li className='post-component'>
            <button>
                <img src={Barry} alt='Barry'/>
                <img src={props.image} alt={props.name}/>
                <p>Barry</p>
                <p>{props.name}</p>
            </button>
...
```

You inserted JavaScript into the JSX markup using {}. This syntax is called a *JSX expression*. JSX expressions are evaluated and then rendered along with the other JSX.

Look in the DevTools again and select the **Post** component. Now you can see details about the new props within the component (Figure 2.14).

Figure 2.14 Viewing **Post** props in the DevTools

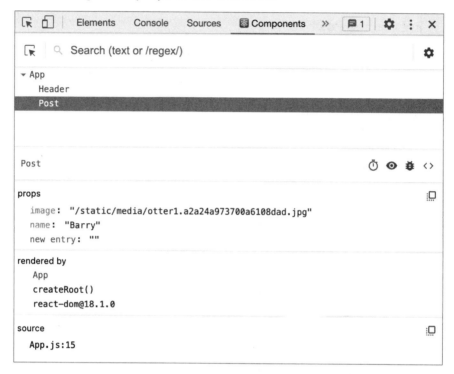

The image prop shows the string path used as the src for the <img> tag. The name prop shows the string used to display the otter's name in the post.

Now that the component can take in dynamic information, it is no longer limited to one use.

Reusing a Component

Replace the other list items in App.js with the **Post** component, using props to provide each otter's image and name.

Listing 2.7 Reusing the **Post** component (App.js)

```
...
function App() {
  return (
    <div>
      <Header />
      <ul className='post-list'>
        <Post image={Barry} name='Barry' />
        <li className='post component'>
          <button>
            <img src={Robin} alt='Robin'/>
            <p>Robin</p>
          </button>
        </li>
        <li className='post component'>
          <button>
            <img src={Maurice} alt='Maurice'/>
            <p>Maurice</p>
          </button>
        </li>
        <li className='post component'>
          <button>
            <img src={Lesley} alt='Lesley'/>
            <p>Lesley</p>
          </button>
        </li>
        <li className='post component'>
          <button>
            <img src={Barbara} alt='Barbara'/>
            <p>Barbara</p>
          </button>
        </li>
        <Post image={Robin} name='Robin' />
        <Post image={Maurice} name='Maurice' />
        <Post image={Lesley} name='Lesley' />
        <Post image={Barbara} name='Barbara'/>
      </ul>
...
```

You can immediately see one benefit of this approach: The code is much shorter and easier to read. Also, to change the way posts are structured or how they appear on Ottergram, now you can make just one edit to the **Post** component, instead of having to edit each list item individually.

You will see this for yourself in a moment. First, save your changes and check your browser to make sure everything is working as before. Now you will see the same charming otter posts, and the DevTools will show that you are seeing them in a series of **Post** components (Figure 2.15).

Figure 2.15 Multiple components

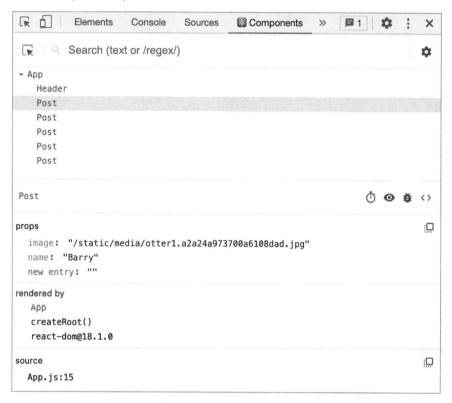

Let's jazz things up a bit. The otter's names should stand out more. Thanks to your **Post** component, you can add styling to all the posts with one change.

In your stylesheet, App.css, add a new style rule for the class post-name to make the text larger and bold.

Listing 2.8 Adding style for post-name (App.css)

```css
...
.selected-item p {
  display: flex;
  justify-content: center;
  font-size: 2.5em;
}

.post-component .post-name {
  font-weight: bold;
  font-size: 2em;
}
```

Now, in your **Post** component, add post-name as a className to the paragraph element.

Listing 2.9 Adding a new className (Post.js)

```
function Post(props) {
    return (
        <li className='post-component'>
          <button>
            <img src={props.image} alt={props.name}/>
            <p>{props.name}</p>
            <p className="post-name">{props.name}</p>
          </button>
...
```

Save your files and return to your browser. Check out the names of each otter (Figure 2.16).

Figure 2.16 Bold otter names

Even though you added the className only one time, the change shows up for each **Post** component. This is much better than manually adding the class to each individual element.

Object destructuring

As it is written, the props object does not give you a lot of insight into what data the component expects. Because the props argument is a JavaScript object, you can destructure it to get the individual props.

Destructuring the props in the component signature is useful for future developers using the component. It helps provide documentation for what data the component needs. It also makes the code easier to read by eliminating the props prefix.

Destructure the props in Post.js.

Listing 2.10 Destructuring props (Post.js)

```
function Post(props) {
function Post({ image, name }) {
    return (
        <li className='post-component'>
          <button>
            <img src={props.image} alt={props.name}/>
            <img src={image} alt={name}/>
            <p className="post-name">{props.name}</p>
            <p className="post-name">{name}</p>
          </button>
...
```

Save your file and check Ottergram in the browser to confirm that everything still looks the same.

Rendering Lists

The **Post** component has streamlined your list item code in App.js. But adding posts one at a time is still somewhat tedious. And if you were working with more than a small list of otters, adding each post could easily become an impossible task.

There is a better way.

In a real-world app, the items you add to a list will probably be related to each other in some way. The data will likely be grouped in an array or another structure, and it might come from an external source or from a data set within your app.

And when you want to render data from a list of individual components, React has tools to help you.

To see how this works, begin modeling a more realistic setup by creating an array with the data you currently have. (Although it would be most true to life for your data to come from an external source or a separate data file, go ahead and hardcode your array in App.js.)

Listing 2.11 Creating an array of otters (App.js)

```
...
import Barbara from './otters/otter5.jpg';

const ottersArray = [
  { image: Barry, name: 'Barry' },
  { image: Robin, name: 'Robin' },
  { image: Maurice, name: 'Maurice' },
  { image: Lesley, name: 'Lesley' },
  { image: Barbara, name: 'Barbara' },
];

function App() {
...
```

Now you can replace the repetitive code that creates the **Post** components. Use {} to insert JavaScript into your JSX markup. Within the JavaScript braces, use the **Array.map** function to iterate over the items in the array and return a **Post** component for each one.

Listing 2.12 Using **map** to render each post (App.js)

```
...
function App() {
  return (
    <div>
      <Header />
      <ul className='post-list'>
        <Post image={Barry} name='Barry' />
        <Post image={Robin} name='Robin' />
        <Post image={Maurice} name='Maurice' />
        <Post image={Lesley} name='Lesley' />
        <Post image={Barbara} name='Barbara'/>
        {ottersArray.map((post) => (
          <Post
            image={post.image}
            name={post.name}
          />
        ))}
      </ul>
...
```

Although there are several ways to iterate through an array in JavaScript, it is conventional to use **map** when rendering components. This is because the **map** function returns a new array, and React knows to use the elements in the returned array as children of the parent <div>.

Why break down each post into image and name and pass those as separate props?

The **Post** component is primarily about presentation. Although the post item contains only two properties right now, eventually you might decide to add more. It is best not to couple components to the format of other data, because doing so limits their reusability. Instead, pass **Post** only the information it needs to render.

Keys

Save your file and switch to the browser. Though Ottergram looks the same, there is a problem.

Using the >> in the DevTools menu bar, open the Console tab. At the bottom of the console, you will see a red warning (Figure 2.17).

Figure 2.17 Key warning in the browser

```
⊗ ▶Warning: Each child in a list should      react-jsx-dev-runtime.development.js:97
  have a unique "key" prop.

  Check the render method of `App`. See https://reactjs.org/link/warning-keys for
  more information.
      at Thumbnail (http://localhost:3000/static/js/bundle.js:217:5)
      at App
```

What happened? As the warning says, you should include a *key* as a prop for each child in the list.

A key is a value that uniquely identifies a component. React uses keys so that when an item in a list is added, removed, or changed, it can render only that item and not the full list.

Imagine an application that renders a list of thousands of items. If the user wants to change a single item, React uses the key attribute to determine which item it needs to update instead of re-rendering the entire list.

Each key must be unique among its siblings and must be consistently associated with the same piece of data. Using the same key more than once in an array results in a duplicate key warning, similar to the warning you see here, and might have unintended side effects.

You cannot insert random values as the keys. Although random values might be unique, they can change each time React re-renders the components, negating any built-in optimizations.

Similarly, the array index is not a good value to use for the key because it can change. For example, when you remove an item from the front of an array, the indexes of the following items shift by one. This means the array index is not guaranteed to consistently identify the same component.

Often, databases are built so that each element has a key or ID, which you can use as the component key in React. To simulate this, add an ID to each item in the otters array. Then, use the ID to add a key to each of the **Post** components:

Listing 2.13 Adding a key to each post (App.js)

```
...
const ottersArray = [
  { image: Barry, name: 'Barry' },
  { image: Barry, name: 'Barry', id: 1 },
  { image: Robin, name: 'Robin' },
  { image: Robin, name: 'Robin', id: 2 },
  { image: Maurice, name: 'Maurice' },
  { image: Maurice, name: 'Maurice', id: 3 },
  { image: Lesley, name: 'Lesley' },
  { image: Lesley, name: 'Lesley', id: 4 },
  { image: Barbara, name: 'Barbara' },
  { image: Barbara, name: 'Barbara', id: 5 },
];

function App() {
  return (
    ...
      {ottersArray.map((post) => (
        <Post
          key={post.id}
          image={post.image}
...
```

Save your file and head back to the browser. Reload the page; the red warning should disappear from the console.

Use the >> in the DevTools menu bar to switch to the Components tab. The new keys appear next to each component (Figure 2.18).

Figure 2.18 Keys in the Components tab

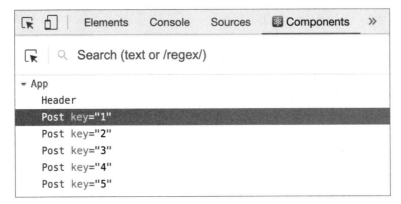

Now switch to the Elements tab. Drill down so you can see the <li> that makes up a list item. The rendered elements do not reference any keys (Figure 2.19).

Figure 2.19 No keys in the Elements tab

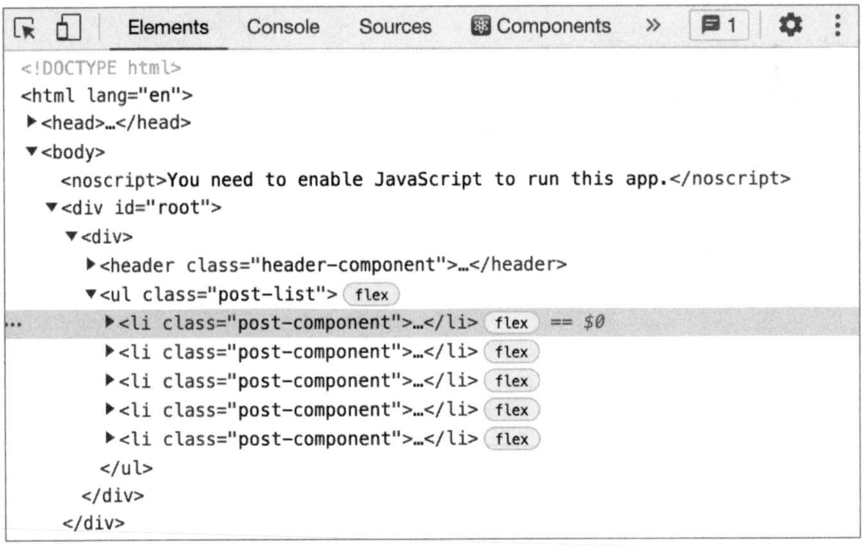

The key is a tool that React uses to optimize performance. It is not added to the HTML and does not appear in the Chrome DevTools tabs.

Conclusion

Your app is on its way to being otter-ly amazing. You broke down the Ottergram application into individual components and can see those components and their props in the React DevTools. And you are set up to render large arrays of data with just a few lines of code.

In the next chapter, you will continue to build on what you have learned and give users the ability to interact with your app by highlighting their favorite otter.

For the More Curious: Testing Prop Changes in the DevTools

The React DevTools allow you to try out changes to props and immediately see the results in your app. This can be a helpful tool when working with dynamic data.

In the props section of the Components tab, select the value of the prop you want to edit and replace it with a new value (Figure 2.20).

Figure 2.20 Editing the name prop in the DevTools

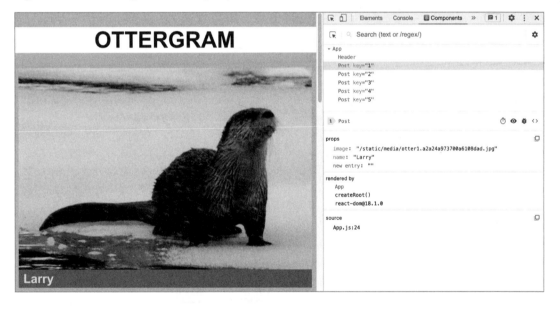

Any changes you make in the React DevTools are only temporary. They do not affect your code base, and they go away as soon as you refresh the page.

Bronze Challenge: Footer

Time to take some credit for your work! Under the list of posts, add a footer component that says Built by: *Your Name*.

Feel free to style the footer however you like.

Silver Challenge: Canarygram Footer

This challenge builds on the Canarygram challenge from Chapter 1.

First, update your Canarygram code base to use organized components, like you did with Ottergram.

Next, add a footer to Canarygram. The canaries heard about the new footer feature, but they want their own spin on it. The footer should have links to the Wikipedia pages for two different types of canaries:

- en.wikipedia.org/wiki/Atlantic_canary
- en.wikipedia.org/wiki/Yellow_canary

3

User Events

Ottergram now displays otters' images and names, and that is great. However, users expect more from a modern application. Users want to be able to *interact* with your website. For example, it would be nice if users could click one of the post items to showcase a special otter.

In this chapter, you will implement this functionality using an *event handler*. Event handlers let React know what to do when a user event, such as a button click, occurs. Handling events in React is similar to handling events in standard HTML and JavaScript   with a few differences, which we will discuss along the way.

By the end of this chapter, you will be able to select different posts and see in the Console tab that you have clicked them. And you will have built a new component to display the featured post, like Figure 3.1:

Figure 3.1 Barry takes center stage

The list of posts, each containing an image and an otter name, will be on the left, and the featured otter will be displayed on the right.

In the next chapter, you will finish your work on Ottergram by allowing the user to click any otter post to feature it.

Adding SelectedItem

Before adding an event handler, you will build a new **SelectedItem** component to display the featured otter.

You will build **SelectedItem** the same way that you built **Header** and **Post**. Start by creating a new file in the components directory called SelectedItem.js (Figure 3.2).

Figure 3.2 New SelectedItem.js file

Inside the file, write and export a component function. Similar to the **Post** component, your new **SelectedItem** component will take in the image and name as props. Return a `<div>` that contains the name and image, and include an appropriate class name for styling:

Listing 3.1 Creating the **SelectedItem** component (SelectedItem.js)

```
function SelectedItem({ image, name }) {
    return (
        <div className='selected-item'>
            <p>{name}</p>
            <img src={image} alt={name} />
        </div>
    )
}

export default SelectedItem;
```

Switch to App.js. To make the new **SelectedItem** component render in the correct position on the page, you will need some additional styling. Add a `<div>` around the `<ul>` post list with a className of app-content.

Listing 3.2 Using a content wrapper (App.js)

```
...
function App() {
  return (
    <div>
      <Header />
      <div className='app-content'>
        <ul className='post-list'>
          ...
        </ul>
      </div>
    </div>
...
```

(To fix the indentation of the lines between the new `<div>`'s opening and closing tags, you can take advantage of a Visual Studio Code shortcut: Highlight all the lines you want to indent and press the Tab key.)

Now you are ready to add your **SelectedItem** component to App.js. Import the new component at the top of the file and add the component tag directly under the closing tag for the <ul>.

For now, use the first item in the otter array as the featured otter by passing along its image and name.

Listing 3.3 Adding the **SelectedItem** component (App.js)

```
...
import Post from './components/Post';
import SelectedItem from './components/SelectedItem';
import Barry from './otters/otter1.jpg';
...
function App() {
  return (
    ...
      <ul className='post-list'>
        ...
      </ul>
      <SelectedItem
        image={ottersArray[0].image}
        name={ottersArray[0].name}
      />
    </div>
...
```

Save your files and check out the browser. Now Ottergram features a special otter (Figure 3.3).

Figure 3.3 Viewing the selected otter in the browser

Try clicking other post items in the browser.

Nothing happens. Barry the otter is still featured.

React still does not know what to do when the user clicks an item. Let's start fixing that by adding an event handler to the **Post** component.

User Events

Your component can listen for many user events, including pressing a key, moving the mouse, or submitting a form. You will listen for a click event – specifically, when the user clicks the button in **Post**.

In Post.js, create a function called **handleClick**, defining it in the body of the component function. This is the callback function that will execute every time a user clicks the button in a **Post** component. This function will have one parameter, the event.

For now, keep the function simple. Return a **console.log** statement that prints the event.

Listing 3.4 Adding a function to handle click events (Post.js)

```
function Post({ image, name }) {

    const handleClick = (event) => {
      return console.log(event)
    }

    return (
...
```

The next step is to listen for the user's click and fire the **handleClick** function.

React event listeners are very similar to event listeners in vanilla JavaScript: Both give you access to the event details. In **handleClick**, you can see that the function takes the event as a parameter.

One difference is that React uses camelCase for naming events. For example, the JavaScript **onclick** becomes **onClick** in React.

Add an **onClick** attribute to the <button> tag and set it equal to the **handleClick** prop. This will bind the function you created to the user event click on the button.

Listing 3.5 Setting the **onClick** attribute equal to the new function (Post.js)

```
function Post({ image, name }) {
    ...
    return (
        <li className='post-component'>
          <button>
          <button onClick={handleClick}>
            <img src={image} alt={name}/>
...
```

Save your files. In your browser, open the DevTools and select the Console tab. (If you do not see the Console tab, click >> in the menu bar to find it.) Click any of the otter posts. A log statement appears in the console each time you click (Figure 3.4).

Figure 3.4 Viewing console logs in the browser

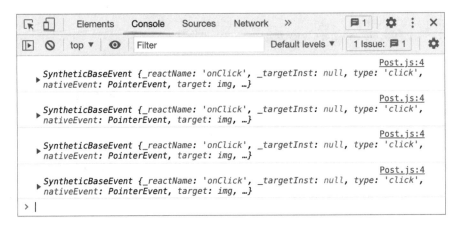

The console logs the click event as **SyntheticBaseEvent**. Because browsers have some slight differences in how they handle events, React uses **SyntheticBaseEvent** as a wrapper around native events to ensure that events behave the same across all browsers. You will learn more about events in Chapter 13.

Passing Parameters

Currently, you log the event to the console to test that the event handler works. In a more complex application, you might use the event's **preventDefault** function to avoid side effects, such as navigation or form submission, when the user clicks a button. But clicking the otter button does not cause any side effects, so you will not need to use the event.

Instead, it will be more helpful to log the name of the otter.

In React, you often need to pass parameters to the event handler. Therefore, although **handleClick** can already access the otter name from the props, you will pass name to it as a parameter. In Post.js, update **handleClick** to accept otterName as a parameter, then log this name to the console. In the **onClick** handler, pass name to the **handleClick** function.

(This code change will produce unexpected results. You will fix it in the next section.)

Listing 3.6 Passing the otter's name (Post.js)

```
function Post({ image, name }) {

    const handleClick = (event) => {
    const handleClick = (otterName) => {
      return console.log(event)
      return console.log('You clicked ' + otterName)
    }

    return (
        <li className='post-component'>
        <button onClick={handleClick}>
        <button onClick={handleClick(name)}>
            <img src={image} alt={name}/>
...
```

Save your file, refresh your browser, and check out the Console tab (Figure 3.5).

Figure 3.5 All otter names in the console

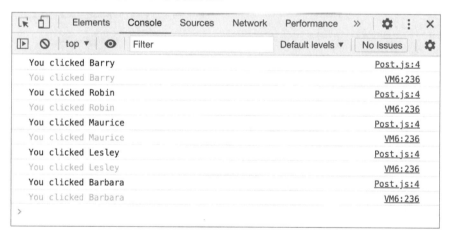

The console prints out all the otters' names before you click anything. What is happening here?

As each **Post** component renders, it calls the **handleClick** function. React executes the content inside curly braces, so {handleClick(name)} executes the **handleClick** function and binds the *result* to **onClick**, rather than binding the function itself.

This is a common mistake developers make in React. To fix it, you need to pass a function. You can do this by creating an anonymous function inline. Then, you bind the new function to **onClick** so it executes only when the user clicks the button.

Refactor your code to use an anonymous arrow function.

Listing 3.7 Refactoring to use an arrow function (`Post.js`)

```
function Post({ image, name }) {
    ...
    return (
        <li className='post-component'>
            <button onClick={handleClick(name)}>
            <button onClick={() => handleClick(name)}>
                <img src={image} alt={name}/>
...
```

Save your file and refresh your browser. Watch the console as you click a few posts. Now the console logs an otter's name only when you click that otter's post (Figure 3.6).

Figure 3.6 Otter names in the console

Conclusion

Congratulations!

You added a new component that shows off a selected otter, and you implemented an **onClick** event handler that fires every time a user clicks on the button element.

There is still one more step: When the user clicks a new otter, you need to update the otter displayed in the **SelectedItem** component. In the next chapter, you will implement state in React and get started with React hooks to tackle this issue.

For the More Curious: Alternate file-naming conventions

You have been naming your component files using PascalCase. This is the most common component filename convention, and it is the style that the Create React App template uses. However, React allows you to find a style that works best for your project and team. You can also use camelCase, snake_case, or kebab-case.

Also, you are using the `.js` extension for all files that use JavaScript. Out in the wild, you might also see the `.jsx` extension for files that contain JSX. Although this is not required, it is useful if you want to designate which files contain JSX.

For the More Curious: Detaching Event Handlers

In JavaScript, you might have come across code that looks like this:

```
EventTarget.addEventListener()
EventTarget.removeEventListener()
```

Neglecting to remove an event listener after attaching it can result in unexpected behavior or memory leaks.

Although it is possible to add and remove event listeners manually in React, the best practice is to bind the event handler using the component attributes, as you did in this chapter. React automatically attaches the click event handler to the component when the page loads, updates it with any changes during the lifecycle of the component, and detaches it when the user leaves the page.

Letting React worry about this for you saves you a lot of effort and ensures that there are no issues resulting from event handlers that you attached but never detached.

Bronze Challenge: Hello, Goodbye

As we mentioned earlier, React provides many event handlers for your components. For example, there are event handlers that can tell you when a user hovers their mouse over one of your components and when they move away.

Use these events to log Hello, {otterName} when the mouse enters a **Post** component and Goodbye, {otterName} when the mouse leaves that component.

Hint: You will want to use the **onMouseEnter** and **onMouseLeave** events, which work similarly to **onClick**.

You can read about all the available events at reactjs.org/docs/events.html.

Silver Challenge: Canary Alert

Continue to apply what you have learned to Canarygram by setting up a **SelectedPost** component to feature a star canary. Feel free to play around with the styling.

Although the selected post feature is not quite finished, the canaries want their app in the hands of their alpha users right away. Simple logging is not enough for them. Instead, when a user clicks a post, show an alert, using

```
window.alert('You clicked ' + canaryName);
```

so they can see that they have clicked the post without having to open the DevTools console.

4

State

While it is great that Barry the otter is getting some time to shine, all the otters should have equal opportunities for fame. Your app currently listens for user events and responds by logging the name of the otter that the user clicks. In this chapter, you will finish up Ottergram by adding *state* to keep track of and display the featured otter.

This chapter introduces React *hooks*, a powerful tool for managing state in a component. You will continue to learn about hooks throughout this book, so do not worry about mastering them right away. In this chapter, you will focus on using the **useState** hook to manage a component's state.

By the end of this chapter, your Ottergram application will be complete (Figure 4.1).

Figure 4.1 Completed Ottergram

What Is State?

You have been using props to pass data to your React components. A component can take the information it receives through props and render that information onscreen.

The information passed using props is external to a component. But what about internal data?

When a component needs to manage information internally, that information is called the component's *state*. A component can create, update, and use an object to manage its own state.

React ensures that what you return from your component matches what renders onscreen. When a component's state changes, it triggers React to re-render the component and its children, updating the UI to match the new data.

Internally, React maintains a virtual Document Object Model, or *DOM*. After re-rendering, React compares the old DOM and a new virtual DOM to determine what needs to change in the real DOM. Then, it updates the real DOM in the browser, which updates what users see onscreen.

Using the virtual DOM is a performance improvement in React, since updating the real DOM is slower than updating the virtual DOM. By minimizing the number of updates made to the real DOM, React can load the needed changes more quickly.

We say that React is *declarative* because you declare the new state you want to display onscreen, and React handles the job of getting it there.

useState

The tool you use to access a component's state is a React hook called `useState`.

Until React 16.8 introduced React hooks, all components with internal state had to be written as classes. An advantage of class components is that they do not automatically re-render when their parent component re-renders, the way functional components do. However, class components are generally more complex and contain more boilerplate code than functional components.

Hooks provide functional components (such as the ones you have been creating) with access to state and other React features, largely eliminating the need for complex classes. You can read more about functional and class components in the section called "For the More Curious: Components – Functions vs Classes" near the end of this chapter. And there are additional tools you can use to protect against automatic re-renders in functional components, which you will learn about in Chapter 19.

At their core, hooks are JavaScript functions that accept arguments and return specific values. The `useState` hook takes one argument: the initial state value. It returns an array with two values: the current state value and a function for updating the state. (Incidentally, all hooks in React have names that begin with use – this makes them easy to identify.)

Open `App.js` in Visual Studio Code.

Add a piece of state called `selectedPostName` using the **useState** hook. Later, you will use `selectedPostName` with the `ottersArray` to find the currently selected otter. For now, set the initial value of the state to `Barry` to select Barry the otter.

Listing 4.1 Creating the `selectedPostName` state (`App.js`)

```
import { useState } from 'react';
import './App.css';
...
function App() {
  const [selectedPostName, setSelectedPostName] = useState('Barry');

  return (
...
```

You import **useState** from React so that you can use it in the component. You must always import React hooks before you can use them.

Then you use array destructuring to get two items from the returned array: the current state value and the function that updates it. Without array destructuring, you would need several lines of code:

```
const selectedPostState = useState('Barry');
const selectedPostName = selectedPostState[0];
const setSelectedPostName = selectedPostState[1];
```

It is conventional to take advantage of array destructuring when creating state. Destructuring makes your code easier to write and to read.

Though you can name the variables created from the array whatever you want, it is a best practice for the name of the update function to start with the word `set`, followed by the state name. This makes it easy to see that the state and its update function are related.

Save your file, make sure your development server is running, and switch to the browser. Open the Components tab in the React DevTools and inspect the **App** component. You now have new information available to you about the component: You can see the component's state in the hooks section (Figure 4.2).

Figure 4.2 Viewing state in the React DevTools

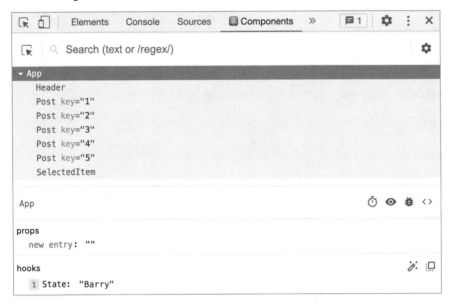

A component can pass down a state value as a prop to another component. As the next step toward displaying the selected otter, update the props for **SelectedItem** to use the state.

Listing 4.2 Using `selectedPostName` to show the featured otter (`App.js`)

```
...
function App() {
  const [selectedPostName, setSelectedPostName] = useState('Barry');
  const selectedPost = ottersArray.find(otter => otter.name === selectedPostName);

  return (
    ...
      </ul>
      <SelectedItem
        image={ottersArray[0].image}
        image={selectedPost.image}
        name={ottersArray[0].name}
        name={selectedPost.name}
      />
...
```

Here, you add a new variable: `selectedPost`. Since the state contains only the name of the otter, you use the **Array.find** method to find the array item with a matching name. You then use `selectedPost` to pass along the correct props.

However, because the value of `selectedPostName` is currently hardcoded as `Barry`, Barry will remain the featured otter until the state updates.

Updating State

Recall that **useState** returns your update function, **setSelectedPostName**. You will use this function to update the state value to a new ID when the user clicks a **Post** component. **setSelectedPostName** will take one argument, the updated state value, and use it to replace the existing state value.

But there is a problem: Although the click handler lives in the **Post** component, the state and the function to update it live in App.js.

No worries!

You can also pass functions as props. You will pass **setSelectedPostName** as a prop to the **Post** component. The **Post** component can then call **setSelectedPostName** each time the user clicks a post.

Add a **setSelectedPostName** attribute to the **Post** component in App.js. Set it equal to the update function returned from **useState**.

Listing 4.3 Passing **setSelectedPostName** as a prop to **Post** (App.js)

```
...
function App() {
  ...
  return (
    ...
      <ul className='post-list'>
        ...
            image={post.image}
            name={post.name}
            setSelectedPostName={setSelectedPostName}
        />
...
```

Now, in Post.js, you have access to the **setSelectedPostName** update function. Add it to the destructured props. Replace the **handleClick** function with a call to **setSelectedPostName**, still passing the name as an argument.

Listing 4.4 Using **setSelectedPostName** in **Post** (Post.js)

```
function Post({ image, name }) {
function Post({ image, name, setSelectedPostName }) {

    const handleClick = (otterName) => {
      return console.log('You clicked ' + otterName)
    }

    return (
        <li className='post-component'>
          <button onClick={() => handleClick(name)}>
          <button onClick={() => setSelectedPostName(name)}>
            <img src={image} alt={name}/>
...
```

Save your files and return to the browser. Click different **Post** components. The selected otter updates each time you click a new **Post**.

Conclusion

Congratulations! Your first React application is complete. You built React components and used props and state to display data in Ottergram. You will continue to build on what you have learned in your next application.

But for now, take a deep breath. You did it!

For the More Curious: Components - Functions vs Classes

Although most newer React applications use functional components, you will probably come across class components at some point.

As we have said, writing a component as a class is still valid React code. This is how Ottergram's **Post** component would look as a class component.

```jsx
import React from "react";

class Post extends React.Component {
    constructor(props) {
        super(props);
        this.state = null;
        this.handleClick = this.handleClick.bind(this);
    }

    handleClick() {
        this.props.setSelectedPostName(this.props.name);
    }

    render() {
        return (
            <li className='post'>
                <button onClick={this.handleClick}>
                    <img src={this.props.image} alt={this.props.name} />
                    <p>{this.props.name}</p>
                </button>
            </li>
        )
    }
}
```

Class components extend **React.Component** and return JSX inside a method called **render**. Although the **render** method is the only required method for class components, you can also add other actions as methods.

In this version of the **Post** component, the event handler, **handleClick**, is a class method rather than an inline handler. Inline click handlers are much more common in functional components than class components, where they are frequently class methods.

Class components also have access to several other built-in methods. These include component lifecycle methods, such as **componentDidMount**, **componentDidUpdate**, and **componentWillUnmount**, which developers use to control component behavior during the React render cycle. Although functional components do not have access to these lifecycle methods, you can achieve similar behavior using hooks.

Notice the use of the keyword `this` in this class-based version of **Post**. `this` is a special, reserved word in JavaScript, used to contain contextual data.

In class components, `this` often refers to the value of the class object. However, functions or methods inside the class, including the constructor, can return different values of `this`, depending on the scope.

In this class-based **Post** component, `this.props` gives you access to the component's props. Similarly, `this.state` returns the current value of the component's state. (In this example, the state value is null.)

You must bind the **handleClick** method to the class in the constructor. **handleClick** accesses the value of `this` inside the function when calling **this.props.setSelectedPostName**. Binding the method ties the value of `this` to the class object, rather than to the method itself. Otherwise, `this.props` would be undefined because the method does not have `props`.

Although you can also access `this` in functional components, you would almost never use it. In functions, the value of `this` depends on how you call the function and whether you enable strict mode.

`this` has always been confusing to learn and talk about. Its complexity has led to many difficult-to-find bugs. Thankfully, functional components use `this` only sparingly. We recommend that you minimize your use of `this` to avoid unintended behavior.

Gold Challenge: Canary Shuffle

Note: You can work on this challenge in a copy of Ottergram if you have not been building Canarygram.

The canaries have asked for one last feature: Each of them would like a chance to be the first post displayed in the list of posts.

Add a Shuffle button that will reorder the canaries' posts. The first post should move to the last spot, and the other posts should move up one spot.

In addition to creating another `<button>` and click event handler, you will need to create a new state value in App.js that holds the `canariesArray`.

Hint: For React to pick up changes to the state value, you will need to pass a new array to the **setState** function instead of mutating the original array. One way to create a new array is with the spread operator (`...`).

If you get stuck, you can ask questions in the forum for this book at forums.bignerdranch.com.

5

Linting

In this chapter, you will set up the Code Café application, which you will build over the next 15 chapters.

Code Café will be an e-commerce site that features food and drinks for sale. When the application is complete, users will be able to add items to their carts, edit their carts, check out, and submit their orders. You will also add authentication to allow users to log in to the site.

Figure 5.1 shows a preview of the application's completed home page.

Figure 5.1 Completed Code Café

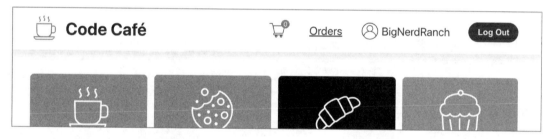

You already have experience setting up a React project, so this chapter will give you the opportunity to practice what you have learned.

In addition to the basic setup process you saw with Ottergram, you will set up JavaScript *linting* for Code Café. A linter is a tool that helps enforce code styles and detect potential errors. You will frequently see developers use linting in React production code. The linting rules you set up here will familiarize you with what linters can offer and help you troubleshoot when you run into warnings or errors in the future.

By the end of this chapter, you will have a new React project that you will be able to see running in the browser. You will also have installed a linting tool and fixed any code errors it has found.

Creating a Project

Begin by creating a new project using Create React App. In your terminal, open a new tab or window and navigate to your react-book projects folder. Use the create-react-app tool to create a new React application called code-cafe:

```
npx create-react-app code-cafe
```

When the script is complete and you see the success message in your terminal, navigate to the new project. Remember that Create React App creates your application in a subdirectory named for your project title, so change your terminal to that directory with the cd command:

```
cd code-cafe
```

Next, go ahead and start the development server by running

```
npm start
```

The tool might open the new application in a browser window for you. If it does not, open a new Chrome window and go to http://localhost:3000 to view the default React application (Figure 5.2).

Figure 5.2 Create React App

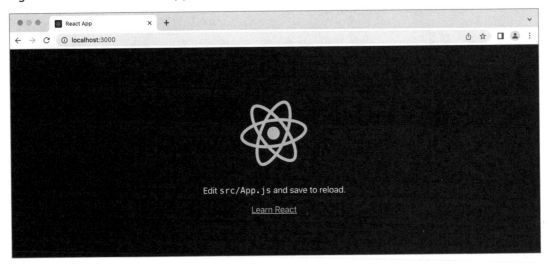

Running npx create-react-app automatically installs the latest version of Create React App. If the differences between your version of Create React App and the code you see in the book are confusing, copy the solution code for this chapter from your downloaded resources file (resources/solutions/05-linting) and use that code when proceeding to the next chapter.

Updating the Title and Favicon

First things first: You will update the default title and image that Create React App generated. As you learned in Chapter 1, the title and favicon give users visual cues about your application when they are navigating across the web.

You will follow the same process to update these items that you used for Ottergram, so feel free to try it on your own before looking at the steps and code below. (The favicon file is provided for you in your downloaded resources file.) Remember that you might need to manually refresh your browser to see the updated title and favicon.

In Visual Studio Code, open the code-cafe project folder by selecting File → Open Folder... in the top navigation bar and then choosing code-cafe from your react-book projects folder (Figure 5.3).

Figure 5.3 Opening the Code Café folder

Once the project is open, make sure the explorer pane is visible so you can navigate between files easily. If the explorer is not visible, toggle it by clicking the top icon in the left sidebar (Figure 5.4).

Figure 5.4 Toggling the explorer

Start by updating the title so that the name of your application appears on the browser tab: Open `public/index.html` and change the text in the `<title>` tag to read Code Café.

Listing 5.1 Updating the application title (`index.html`)

```
<!DOCTYPE html>
<html lang="en">
  <head>
    ...
    <!--
      Notice the use of %PUBLIC_URL% in the tags above.
      ...
    -->
    <title>React App</title>
    <title>Code Café</title>
  </head>
...
```

Now users will see the correct title when they navigate to your site (Figure 5.5).

Figure 5.5 Title on the browser tab

Next, update the favicon.

All the icons you will need for Code Café, including the favicon, are in your downloaded resources file.

In your device's file explorer, copy the `favicon.ico`, `logo192.png`, and `logo512.png` files from `code-cafe-resources` and use them to replace the files with the same names in your project's `public` directory.

Refresh your browser to see your new icon, now nicely representing Code Café (Figure 5.6).

Figure 5.6 Favicon on the browser tab

Good – you have customized your site info so users can find Code Café.

Linting Overview

Before you jump into building Code Café, you will configure *ESLint* and add linting rules to your application.

ESLint is a popular JavaScript linter that is automatically included in projects created with Create React App.

Most React projects and teams you work on will have a set of linting rules developers must adhere to. A linter provides two main benefits:

1. It flags code that is not consistent with style rules.

   Whether working on a team or as an individual, you will likely want consistency across your code base. Setting up style rules helps ensure uniformity and enforce code patterns, which in turn make your project easier to maintain.

2. It provides immediate feedback when it detects potential errors, so you can correct the code before the application runs.

This is helpful because JavaScript is a *dynamically typed* language. When you create a variable, JavaScript does not assign the variable type until the browser uses the variable. Although this increases the flexibility of JavaScript, it also introduces the potential for *runtime errors*. These are errors that do not occur until the application is running in the browser.

Think back to Ottergram. You observed a couple of errors in the Chrome console. Those were runtime errors.

Linting flags code during the development process to catch and prevent runtime errors.

Setting up a linter in Code Café will emulate working in a production environment.

Linting Rules

To use ESLint, you must choose and configure the rules you want to use.

ESLint has hundreds of rules you can enable. For example, ESLint can perform inspections for unused or missing variables, which can indicate misspelled words or incorrect import statements that will lead to errors.

ESLint can also enforce the use of semicolons in code. Look at the function below:

```
const sum = () => {
  return
    (
      2 + 1
    );
}
```

At first glance, it appears that the function **sum** returns the value of 2 + 1, which is 3. However, because of JavaScript's automatic semicolon insertion, this code actually evaluates as

```
const sum = () => {
  return;
    (
      2 + 1
    );
}
```

With the addition of the semicolon after the `return` keyword, **sum** returns `undefined` and never evaluates the remaining code.

With the `semi` rule enabled, ESLint will point out the missing semicolon after the `return` keyword, alerting you to a potential problem. You can then rewrite the function to work as intended:

```
const sum = () => {
  return (
    2 + 1
  );
}
```

So, do you need to sort through the hundreds of available rules to find the ones you want to apply? Thankfully, no. There are many preconfigured rule sets available to save you time and effort. You will see how this works in a moment.

Open a new terminal window and navigate to the code-cafe directory. Run the following command to see the ESLint configurations included with Create React App:

```
npm ls eslint
```

The output will look similar to this:

```
└─┬ react-scripts@5.0.1
  ├─┬ eslint-config-react-app@7.0.1
  │ ├─┬ @babel/eslint-parser@7.18.9
  │ │ └── eslint@8.23.0 deduped
  │ ├─┬ @typescript-eslint/eslint-plugin@5.36.2
  │ │ ├─┬ @typescript-eslint/type-utils@5.36.2
  │ │ │ └── eslint@8.23.0 deduped
  │ │ ├─┬ @typescript-eslint/utils@5.36.2
  │ │ │ └── eslint@8.23.0 deduped
  │ │ └── eslint@8.23.0 deduped
  │ ├─┬ @typescript-eslint/parser@5.36.2
  │ │ └── eslint@8.23.0 deduped
  │ ├─┬ eslint-plugin-flowtype@8.0.3
  │ │ └── eslint@8.23.0 deduped
  │ ├─┬ eslint-plugin-import@2.26.0
  │ │ └── eslint@8.23.0 deduped
  │ ├─┬ eslint-plugin-jest@25.7.0
  │ │ ├─┬ @typescript-eslint/experimental-utils@5.36.2
  │ │ │ └── eslint@8.23.0 deduped
  │ │ └── eslint@8.23.0 deduped
  │ ├─┬ eslint-plugin-jsx-a11y@6.6.1
  │ │ └── eslint@8.23.0 deduped
  │ ├─┬ eslint-plugin-react-hooks@4.6.0
  │ │ └── eslint@8.23.0 deduped
  │ ├─┬ eslint-plugin-react@7.31.8
  │ │ └── eslint@8.23.0 deduped
  │ ├─┬ eslint-plugin-testing-library@5.6.3
  │ │ └── eslint@8.23.0 deduped
  │ └── eslint@8.23.0 deduped
  ├─┬ eslint-webpack-plugin@3.2.0
  │ └── eslint@8.23.0 deduped
  ├─┬ eslint@8.23.0
  │ └─┬ eslint-utils@3.0.0
  │   └── eslint@8.23.0 deduped
  └─┬ react-dev-utils@12.0.1
    └─┬ fork-ts-checker-webpack-plugin@6.5.2
      └── eslint@8.23.0 deduped
```

At its base, ESLint provides rules for writing JavaScript code. You can add rules via plugins, which are special files that add rules not included in the default eslint package.

eslint-config-react-app is listed directly under react-scripts and contains a number of plugins as dependencies. This file configures some basic ESLint rules as well as the default rule settings for the plugins it contains. eslint-config-react-app and its plugin dependencies are published as npm packages, and you can find a list of rules they provide on the npm website at www.npmjs.com/package/eslint-config-react-app.

Although eslint-config-react-app is useful for writing React code, it is not as strict as other rule sets. Its focus on React means that there are several JavaScript lint rules it does not enforce. This leaves the potential for problems to arise.

In addition to this configuration, you will use a popular set of ESLint rules put together by Airbnb. Airbnb's rule set includes rules for React and JavaScript, such as the semi rule from the example above. Though this rule set is opinionated, the preset lint rules will eliminate formatting discrepancies and result in code that is easy to read.

Like eslint-config-react-app and its included plugins, the Airbnb rule set is published on npm. The style guide available at github.com/airbnb/javascript provides more information on each rule.

Installing and configuring Airbnb's ESLint

To add the Airbnb-configured rule set to the included ESLint configuration, install it by running the following command in the same terminal window you used earlier:

```
npm install eslint-config-airbnb@19.0.4
```

There is no need to install additional plugins, because Airbnb's rule set uses the same ones included with Create React App.

Linting packages update frequently, with their developers adding or removing default linting rules. The command above specifies the version number of the package with the syntax eslint-config-airbnb@version.

As you work through Code Café, using this version will ensure consistency between your code and what you see in the book. Generally, in your own development work, you will want to install the most recent versions of packages, using just the package name without a version number.

When the installation is complete, you might see output like this warning about vulnerabilities:

```
6 high severity vulnerabilities

To address all issues (including breaking changes), run:
  npm audit fix --force

Run `npm audit` for details.
```

npm audit runs behind the scenes each time npm installs a new package. Although you should never ignore security warnings, npm audit often flags items that are not applicable to your project or are false positives. In this case, because the code is running on only your machine and you are the only one accessing the website, you can continue without further action.

If you are concerned and want to investigate further, run the npm audit command again locally to list the security vulnerabilities that npm identified when it installed the package.

npm audit also gives you the option to fix any problems with the command npm audit fix --force. Running this command will likely force updates to other dependencies in your project, causing new vulnerabilities or errors that will make it difficult to follow along in the book. If you choose to run this command, we recommend that you first make a backup of your project by copying the files or using Git, so you can revert if needed.

Next, open package.json in Visual Studio Code. The package you just installed is included under dependencies:

```
{
  "name": "code-cafe",
  "version": "0.1.0",
  "private": true,
  "dependencies": {
    "@testing-library/jest-dom": "^5.16.5",
    "@testing-library/react": "^13.4.0",
    "@testing-library/user-event": "^13.5.0",
    "eslint-config-airbnb": "^19.0.4",
    "react": "^18.2.0",
    "react-dom": "^18.2.0",
    "react-scripts": "5.0.1",
    "web-vitals": "^2.1.4"
  },
  "scripts": {
    ...
}
```

Could you have manually added the new package dependency to package.json? Yes, but it is not recommended. Using the npm install command to add dependencies ensures that you do not accidentally introduce conflicts between package.json and package-lock.json (which, you might recall, includes the version numbers of every installed dependency).

Although you have added the Airbnb rule set as a dependency to Code Café, you still need to configure it so you can use it in your project.

In package.json, take a look at the eslintConfig setup, below the dependencies and scripts sections. The configuration files listed in this section provide the rules and options that ESLint will use to flag potential problems.

```
"eslintConfig": {
    "extends": [
      "react-app",
      "react-app/jest"
    ]
},
```

The extends property points to any configuration files that should be included when ESLint runs.

The two configuration files that are extended here, react-app and react-app/jest, relate to the eslint-config-react-app rule set that Create React App added. Although react-app/jest is included with eslint-config-react-app, you must explicitly extend it to use it.

Similarly, eslint-config-airbnb contains both the airbnb configuration file, which contains Airbnb's default style rules, and another file called airbnb/hooks, which includes additional rules for React hooks.

Add both `airbnb` and `airbnb/hooks` to the list of configuration files to extend.

Listing 5.2 Extending Airbnb's ESLint (`package.json`)

```
...
"eslintConfig": {
  "extends": [
    "react-app",
    "react-app/jest"
    "react-app/jest",
    "airbnb",
    "airbnb/hooks"
  ]
},
...
```

Now ESLint will include Airbnb's linting rules.

Running ESLint

Now that you have ESLint configured with the rule sets you want to use, you can use it to identify potential problems.

By default, Create React App does not include a script for running the linter. To run it manually, target the project ESLint file by executing the following command in your terminal:

```
node_modules/.bin/eslint src --max-warnings=0
```

In addition to specifying the `eslint` path, this script adds two parameters, `src` and `max-warnings`.

`src` specifies that ESLint should check files in only the `src` directory. (Remember, ESLint is a JavaScript linter.)

As for `max-warnings`, ESLint has two levels of checks: warnings and errors. By default, if ESLint finds any errors, it will exit with an error status. If there are warnings but no errors, the lint check will resolve successfully.

Adding the `max-warnings` option forces ESLint to exit with an error status if the number of warnings exceeds the value you set. Because you set `max-warnings` to `0`, ESLint will exit with an error status if it finds any warnings or errors. Though engineering teams each handle warnings differently, it is common to limit the number of lint warnings in production code.

Typing out this entire command every time you want to run the linter would be cumbersome, so you will add a script to make life simpler.

In `package.json`, find the `scripts` section and add a new script called `lint` to run `eslint`.

Listing 5.3 Adding a `lint` script (`package.json`)

```
...
"scripts": {
  "start": "react-scripts start",
  "build": "react-scripts build",
  "test": "react-scripts test",
  "lint": "eslint src --max-warnings=0",
  "eject": "react-scripts eject"
},
...
```

Because `react-scripts` includes `eslint`, you do not need to specify the file path in this script.

Now you can use the command `npm run lint` in the terminal to run ESLint and check your code style. Try it out.

Oops, you already have lint errors! Why?

Take a look at the errors in your terminal. Your output might be slightly different, depending on your version of Create React App. (Also, we have broken each line of output to fit on the printed page.)

```
/.../code-cafe/src/App.js
    6:5    error  'React' must be in scope when using JSX
                                             react/react-in-jsx-scope
    6:5    error  JSX not allowed in files with extension '.js'
                                             react/jsx-filename-extension
    7:7    error  'React' must be in scope when using JSX
                                             react/react-in-jsx-scope
    8:9    error  'React' must be in scope when using JSX
                                             react/react-in-jsx-scope
    9:9    error  'React' must be in scope when using JSX
                                             react/react-in-jsx-scope
   10:16   error  `code` must be placed on a new line
                                             react/jsx-one-expression-per-line
   10:16   error  'React' must be in scope when using JSX
                                             react/react-in-jsx-scope
   10:39   error  ` and save to reload. ` must be placed on a new line
                                             react/jsx-one-expression-per-line
   12:9    error  'React' must be in scope when using JSX
                                             react/react in jsx-scope

/.../code-cafe/src/App.test.js
    5:10   error  'React' must be in scope when using JSX
                                             react/react-in-jsx-scope
    5:10   error  JSX not allowed in files with extension '.js'
                                             react/jsx-filename-extension

/.../code-cafe/src/index.js
    9:3    error  JSX not allowed in files with extension '.js'
                                             react/jsx-filename-extension
   11:22   error  Missing trailing comma
                                             comma-dangle

/.../code-cafe/src/reportWebVitals.js
    1:25   error  Expected parentheses around arrow function argument
                                             arrow-parens
    3:32   error  Expected a line break after this opening brace
                                             object-curly-newline
    3:74   error  Expected a line break before this closing brace
                                             object-curly-newline

✖ 16 problems (16 errors, 0 warnings)
  6 errors and 0 warnings potentially fixable with the `--fix` option.
```

The problem is that Create React App does not adhere fully to the lint rules from Airbnb that you configured. ESLint has identified 16 problems in the code and listed them by file.

Several of the errors that ESLint identified are related to just two rules: `react/react-in-jsx-scope` and `react/jsx-filename-extension`. In a moment, you will learn why these rules exist and how to modify them. For now, ignoring those two rules leaves six other errors to review.

The ESLint output shows the file and line number where the error occurs. Open `src/App.js`. ESLint identified two errors on line 10 in this file, both related to the rule `react/jsx-one-expression-per-line`.

Take a look at line 10:

```
Edit <code>src/App.js</code> and save to reload.
```

This line is triggering errors because the `<code>` element is on the same line as the text, instead of being on its own line.

Update the code so that each expression is on its own line.

Listing 5.4 Fixing the ESLint `jsx-one-expression-per-line` error (App.js)

```
...
function App() {
  return (
    <div className="App">
      <header className="App-header">
        <img src={logo} className="App-logo" alt="logo" />
        <p>
          Edit <code>src/App.js</code> and save to reload.
          Edit
          {' '}
          <code>src/App.js</code>
          {' '}
          and save to reload.
        </p>
...
```

JSX removes whitespace between lines. To make the text render correctly, you add lines of code with strings containing a space. This is a workaround you will see out in the wild.

Run the lint command again (`npm run lint`). The errors related to `react/jsx-one-expression-per-line` disappear from `src/App.js`:

```
/.../code-cafe/src/App.js
   6:5   error  'React' must be in scope when using JSX
                                                 react/react-in-jsx-scope
   6:5   error  JSX not allowed in files with extension '.js'
                                                 react/jsx-filename-extension
   7:7   error  'React' must be in scope when using JSX
                                                 react/react-in-jsx-scope
   8:9   error  'React' must be in scope when using JSX
                                                 react/react-in-jsx-scope
   9:9   error  'React' must be in scope when using JSX
                                                 react/react-in-jsx-scope
  10:16  error  'React' must be in scope when using JSX
                                                 react/react-in-jsx-scope
  12:9   error  'React' must be in scope when using JSX
                                                 react/react-in-jsx-scope

/.../code-cafe/src/App.test.js
  5:10  error  'React' must be in scope when using JSX
                                                 react/react-in-jsx-scope
  5:10  error  JSX not allowed in files with extension '.js'
                                                 react/jsx-filename-extension

/.../code-cafe/src/index.js
   9:3   error  JSX not allowed in files with extension '.js'
                                                 react/jsx-filename-extension
  11:22  error  Missing trailing comma
                                                 comma-dangle

/.../code-cafe/src/reportWebVitals.js
  1:25  error  Expected parentheses around arrow function argument
                                                 arrow-parens
  3:32  error  Expected a line break after this opening brace
                                                 object-curly-newline
  3:74  error  Expected a line break before this closing brace
                                                 object-curly-newline

✖ 14 problems (14 errors, 0 warnings)
  4 errors and 0 warnings potentially fixable with the `--fix` option.
```

Now open `src/index.js` and notice that line 11 is missing a trailing comma – which the `comma-dangle` rule requires, as the output above indicates. Do not fix this error yet. Instead, open `src/reportWebVitals.js` and review lines 1 and 3 for the errors indicated in the output.

(If you are not sure why any of the lines flagged in the output violates a rule, you can find more information on the rules in the ESLint documentation: eslint.org/docs/latest/rules.)

Auto-fixing errors

Many ESLint rules can go beyond simply flagging violations and actually reformat the code to be valid. This is called *auto-fixing*, and you trigger it by passing ESLint the `--fix` flag.

ESLint tells you how many errors and warnings are potentially fixable using `--fix`. In this case, ESLint can auto-fix all four errors you just reviewed.

Use `npm` to run the `lint` command and fix the errors, like this:

```
npm run lint -- --fix
```

What is the extra -- for? It tells `npm` to pass all the arguments that follow it to the command being executed. In this case, `--fix` is a parameter that npm passes to the `eslint` command.

Using the `--fix` argument fixes the four errors you just reviewed. Open `src/index.js` to verify that ESLint added a comma to line 11. ESLint also modified `src/reportWebVitals.js`, adding parentheses around the function argument in line 1, and adding line breaks further down in the file.

Why bother running `npm run lint` to see the errors and warnings? Why not just run `npm run lint -- --fix` to make fixable errors go away? Sometimes, auto-fixing can change code that you do not want to change. Always look over the list of errors before auto-fixing them.

After ESLint makes those fixes, the output tells you there are still 10 errors remaining.

```
/.../code-cafe/src/App.js
   6:5   error  'React' must be in scope when using JSX
                                          react/react-in-jsx-scope
   6:5   error  JSX not allowed in files with extension '.js'
                                          react/jsx-filename-extension
   7:7   error  'React' must be in scope when using JSX
                                          react/react-in-jsx-scope
   8:9   error  'React' must be in scope when using JSX
                                          react/react-in-jsx-scope
   9:9   error  'React' must be in scope when using JSX
                                          react/react-in-jsx-scope
  12:11  error  'React' must be in scope when using JSX
                                          react/react-in-jsx-scope
  16:9   error  'React' must be in scope when using JSX
                                          react/react-in-jsx-scope

/.../code-cafe/src/App.test.js
  5:10  error  'React' must be in scope when using JSX
                                          react/react-in-jsx-scope
  5:10  error  JSX not allowed in files with extension '.js'
                                          react/jsx-filename-extension

/.../code-cafe/src/index.js
  9:3  error  JSX not allowed in files with extension '.js'
                                          react/jsx-filename-extension

✖ 10 problems (10 errors, 0 warnings)
```

The remaining errors that ESLint has identified are related to just two rules: `react/react-in-jsx-scope` and `react/jsx-filename-extension`.

Overriding ESLint rules

What happens if you disagree with an ESLint rule? You can modify ESLint rules for specific chunks of code or for entire files.

To disable a rule for one line of code, add a comment directly above the line with this syntax:

```
/* eslint-disable-next-line [rule-name] */
```

You can put a similar comment at the top of a file to disable a rule for the entire file:

```
/* eslint-disable [rule-name] */
```

Both of these options exempt a particular section of code, leaving the rule in place. (Other options for modifying ESLint rules are also available. For more information, see the documentation at eslint.org/docs/latest/user-guide/configuring/rules.)

Alternatively, ESLint allows you to override default rules or to set your own rules at the application level by adding a `rules` section inside `eslintConfig`.

Which brings us back to the two ESLint rules that are the source of all your remaining errors: `react/react-in-jsx-scope` and `react/jsx-filename-extension`.

The first states that "React must be in scope when using JSX." In previous versions of React, you had to import React into any file returning JSX. The `react/react-in-jsx-scope` rule flags any files that contain JSX but do not have the React import. Recent versions of React have changed how JSX compiles and made this rule obsolete, so you will turn it off.

The second error, `react/jsx-filename-extension`, states: "JSX not allowed in files with extension .js." Airbnb's default setting for this rule requires that any file containing JSX end with the `.jsx` extension. However, Create React App generates files with the `.js` extension, and you will follow that convention for the files you create in this book. You will override this rule as well, so that you can include JSX markup in files with either extension.

Now add these two rules to the `eslintConfig`:

Listing 5.5 Overriding JSX rules (`package.json`)

```
...
"eslintConfig": {
  "extends": [
    ...
+
  ],
  "rules": {
    "react/react-in-jsx-scope": "off",
    "react/jsx-filename-extension": [
      "warn",
      {
        "extensions": [
          ".js",
          ".jsx"
        ]
      }
    ]
  }
},
...
```

Rules are listed as key-value pairs, where the key is the name of the rule, and the value is the rule setting. If there are additional options, as is the case with the `react/jsx-filename-extension` rule, the value is an array, where the first item is the rule setting, followed by any options.

You turn the `react/react-in-jsx-scope` rule off, because it is obsolete. But instead of turning the `react/jsx-filename-extension` rule completely off, you set it to warn you if a file containing JSX does not end in either the `.jsx` or `.js` file extension.

Save the file and check for lint errors again with `npm run lint`. Now there are no errors or warnings. Doesn't that feel good?

Before moving on, you need to override one more rule. You will turn off a rule called `no-console`, which flags any **console.log** statements that you include in your code.

In a production environment, teams often disable logs to the console. Instead, they use a separate logging package, such as Sentry, to store and search through logs in the cloud. Since Code Café will be running on only your machine, you will not use a logging package. Instead, you will use **console.log** statements for debugging. Turning the `no-console` rule off allows you to use **console.log** statements without linting errors.

Make this change in `package.json`:

Listing 5.6 Configuring Airbnb's ESLint (`package.json`)

```
...
"rules": {
  "react/react-in-jsx-scope": "off",
  "react/jsx-filename-extension": [
    "warn",
    {
      ...
    }
  ],
  "no-console": "off"
}
...
```

The `no-console` rule does not use the `react` prefix, unlike the other rules, because it comes from the `eslint` rule set and not from a plugin.

Installing the ESLint Extension in Visual Studio Code

Running scripts in the terminal to find and fix potential code errors is helpful. But wouldn't it be nice to see errors in real time as you type? Good news: You can, with the ESLint extension in Visual Studio Code.

Install the extension from the Visual Studio website: marketplace.visualstudio.com/items? itemName=dbaeumer.vscode-eslint.

Once the installation is complete, make sure the extension is enabled (Figure 5.7).

Figure 5.7 Adding the ESLint extension to Visual Studio Code

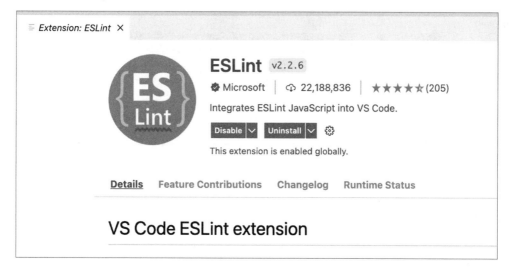

VS Code ESLint extension

Now try it out: Open `src/App.js` and delete the semicolon at the end of the second line, `import './App.css';`.

A small red squiggle appears where the semicolon should be. Hover over the marker to see a pop-up with information from ESLint (Figure 5.8).

Figure 5.8 ESLint missing semicolon warning

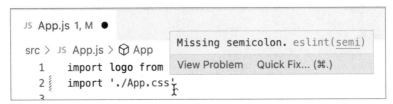

Though you can click Quick Fix... in the pop-up to fix the error, do not fix it just yet.

You should also see a problem indicator in the bottom left of the Visual Studio Code window (Figure 5.9).

Figure 5.9 One problem

Click the error icon to open the problems pane, which shows information about all the errors and warnings found (Figure 5.10).

Figure 5.10 Problems pane

If you do not see the red squiggle or the problem indicator, do not despair. Sometimes it takes a few seconds for them to show up.

Now to fix that pesky semicolon error. The ESLint extension allows you to auto-fix all the errors and warnings in the document from the *actions menu.*

Open the actions menu by pressing Command-Shift-P (Ctrl-Shift-P). Begin typing "eslint" in the search box until you see ESLint: Fix all auto-fixable Problems (Figure 5.11). Select this action.

Figure 5.11 ESLint action menu

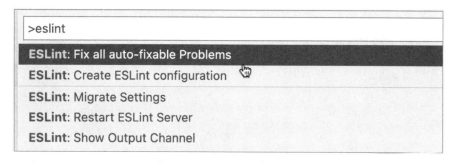

The semicolon reappears in App.js. The problems pane reports that no problems have been detected. Success!

Save your freshly fixed file. You can close the problems pane by clicking the X in its top-right corner.

Conclusion

Having ESLint configured in your application will help you identify and fix potential problems as you build your app. In the next chapter, you will get practice building components as you lay the foundation for Code Café.

For the More Curious: Shortcuts to Running ESLint in Visual Studio Code

Running the ESLint extension from the actions menu is a little tedious. There are a couple ways to streamline auto-fixing your files: creating a keyboard shortcut and setting Visual Studio Code to auto-fix whenever you save files.

Using these methods, you will probably perform lint checks more frequently, allowing you to fix problems as they arise instead of having a bunch of issues to deal with at the end of the development process.

Bear in mind that if you want to review errors and warnings before they are fixed, you must review them before using either of these auto-fixing methods.

To add a keyboard shortcut, open the Keyboard Shortcuts preferences by selecting Code →
Preferences → Keyboard Shortcuts in Visual Studio Code's menu bar. In the keybindings search bar at
the top, enter "eslint." Then, hover over the row for ESLint: Fix all auto-fixable Problems and click the
+ to its left (Figure 5.12).

Figure 5.12 ESLint keyboard shortcuts

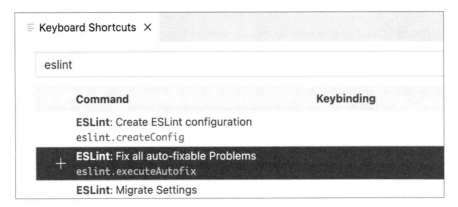

Enter a keybinding that will work for you, such as Command-Shift-A. The pop-up will warn you if
the combination you enter is already assigned to another action. Try again until you find one that is
unassigned, and press Return to set it.

Note that Visual Studio Code supports chords – two separate keystroke combinations entered in
sequence, such as Command-Shift-A Command-Shift-A. If you enter one combination after another,
the second combination will be appended to the first to make a chord. If you do not want the chord,
enter the new combination again to set it as the single-combination shortcut.

To exit the keybinding entry pop-up without assigning a shortcut, click anywhere outside the pop-up.

To enable auto-fix on save, open Visual Studio Code's settings by selecting Code → Preferences →
Settings.

The settings window has two tabs: User and Workspace. Settings on the User tab apply globally; those
on the Workspace tab apply only to the current workspace, or project.

In the Workspace tab, begin typing "code actions on save" and click Edit in settings.json when it appears.

When settings.json is open, Visual Studio Code suggests options to add source.fixAll or source.organizeImports (Figure 5.13).

Figure 5.13 Editing settings.json

Ignore these suggestions and add the code below instead. (If you do use the suggestion to add source.fixAll, you will need to modify the value to include .eslint and ensure it is set to true.)

Add two properties to settings.json:

Listing 5.7 Enabling auto-fix on save (settings.json)

```
{
  "editor.codeActionsOnSave": {
    "source.fixAll.eslint": true
  }
  },
  "eslint.validate": [
    "javascript"
  ]
}
```

Save the file when you are done.

Setting up a keyboard shortcut or auto-fix on save – or neither – is a personal preference. For the purposes of this book, it is up to you. But however you prefer to use linting, it is a tool we recommend for all your projects to help you avoid errors and write consistent, easy-to-maintain code.

For the More Curious: Linting Before Committing

It can also be helpful for ESLint to run automatically as a final check before you commit your code. Some npm packages can ensure that everyone on a project lints before committing. For example, husky helps ensure Git hooks such as pre-commit are installed for everyone on the project. You can read more about it at www.npmjs.com/package/husky.

Although linting the whole project works for small projects, it can be painfully slow for larger projects. Another npm package, lint-staged, runs ESLint on only the files that are staged to be committed. This makes the pre-commit hook much faster. You can find out more about lint-staged at www.npmjs.com/package/lint-staged.

6

Prop Types

Now that your application is set up, you are ready to begin building Code Café.

When you worked on Ottergram, you built it using components – reusable JavaScript functions that return React elements. Components are key to building scalable React applications, so understanding how they work is crucial.

Building your own components is an important skill for React developers. In this chapter, you will reinforce what you learned from building Ottergram by creating and using components for Code Café.

Another important aspect of React development is using components that other developers have built – and building components that other developers will use. Knowing the exact props that a component needs can be difficult, especially when it needs many of them. And passing incorrect props to a component can lead to errors in the application.

To make components easier to work with, you can assign *prop types* to your component props. A prop type defines the data type, such as `string` or `number`, required for a given prop. (If you have experience with typed function parameters in TypeScript or other languages, prop types will likely feel familiar.)

Prop types serve as documentation to help future developers know how to use your component. They also give you some automatic checks for compatibility between the type required for a component's prop and the actual prop being passed in, as you will see in a moment.

By the end of this chapter, Code Café will have three components: a **Header** component proudly proclaiming the name of the site, a **Home** component that renders when a user first navigates to your site, and a **Thumbnail** component you will use multiple times to display a list of items available for purchase (Figure 6.1). And you will use the prop-types library to document all the props your components use.

Figure 6.1 Code Café at the end of this chapter

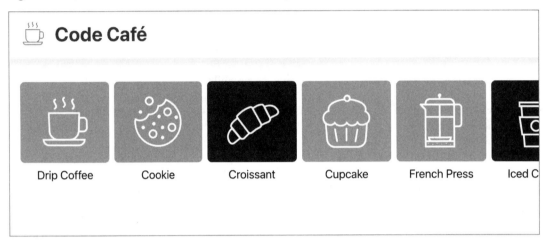

When building each new component, try reading through the instructions and writing the code on your own. Then compare your code with ours.

There may be some differences, even if your component works as expected. In development, there is often more than one way to do things! But to follow along with future code listings in the book, we recommend that you adjust your code to match what you see here.

It is OK if you still have questions about components when you reach the end of this chapter. Building components is a fundamental skill, and you will have more opportunities to practice as you continue to work on Code Café.

Adding Resources

You will need some images and other resources for your components. They are in the resources file you downloaded in The Necessary Tools.

Make a place for these resources by setting up a new `items` folder in the `src` directory: In Visual Studio Code, select `src` and click the New Folder icon at the top of the explorer (Figure 6.2).

Figure 6.2 Adding a folder

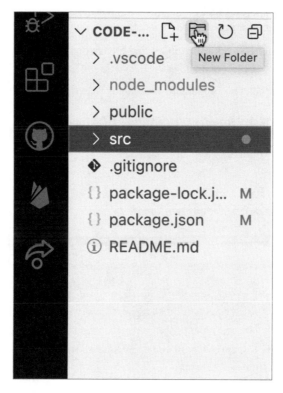

Name the new folder `items`. Now, using your device's file explorer, copy all the files from `code-cafe-resources/items` to `src/items`.

Next, create an `images` folder in the `src` directory and copy all the files from `code-cafe-resources/images` to `src/images`.

Finally, create a `src/components` folder. This is where you will house the components you build.

Header Component

As in Ottergram, your first component for Code Café will be its header.

Ottergram's header component was simple – just the app's name, with some styling. Code Café's header component will start off with the app's name and an image of a coffee cup. Later, you will make it more complex.

Create a file called Header.js inside src/components.

In the new file, create and export a function that returns the header image and text. The coffee cup image is in the images folder you just created: src/images/logo.svg.

(It is not unusual to encounter ESLint errors about line breaks or indentation in your file. Do not panic! We will discuss these issues in a moment.)

Once you have written your header component, compare it with the code shown below:

Listing 6.1 Creating the **Header** component (Header.js)

```
import CoffeeLogo from '../images/logo.svg';

function Header() {
  return (
    <header>
      <img src={CoffeeLogo} alt="coffee logo" />
      <h1>Code Café</h1>
    </header>
  );
}

export default Header;
```

Whitespace issues

You might have gotten some ESLint errors in your new **Header** file. Let's go over three common issues and how to fix them. First is this error:

```
Expected linebreaks to be "LF" but found "CRLF".        eslint(linebreak-style)
```

What is this about?

By default, Windows uses two characters for a new line: a carriage return (CR) plus a line feed (LF). Unix systems use just an LF and might display an extra blank line when both CR and LF are used. (On some old printers, a carriage return moved the printhead to the left margin, without advancing the paper, while a line feed advanced the paper one line.)

Visual Studio Code allows you to choose whether pressing Return results in just an LF, or a CR plus an LF. Although the code looks the same in the code editor, the hidden characters representing the line endings are different.

The Airbnb ESLint configuration is more picky than Visual Studio Code: It requires LFs only, to keep code consistent across operating systems and code editors.

So how do you fix this error if you see it? Take a look at Visual Studio Code's status bar, at the bottom of the window (Figure 6.3). It indicates, using LF or CRLF, what Visual Studio Code currently uses for new lines.

Figure 6.3 Visual Studio Code's status bar

If you see CRLF, click it. In the pop-up window, select LF (Figure 6.4).

Figure 6.4 Updating the current file's end-of-line sequence

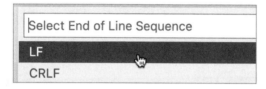

This change affects only your current file. Change the setting globally by selecting Code → Preferences → Settings in the menu bar. Search for "eol" (for "end of line") and change the setting to \n (which is the regex equivalent of LF) (Figure 6.5).

Figure 6.5 Updating the end-of-line settings

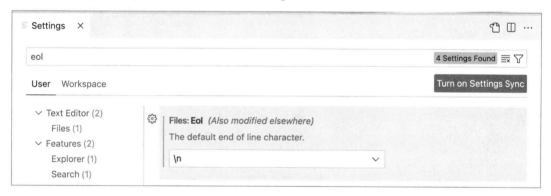

(Though this global change automatically applies the setting to new files, it does not edit existing files. That is why you used the status bar to make the change in Header.js.)

Similarly, Visual Studio Code's default setting for tab size (the number of spaces used for an indent made with a tab character) might be clashing with your ESLint rules. If so, you will see an error like this:

```
Expected indentation of x space characters but found y.  eslint(react/jsx-indent)
```

Visual Studio Code allows 2 or 4 spaces for an indent; ESLint requires 2. To change Visual Studio Code's setting, click Spaces: 4 in the status bar. Then, click Indent Using Spaces. Finally, click 2. This will change the settings for Header.js.

To update the setting globally, open Settings again (Code → Preferences → Settings). Search for "tab size" and change the setting appropriately (Figure 6.6).

Figure 6.6 Updating tab size settings

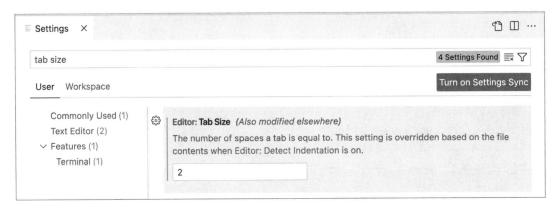

Finally, you might see an error related to the eol-last lint rule, which requires an empty line at the end of each file:

```
Newline required at end of file but not found.            eslint(eol-last)
```

You can add the new line by simply pressing Return after the last line in the file. Or – since this is an auto-fixable error – you can use one of the auto-fix methods discussed in the previous chapter to fix the error and add the new line.

Adding the component to App.js

Save `Header.js`. Now import and add your new header component to `App.js`. While you are there, delete some of the generic code that Create React App generated – you will not need it.

Listing 6.2 Adding the header component to `App.js` (`App.js`)

```
import logo from './logo.svg';
import './App.css';
import Header from './components/Header';

function App() {
  return (
    <div className="App">
    <div>
      <header className="App-header">
        <img src={logo} className="App-logo" alt="logo" />
        <p>
          Edit
          {' '}
          <code>src/App.js</code>
          {' '}
          and save to reload.
        </p>
        <a
          className="App-link"
          href="https://reactjs.org"
          target="_blank"
          rel="noopener noreferrer"
        >
          Learn React
        </a>
      </header>
      <Header />
    </div>
    ...
```

Save your files, start your development server (if it is not already running), and check your browser. You will see your new component displayed on the page and listed in the React DevTools Components tab (Figure 6.7).

Figure 6.7 Viewing the header in the browser

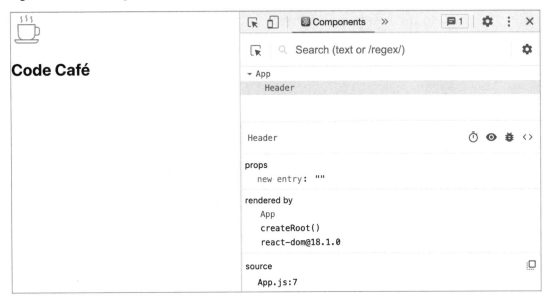

Styling the header

Although the component renders to the screen, it does not look like a header. It needs some styling.

In Ottergram, all the styles were in a single file, App.css. That worked because Ottergram was small enough that you did not need to worry about organizing your styles.

But in larger, more complex apps, you will often see stylesheets for individual components. Breaking styles up by component helps keep your code base organized and maintainable. That is what you will do here.

In the `components` folder, create a file called `Header.css`. Add styles for the header's image and text, using `header-component` as the class name for the selectors.

Listing 6.3 Creating header styles (`Header.css`)

```css
.header-component {
    display: flex;
    margin-bottom: 10px;
    box-shadow: 0px 9px 13px rgb(0 0 0 / 5%);
    align-items: center;
    padding: 0 20px;
}

.header-component img {
    height: 50px;
    width: 50px;
}

.header-component h1 {
    font-size: 36px;
    font-weight: 700;
    color: #674836;
    margin-left: 15px;
}
```

Now add the `header-component` class name to your component in `Header.js`. Remember to import the stylesheet at the top of the file.

Listing 6.4 Using header styles (`Header.js`)

```js
import CoffeeLogo from '../images/logo.svg';
import './Header.css';

function Header() {
  return (
    <header>
    <header className="header-component">
      <img src={CoffeeLogo} alt="coffee logo" />
...
```

Save your files and reload Code Café in the browser. The header looks a lot better, and you have now finished the first component of your new application (Figure 6.8).

Figure 6.8 Viewing the styled header in the browser

Thumbnail Component

Now you have a nice header that shows the name of your shop. The next step is to list the items for sale at Code Café.

At the beginning of this chapter, you added a folder called src/items. This folder has the image files for all the available items, as well as a helper file called index.js.

Open index.js and take a look at what it does. After it imports the image files, it exports two variables: itemImages and items.

itemImages is an object made up of key-value pairs, where the key is the imageId and the value is the corresponding image. Hyphenated object properties, such as the multi-word imageIds, are wrapped in single quotes. Importing this object into any file will give you access to all the images – without having to import each one individually.

The second variable, items, is an array of the items available for sale. It represents the information that you would normally store in a database, including details about each item such as the title, price, imageId, and itemId. Eventually, you will replace this variable with a call to an API. But for now, you will use this mock data so you can continue to focus on your React skills.

Your app will display each item in a **Thumbnail** component. Clicking a **Thumbnail** will route the user to a details page for the item. You will add the routing functionality later; for now, you will focus on displaying the **Thumbnail** components on the page.

Create the component file and corresponding CSS file in the components directory. Name the files Thumbnail.js and Thumbnail.css.

Add the styles for the component to `Thumbnail.css` first:

Listing 6.5 Adding thumbnail styles (Thumbnail.css)

```css
.thumbnail-component {
    display: flex;
    flex-direction: column;
    width: 100%;
    text-decoration: none;
    color: black;
}

.thumbnail-component div {
    background-color: #B9A28D;
    border-radius: 8px;
    display: flex;
    justify-content: center;
    align-items: center;
    padding: 20px 40px;
}

.thumbnail-component img {
    height: 106px;
    width: 106px;
}

.thumbnail-component p {
    display: flex;
    width: 100%;
    justify-content: center;
    align-items: center;
    margin: 9px 0 0;
    font-size: 21px;
    text-align: center;
    white-space: nowrap;
}
```

Now build the component in `Thumbnail.js`, using the `thumbnail-component` class name. Remember to export the component after you create it. (This component will have ESLint errors. You will fix them in the next step.)

Listing 6.6 Creating the **Thumbnail** component (Thumbnail.js)

```js
import './Thumbnail.css';

function Thumbnail({ image, title }) {
  return (
    <a
      href="#todo"
      className="thumbnail-component"
    >
      <div>
        <img src={image} alt={title} />
      </div>
      <p>{title}</p>
    </a>
  );
}

export default Thumbnail;
```

The component returns an anchor element (<a>) because the **Thumbnail** component will eventually route the user to another screen. Inside the anchor tag, the component displays the item image and the item title. Nesting the image and title inside the anchor element means that the user can click anywhere on the component to trigger the routing action.

There is an extra <div> tag wrapping the item image; it is there to add some styling. Finally, the title and image variables are passed to the component as props.

Prop Types

The **Thumbnail** component has two props: an image and a title. And ESLint has a rule that requires all props to have a declared *prop type*.

ESLint will attempt to validate the prop types of each component in your app. You have not added any prop types yet, so it will alert you that they are all missing: As you have seen before, ESLint underlines problem areas with a squiggly red line. In Thumbnail.js, it underlines the component props – image and title.

Hover over each prop, and you will see the same error telling you that the prop is missing in props validation (Figure 6.9).

Figure 6.9 ESLint prop types error

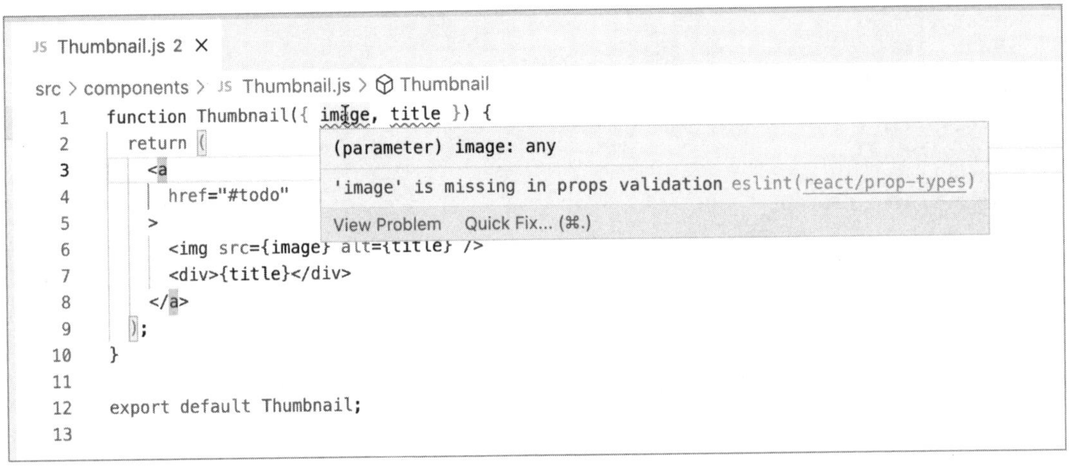

In this case, ESLint cannot validate your props because you have not defined their prop types yet. Providing prop types is useful later in the development process because you will get specific errors in the browser console if a component's props are missing or of a different type. This can greatly speed up debugging.

Installing the prop-types library

The first step to using prop types (and fixing these errors) is to install the prop-types library.

prop-types is a library built and maintained by the React team. With it, you can define the type of each prop in a component. It also serves as a runtime check to ensure compatibility between the prop types defined for a component and the props passed to the component.

You will need to run a new command in your terminal to install the library. Since you already have Code Café running, you have two options: open a new window or tab, or stop and restart your server. Either way is fine; just make sure you have the server running again when you are done.

Install the new library with the following command:

```
npm install --save prop-types@15.7.2
```

Thumbnail Prop Types

Now you can fix the errors in your **Thumbnail** component.

At the top of Thumbnail.js, import PropTypes from the newly installed prop-types library so that you can access the type definitions. The ESLint rule import-order specifies that you must import external libraries before other files, so place this import before the stylesheet.

Then add prop type documentation to the **Thumbnail** component.

Listing 6.7 Adding PropTypes to the **Thumbnail** component (Thumbnail.js)

```
import PropTypes from 'prop-types';
import './Thumbnail.css';

function Thumbnail({ image, title }) {
  ...
}

Thumbnail.propTypes = {
  image: PropTypes.string.isRequired,
  title: PropTypes.string.isRequired,
};

export default Thumbnail;
```

You declare both props as PropTypes.string, indicating that they are expected to be string values.

It might be surprising that you declare the image prop as the string type. This is because its value points to an imported image. When an image is imported as a variable, the result is either a string path pointing to the image location or an inline Base64-encoded string, depending on the webpack configuration. Details on how to edit the configuration are at the end of this chapter.

You add .isRequired at the end of the type definition to specify that the props are required by the component. When a prop is marked as required, an error will warn you if the parent component does not provide the prop.

Now future developers will know that **Thumbnail** expects an image and a title, both in string format.

Rendering Items

Now that you have built the **Thumbnail** component and identified the needed prop types, it is time to use it to render the items in the browser.

Switch to App.js. You will need both the items and itemImages variables that items/index.js exports, so import those at the top of the file.

As we mentioned earlier, items is an array of item objects containing the item title, imageId, itemId, and price. Use the array **map** method to iterate over the items array and return a **Thumbnail** for each item. Use the item object to define the **Thumbnail** props: image and title. Find the image by using the item's imageId to locate the corresponding value in itemImages. The title is the item's title.

Each item will need a key. The itemId for each item is unique, so you can use it as the key.

Listing 6.8 Rendering the item array (App.js)

```
import './App.css';
import Header from './components/Header';
import Thumbnail from './components/Thumbnail';
import { items, itemImages } from './items';

function App() {
  return (
    <div>
      <Header />
      {items.map((item) => (
        <Thumbnail
          key={item.itemId}
          image={itemImages[item.imageId]}
          title={item.title}
        />
      ))}
    </div>
...
```

Save your files and check the browser to see all the items being displayed (Figure 6.10).

Figure 6.10 Items displayed in the browser

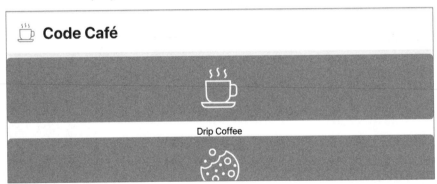

Now customers can see all the items Code Café offers, which is great. But the site does not look very stylish. Currently, the **Thumbnail**s are displayed in a column that is much too wide, and you have to scroll down to see them all. You will fix that shortly.

Home Component

Before you take care of styling your home page, take a step back and look at how you are getting the items onscreen: In App.js, you map over the items array to create an array of **Thumbnail**s.

Normally, App.js is responsible only for top-level data and routing to other components. It is better to encapsulate the details of how a component is built, such as how a **Thumbnail** gets its image and title, in another file.

In this case, you will create a new component called **Home** to render the **Thumbnail**s. You will display this component when the user navigates to your home page or to /. It will also let you add the styling you need for your home page.

In Visual Studio Code, create the files for the **Home** component and its associated CSS stylesheet. Add the styles to Home.css first:

Listing 6.9 Adding home styling (Home.css)

```css
.home-component {
    display: grid;
    grid-template-columns: repeat(auto-fit, minmax(150px, 1fr));
    grid-gap: 32px 10px;
    padding: 32px 20px;
}

.home-component .thumbnail-component:nth-child(3n + 2) div {
    background-color: #9BA699;
}

.home-component .thumbnail-component:nth-child(3n + 3) div {
    background-color: #3F3F40;
}
```

Now, in Home.js, import the stylesheet. Then create the **Home** functional component, which should return a <div> with the home-component class name. Export your newly created component with export default Home;.

Next, you need access to the items array. In the new component, accept the items array as a prop. This will emulate fetching data at the top level of your application. (When you do this, ESLint will flag an error related to prop types in this component. You will address this error in a moment. Also, if you are wondering why you do not import items, we will explain that at the end of this chapter.)

Then, in App.js, copy the code that renders the items:

```jsx
{items.map((item) => (
  <Thumbnail
    key={item.itemId}
    image={itemImages[item.imageId]}
    title={item.title}
  / >
))}
```

Paste this code inside the `<div>` in the **Home** component. (ESLint will flag another error related to prop types. You will fix this in a moment as well.)

Finally, import the `itemImages` object directly into the component. This is a static object and not likely to change.

Your **Home** component should look like this:

Listing 6.10 Creating the **Home** component (Home.js)

```
import Thumbnail from './Thumbnail';
import { itemImages } from '../items';
import './Home.css';

function Home({ items }) {
  return (
    <div className="home-component">
      {items.map((item) => (
        <Thumbnail
          key={item.itemId}
          image={itemImages[item.imageId]}
          title={item.title}
        />
      ))}
    </div>
  );
}

export default Home;
```

Now that **Home** is taking care of rendering the **Thumbnail**s, add the new component to App.js and delete the code you no longer need:

Listing 6.11 Adding the **Home** component (App.js)

```
import './App.css';
import Header from './components/Header';
import Thumbnail from './components/Thumbnail';
import Home from './components/Home';
import { items, itemImages } from './items';
import { items } from './items';

function App() {
  return (
    <div>
      <Header />
      {items.map((item) => (
        <Thumbnail
          key={item.itemId}
          image={itemImages[item.imageId]}
          title={item.title}
        />
      ))}
      <Home items={items} />
    </div>
...
```

So far, you have looked at ESLint errors in your terminal and in Visual Studio Code. ESLint errors also appear in your browser when your app runs in development mode (but not in production). To see what that looks like, open your browser with your app running. An overlay on the screen displays several errors (Figure 6.11).

Figure 6.11 ESLint compilation errors

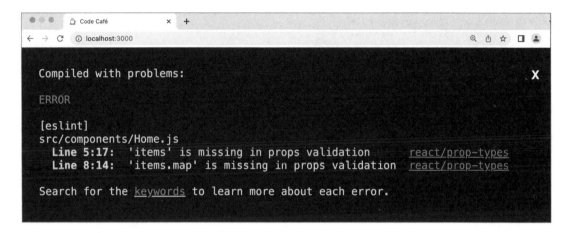

Though the errors shown are also flagged in Visual Studio Code and your terminal, you might not notice them right away. The eye-catching overlay in your browser is hard to miss when there are problems that need your attention. You can close the overlay by clicking the X in the top-right corner.

The **Home** component has only one prop – items – but two errors. ESLint marks both the prop itself and the call to **items.map** with problem squiggles. What is going on?

You intended for the items prop to be an array of objects. But ESLint does not know that, because you have not defined the prop type. So when the **Home** component calls **items.map**, ESLint has no way to verify that items has a method called **map**.

Calling an array method on a variable of a different type usually leads to an error. This is a great example of ESLint mitigating potential errors and identifying ways to make your code more robust.

To fix both errors, you need to define items as an array.

There are two prop types that identify a prop as an array: array and arrayOf. Use PropTypes.array to define a prop as an array of any type; use PropTypes.arrayOf to specify the type of the items inside the array.

To make your code as well documented as possible, use arrayOf to define the *shape*, or the underlying structure, of the objects contained in the array.

Listing 6.12 Adding PropTypes to the **Home** component (Home.js)

```
import PropTypes from 'prop-types';
import Thumbnail from './Thumbnail';
...
function Home({ items }) {
  ...
}

Home.propTypes = {
  items: PropTypes.arrayOf(
    PropTypes.shape({
      itemId: PropTypes.string.isRequired,
      imageId: PropTypes.string.isRequired,
      title: PropTypes.string.isRequired,
      price: PropTypes.number.isRequired,
      description: PropTypes.string,
      salePrice: PropTypes.number,
    }),
  ).isRequired,
};

export default Home;
```

You use PropTypes.shape to specify the shape of the item object.

Each item contains an itemId, imageId, title, and price. The price is a number, and all the other fields are strings. All the keys are required.

A couple of the items also contain the properties description, which is a string, and salePrice, which is a number. These properties are not marked as required, since they are not present in every item.

Save your files and check your browser again. Now that you have defined the types for all your props, you have no more errors.

Reusing Prop Types

You will use the `item` prop type multiple times when building Code Café. To make things easier – and to minimize the risk of errors – you can extract and reuse prop types.

Create a new `src/types` directory. Copy the code for the `item` prop type from **Home** and add it to a new file in the types folder called `item.js`.

Listing 6.13 Exporting the `item` prop type (`item.js`)

```
import PropTypes from 'prop-types';

const ItemType = PropTypes.shape({
  itemId: PropTypes.string.isRequired,
  imageId: PropTypes.string.isRequired,
  title: PropTypes.string.isRequired,
  price: PropTypes.number.isRequired,
  description: PropTypes.string,
  salePrice: PropTypes.number,
});

export default ItemType;
```

You import `PropTypes` here, just as you did in the component file. You also export `ItemType` so you can use it in your components.

Save your file. Now update the copied code in **Home** to use your new variable.

Listing 6.14 Replacing the type of `items` (`Home.js`)

```
...
import './Home.css';
import ItemType from '../types/item';

function Home({ items }) {
  ...
}

Home.propTypes = {
  items: PropTypes.arrayOf(
    PropTypes.shape({
      itemId: PropTypes.string.isRequired,
      imageId: PropTypes.string.isRequired,
      title: PropTypes.string.isRequired,
      price: PropTypes.number.isRequired,
      description: PropTypes.string,
      salePrice: PropTypes.number,
    }),
  ).isRequired,
  items: PropTypes.arrayOf(ItemType).isRequired,
};

export default Home;
```

Now you can use `ItemType` throughout your app, without having to type multiple lines of code and without having to keep the various prop types it contains in sync.

Your code is clean and well organized. Save your files and take a look at Code Café in the browser. Now it is just as well organized as your code (Figure 6.12).

Figure 6.12 Completed components

Prop Mismatch

You have seen what happens if you do not define prop types in a component. But what happens if a component receives props that do not match what it expects?

For example, you just declared that **Home** should receive an array of objects that each have specific fields, including `price`. What happens if the price of an item is missing? To find out, open `items/index.js` and comment out the price of an item, such as the cupcake. Then save the file.

ESLint does not immediately complain, and your website will load. Props validation is a runtime check, so your app still compiles (provided there are no other errors as a result of the mismatch). However, if you check the DevTools console, you will see an error warning you of the missing prop:

> Warning: Failed prop type: The prop `items[0].price` is marked as required in `Home`, but its value is `undefined`.

Next, uncomment the price to restore it, but add single quotes around the value, like `price: '1'`. Save the file again. Now the console shows a different warning:

> Warning: Failed prop type: Invalid prop `items[0].price` of type `string` supplied to `Home`, expected `number`.

Console warnings like these can help minimize the time you spend debugging because you forgot to pass a required prop or passed a value of the wrong type.

Before you move on, undo the changes you made to `items/index.js`.

Conclusion

Your practice building components is paying off: Code Café is looking great.

By defining needed prop types for your components, you make them more robust, increase their reusability, and help prevent errors. You can quickly see what data you need to use a component correctly (and can get instant feedback if you are not using it correctly), saving you time and energy. This is especially true when working on applications with many components and many developers.

For the More Curious: Why Pass Items as a Prop?

Why did you pass the items array as a prop to the **Home** component instead of importing it, like you did with itemImages?

Later, you will load the items from an API. Getting data from an API should happen in only one place, not in every component that uses the data. So passing items as a prop will make the later change more straightforward. The itemImages, on the other hand, will continue to live in your application, so it is safe to import them everywhere.

However, if you did not plan to replace items with data from an API, your code would be cleaner if you imported items in **Home** rather than having an extra prop.

So then why not pass the item object as a prop to **Thumbnail** (like item={item})?

Similar to Ottergram's **Post** and **SelectedItem** components, **Thumbnail** is a presentational component. Passing the whole item object would unnecessarily couple **Thumbnail** to the format of the item.

By passing only title, you give the **Thumbnail** component only the details it needs to render a given item as a thumbnail. (Note that key is a reserved prop that React requires when rendering a list of items with **map**, so even if you were to pass the whole item object to **Thumbnail**, you would still need to specify key separately.)

For the More Curious: Inlining Images

Every server request takes a small amount of extra time beyond the time needed to actually download the data. That extra time is called *latency*. Inlining images helps avoid extra requests to the server, and therefore latency, by encoding images as data URIs in Base64 and then inlining them in the JavaScript or CSS file.

However, increasing the size of JavaScript files makes your application load more slowly. Similarly, increasing the size of CSS files makes your styles load and display more slowly. So there is a trade-off between inlining images to reduce the number of server requests and decreasing the speed at which styles and the whole application load.

By default, Create React App places images of less than 10,000 bytes inline. If you want to change the limit for inlining images, you can do that by setting an environment variable with the name IMAGE_INLINE_SIZE_LIMIT. You can also disable inlining entirely by setting the limit to 0. (You can set the environment variable as part of your build or start command, or add it to the appropriate script in package.json.)

For example, IMAGE_INLINE_SIZE_LIMIT=0 npm run build would build your application without inlining images. (You will learn more about building the application in Chapter 23.)

Only AVIF, BMP, GIF, JPG, and PNG images are inlined; SVG images are not. To import an SVG as a component, Create React App provides special syntax that renders the SVG inline and includes the SVG in your JavaScript files:

```
import { ReactComponent as Logo } from '../images/logo.svg';
```

You can then use the image as a component: `<Logo />`. Note that this means you will need to change how you apply styles to your SVGs.

In this book, we will stick to using SVGs as images.

Bronze Challenge: Add a Prop

Code Café may be expanding into new markets. Update the **Header** component so that you can reuse it to display regional store names. Add a `title` prop and the correct prop type to the **Header** component. Pass "Code Café" (or any other name) as the title, and render it in the header.

7

Styles

When it comes to UI development, form and function go hand in hand. A well-styled UI is important for a successful app.

You have already seen that React makes it easy to add styles by importing CSS and using the `className` keyword in components. In this chapter, you will add more style rules to enhance the design of your application.

By the end of the chapter, Code Café will have a UI that looks good on both mobile devices and desktop browsers and that has some polished features (Figure 7.1). This will set the stage for the order functionality you will begin adding in the next chapter.

Figure 7.1 Hover effect

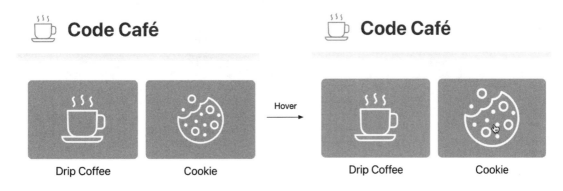

But first, you will take care of some housekeeping and learn about some core style concepts.

Create React App provides a default stylesheet: `App.css`. You are using your own styles, not the default styles, so you no longer need this file.

Delete `App.css`, either by using your file explorer or by right-clicking the file in Visual Studio Code and selecting Delete. Then remove the import for `App.css` from the top of `App.js`.

Listing 7.1 Deleting the `App.css` import (`App.js`)

```
import './App.css';
import Header from './components/Header';
...
function App() {
...
```

Style Scoping

Now for some core style concepts. Recall from Chapter 2 that all CSS has a global scope, meaning that style rules apply throughout your app. This is true even when style rules are split into multiple CSS files.

To see this in action, add a style rule in Header.css that specifies the color for text in <p> tags.

Listing 7.2 Adding color to the **Header** component (Header.css)

```
...
.header-component h1 {
    ...
}

p {
    color: #674836;
}
```

With your development server running, look at your browser. The titles for the thumbnails have changed color (Figure 7.2).

Figure 7.2 Brown thumbnail titles

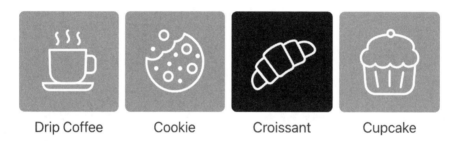

| Drip Coffee   Cookie   Croissant   Cupcake |

What happened?

The thumbnail titles are inside <p> tags in the **Thumbnail** component, not in the **Header** component. But the React build process merges all the CSS together. So setting a style rule for the <p> tag affects <p> tags throughout your app.

This is why you have been prepending all your CSS class names with component names, such as .thumbnail-component and .home-component. This naming convention keeps the class names unique and ensures that your styles apply only where you want them to.

Add specificity to the style rule in Header.css by using the component name.

Listing 7.3 Fixing the style rule (Header.css)

```
...
.header-component h1 {
    ...
}

p {
.header-component p {
    color: #674836;
}
```

Check your browser again. The thumbnail titles are back to the correct color (Figure 7.3).

Figure 7.3 Black thumbnail titles

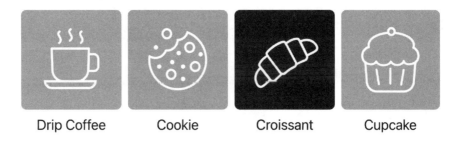

| Drip Coffee | Cookie | Croissant | Cupcake |

(Leave the .header-component p style rule in place. Although it does not do anything at the moment, it will play a role later.)

Responsive Design

The next style concept to consider is *responsive design*, a design approach meant to ensure that your site works across a variety of screen sizes and devices.

Ultimately, Code Café should function and look good on both desktops and mobile devices. Figure 7.4 and Figure 7.5 show the target designs:

Figure 7.4 Desktop design

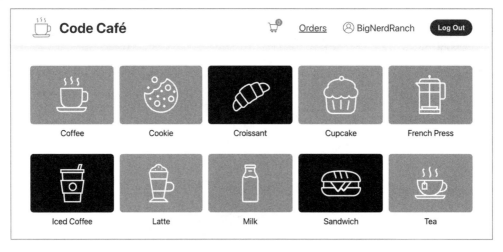

Figure 7.5 Mobile design

The styles you have added so far have taken into account *mobile-first* design. This means that the styles are optimized for smaller screens first. Any additional styling needed for larger screens will be added later.

Mobile-first design is popular with sites that will be used mostly on mobile devices. *Desktop-first* design is still useful when your site will be used primarily on desktops, either because of the demographics of your target audience or because it needs to display a lot of data on the page at once.

Should you grab a mobile device and connect it to verify that your styles work for smaller screens? No need. The DevTools can show you what your site will look like on various screen sizes and under various conditions.

Try it out: Open the DevTools. In the top menu bar, the second icon toggles the device toolbar (Figure 7.6).

Figure 7.6 Toggling the device toolbar

Click the icon to toggle the device toolbar and preview how your website will look on a different device. In the toolbar, click the first dropdown (which has either the name of a mobile device or Dimensions: Responsive) and select iPhone 12 Pro to see how it looks (Figure 7.7).

Figure 7.7 Previewing the site on iPhone 12 Pro

It looks pretty nice, right? Though you still need to add some things to achieve the target design, the elements you have in place look good.

The thumbnails have automatically reorganized themselves to fit the narrower width of a phone screen. If you switch the device in the DevTools to a tablet, such as an iPad Air, you will see that the thumbnails adjust again.

In Chapter 6, you styled the **Home** component with *grid* styling. This means that **Home** uses the CSS Grid Layout element, which creates responsive rows and columns that take up the available space.

Now switch back to the desktop view by toggling the device toolbar off. Compare what you see with the target design above.

The thumbnails are a little small. You need to make them larger – but only on desktops, not on mobile devices.

CSS *media queries* let you create styles that respond to the screen size and other conditions, so that your site looks just right on any screen.

Media Queries

Open Home.css.

In the style rule for .home-component is a rule called grid-template-columns. This rule specifies a minmax width for the columns in the grid:

```
grid-template-columns: repeat(auto-fit, minmax(150px, 1fr));
```

Based on this rule, a column's minimum width is 150px, and the maximum width is 1fr – or one "fraction" of the available space. In this case, that means the columns will expand evenly to take up any extra space.

Add a media query so the columns are slightly larger on larger devices, using 768px as the screen-width breakpoint.

Listing 7.4 Adding a media query to **Home** (Home.css)

```
...
.home-component .thumbnail-component:nth-child(3n + 3) div {
    background-color: #3F3F40;
}

@media (min-width: 768px) {
    .home-component {
        grid-template-columns: repeat(auto-fit, minmax(200px, 1fr));
        padding: 40px 50px;
        grid-gap: 40px 15px;
    }
}
```

A media query tells React, "When the conditions the app is running in match my specified conditions, use the styles defined here instead of the styles defined elsewhere."

Here, the media query says that when the device width is at least 768px, the minimum width of the grid columns should be 200px. It also specifies larger values for the padding (40px on the top and bottom of the component and 50px on the left and right) and grid-gap (40px between the rows and 15px between the columns).

Save the file and check out your browser (Figure 7.8).

Figure 7.8 Thumbnails in the browser

Nice! Now that the thumbnails are a little larger and have a little more elbow room, they look good on the browser screen. Switch to the device view in the DevTools to confirm that the site looks the same as before on a mobile device. The new CSS rules you added apply only when the screen is at least 768px wide.

Now switch back to the desktop view. Although the thumbnails look good, the header could use some attention. The padding you added has shifted the thumbnails over, leaving the header out of alignment. And now that the thumbnails are larger, the header image looks a little small.

Add a media query to Header.css using the same screen-width breakpoint, 768px. Use it to pad the header and increase the size of the image.

Listing 7.5 Adding a media query to **Header** (Header.css)

```
...
.header-component p {
    color: #674836;
}

@media (min-width: 768px) {
    .header-component {
        padding: 0 50px;
    }

    .header-component img {
        height: 60px;
        width: 60px;
    }
}
```

Much better – now everything is aligned again (Figure 7.9).

Figure 7.9 Header in the browser

Hover Effect

It would be stylish to add a hover effect to the thumbnail image so that the image is a bit larger when the mouse is over it.

To accomplish this, you will use the transform property, which can alter the shape, size, rotation, and location of an HTML element without interrupting the flow of the elements around it.

Open Thumbnail.css. Add a CSS rule to make the image scale up when the user hovers over the thumbnail.

Listing 7.6 Adding a transform CSS rule (Thumbnail.css)

```
...
.thumbnail-component p {
    ...
}

.thumbnail-component:hover img {
    transform: scale(1.2);
}
```

The target element for the transformation is the <img> tag – you want the image to get larger, not the entire thumbnail. But you apply the pseudo-class :hover to .thumbnail-component, rather than to the <img> tag, so that the image scales if the mouse is anywhere over the thumbnail, including the text.

transform: scale(1.2) tells the browser to draw the target element at 120% of its original size.

Save the file and test the change in your browser. The images grow larger when you hover over the thumbnail. (The effect is also visible on mobile devices when the user presses and holds a thumbnail.)

Animating the hover effect

Though the transformation properly scales the images, the visual change might look a little jarring. The image jumps abruptly from one size to the next.

Let's use the `transition` property to animate the change. CSS transitions create a gradual change from one visual state to another, which is just what you need to make the transformation more polished.

Listing 7.7 Adding a `transition` CSS rule (`Thumbnail.css`)

```
...
.thumbnail-component img {
    height: 106px;
    width: 106px;
    transition: transform 333ms ease;
}
...
```

The `transition` style rule you added to the `<img>` tag has three parts.

First is the property you are targeting. Here, you tell the browser that it will need to animate changes to the `transform` property.

The second part is the duration of the transition. You specify that this transition should take 333 milliseconds. Feel free to play around with this value to see the effects of longer and shorter durations.

The last value you supply is the *timing function*. By default, the browser uses the `ease` timing function, which makes the transition faster in the middle than at the start or end.

You can add an optional fourth value to `transition`, called `transition-delay`. It allows you to specify when the transition begins. If you omit the value, as you did here, the transition defaults to beginning as soon as it is triggered, with no delay.

Save the file and hover over some thumbnails in the browser to see the transformation happen again. Now the transformation happens gradually and provides just the pop you need (Figure 7.10).

Figure 7.10 Completed hover effect

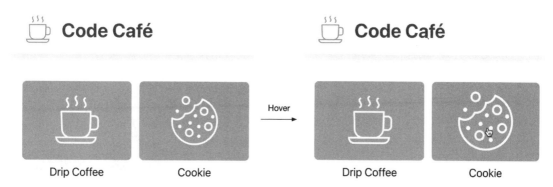

You can also use transitions for other properties, such as `background-color` or `margin`. Targeting `all` animates all style rule changes. You can learn more about transitions, including the other options for timing functions, at developer.mozilla.org/en-US/docs/Web/CSS/CSS_Transitions/Using_CSS_transitions.

Conclusion

Now your components showcase the items for sale at Code Café – and because of the styles you added, they look great.

For the rest of this book, we will provide most of the styles you need so that you can focus on honing your React skills. But feel free to experiment with different style rules along the way. React makes it easy to add styles using the `className` attribute.

Now that you have built your app foundation, it is time to add functionality by fetching data from an API. You will do that in the next chapter.

For the More Curious: Grid Layout

If you are not familiar with CSS Grid Layout, this game is a good introduction to it: cssgridgarden.com.

For the More Curious: Styled Components

Another way to add styles to your components is to use *styled components*. This approach uses an external library to let you write CSS in your JavaScript files. The styles are then automatically scoped to the component. You can read more about styled components at styled-components.com.

For the More Curious: Compiled CSS

Instead of styled components, you can also use a CSS preprocessor such as SCSS, Sass, Less, or Stylus to make scoping the CSS to a single component easier. These options also provide other benefits, such as variables, loops, and functions to generate CSS.

As with using styled components, using a CSS preprocessor requires installing an additional library. You can read about adding Sass/SCSS to Create React App at create-react-app.dev/docs/adding-a-sass-stylesheet.

Silver Challenge: Custom Effect

Adjust the `transform` and `transition` CSS rules to create a different hover effect for the thumbnails.

8

Interacting with a Server

Now that Code Café has a polished, responsive UI, you are ready to add functionality. The site should not just be an online menu with a static collection of items. Instead, it should be the front end for data on a server. By the end of this chapter, Code Café will fetch the items from an API, making it easier to remove out-of-stock items and update prices.

To make this happen, you will first set up a back-end server and then make a network request to load the items from the server.

Setting Up the Server

Your downloaded resources file includes a server for Code Café called `code-cafe-backend`.

Open a new terminal window or tab and navigate to the `code-cafe-backend` directory:

```
cd YOUR_PATH/resources/code-cafe-backend
```

Next, install the dependencies required for the server to run:

```
npm install
```

Then start the server:

```
npm start
```

The console prints `Listening on http://localhost:3030` to let you know the server is up and running (Figure 8.1).

Figure 8.1 The server is listening

```
npm (node)
>>npm start

> rest-api@0.0.0 start
> node app.js

Listening on http://localhost:3030
```

View the running server in your browser by visiting http://localhost:3030 (Figure 8.2).

Figure 8.2 Viewing the server in the browser

In this chapter, you will focus on retrieving the list of items from the API at the endpoint /api/items.

(We will tell you what endpoints to use as you need them. However, if you would like to know all the endpoints on the server, you can see a list in the section called "For the More Curious: Server Endpoints" near the end of this chapter or in the resources/code-cafe-backend/README.md file.)

You can see what the response looks like by navigating to http://localhost:3030/api/items in your browser (Figure 8.3).

Figure 8.3 Items in the browser

```
● ● ●      localhost:3030/api/items      ×   +

←  →  C    ⓘ localhost:3030/api/items

[{"itemId":"coffee","imageId":"coffee","title":"Coffee","price":0.99,"description":"","salePrice":0},
{"itemId":"cookie","imageId":"cookie","title":"Cookie","price":1,"description":"May contain nuts.","salePrice":0.5},
{"itemId":"croissant","imageId":"croissant","title":"Croissant","price":2.5},{"itemId":"cupcake","imageId":"cupcake","title":"Cupcake","price":3},
{"itemId":"french-press","imageId":"french-press","title":"French Press","price":1.75},{"itemId":"iced-coffee","imageId":"iced-coffee","title":"Iced
Coffee","price":1.25},{"itemId":"latte","imageId":"latte","title":"Latte","price":2},{"itemId":"milk","imageId":"milk","title":"Milk","price":0.5},
{"itemId":"sandwich","imageId":"sandwich","title":"Sandwich","price":6},{"itemId":"tea","imageId":"tea","title":"Tea","price":1.5}]
```

The list of items that the server returns will take the place of the items array that you currently import into App.js.

Like the React server, the back-end server will run until you stop it with Control-C. You will need the server running whenever you work on Code Café, so remember to start it each time you work on the project. If you do not, you will get network errors. (And if you do see network errors, check that the server is running and see whether the console has logged any errors.)

Now that you have the server running, you need to set up Code Café to begin interacting with it.

Creating a proxy

Although the servers for Code Café and the back end both run locally, they run on different ports. By default, to protect against cross-site script attacks, the browser blocks API requests to a different origin, including a different port. You need to let your development server know that it is safe to communicate with the back-end server.

You can set up cross-origin resource sharing (CORS) policies to allow communication between different origins. But CORS policies can be complicated to set up properly. If your policies are too lax, they can leave your site open to attacks. If they are too strict, your API will not work from your own front end.

Instead of dealing with the complexities of CORS policies, you will set up Code Café to act as a *proxy* to the back-end server. This way, you will not have to make any allowances for cross-origin sharing.

This is a common pattern, so Create React App makes it easy to set this up in the development servers it creates. Open `package.json` in Code Café and add a proxy.

Listing 8.1 Adding a server proxy (`package.json`)

```
...
  "scripts": {
    ...
  },
  "proxy": "http://localhost:3030",
  "eslintConfig": {
...
```

Save `package.json`. If you are currently running the Code Café development server, stop the process in the terminal with Control-C, and start it again with `npm start`. (Here is a tip: Instead of retyping the start command, you can duplicate the most recently run command in the terminal by pressing the up-arrow key. Press Return to run it.)

Adding an HTTP request library

There is one more step to setting up Code Café's back-end server: You need a way to make HTTP requests.

There are many tools you can use to make HTTP requests in React applications, including the browser's built-in Fetch API. React is not opinionated about this. We like the popular Axios library, because it is a lightweight package that provides a simple syntax for making network calls, working with JSON data, and handling errors.

Go ahead and install Axios. In a terminal separate from the two servers you have running, navigate to your `code-cafe` directory. Then install Axios by running

```
npm install --save axios@0.27.2
```

useEffect

With Axios installed, you are ready to make a request to the server for the list of available items.

When a user visits Code Café, the app should retrieve the list of items from the server and then load them on the screen. This request should happen only the first time the component renders.

How can you trigger this call within your component?

React provides a hook called **useEffect** to perform side effects, such as API calls that are not directly triggered by a user event or action.

The **useEffect** hook takes two arguments:

- the function to be executed
- the *dependency array*

The dependency array is an array of variables that React uses to determine whether it should execute the function supplied to **useEffect**. To avoid stale data, add any values that you use within **useEffect** to the dependency array.

Each time the component renders, React compares the current values of the variables in the array with the values from the previous render. If any value has changed, React executes the function. Otherwise, React skips the function until the next render cycle.

Use the **useEffect** hook in App.js to make an HTTP request to get the list of items.

Listing 8.2 Adding **useEffect** (App.js)

```
import axios from 'axios';
import { useEffect } from 'react';
import Header from './components/Header';
...
function App() {
  useEffect(() => {
    axios.get('/api/items');
  }, []);

  return (
...
```

The first argument you supply to **useEffect** is the callback function. This function uses the Axios library to make a GET request to the API.

The second argument is the dependency array, which should contain all the dependencies of the effect. During each subsequent render, React compares the contents of the dependency array with the previous values. React uses shallow comparisons (that is, reference equality) to determine whether the contents of the array have changed. React executes the callback only if it detects changes within the dependency array.

Here, you use an empty dependency array. There are no values within the array that can change from render to render. This ensures that React will run the callback function only once, after the initial render.

Normally, to keep the code in sync, you must include in the dependency array the values (including functions) that you define within your component and use inside **useEffect**. Because axios is defined outside your component, it is not a part of the dependency array.

(The setter function returned from **useState** is a special case, which you will see in a moment.)

Since the dependency array is empty, it might be tempting to leave it off entirely. However, that would not have the same result. If you do not supply a dependency array at all, the effect runs after each render, which is usually not what you want.

Save your files before moving on.

Confirming the Network Request

Any requests you make from your application are visible in the DevTools. This lets you easily check the status of network requests and helps you debug when things go wrong.

Hop back over to Code Café at http://localhost:3000 in your browser. Open the DevTools and navigate to the Network tab (Figure 8.4).

Figure 8.4 DevTools Network tab

To focus on the HTTP requests, filter the requests by selecting Fetch/XHR (Figure 8.5). This will hide any other requests, such as requests for static files.

Figure 8.5 Filtering network requests

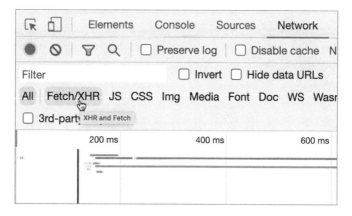

With the DevTools still open, refresh your browser.

You should see a request made to items as the page loads (Figure 8.6).

Figure 8.6 items requests

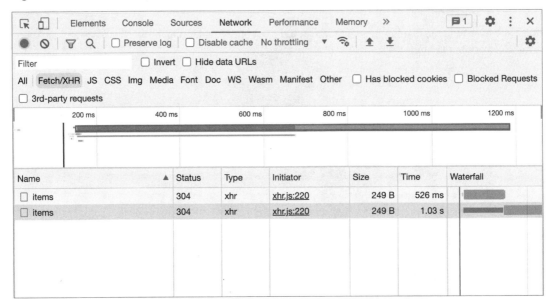

(If the network request is not working, first check that your server is still running. If the server is running and the request is not working, there might be an issue with resolving localhost. In package.json, try replacing

```
"proxy": "http://localhost:3030"
```

with

```
"proxy": "http://127.0.0.1:3030"
```

Then restart your React application and try again.)

But wait – why are there two identical requests?

You might recall from Chapter 1 that Create React App automatically renders your app using React.StrictMode, a developer tool that checks your code for potential problems and provides warnings when issues are detected.

One way this tool tests your components is by mounting a component and then simulating its destruction and re-creation immediately afterward. Because of this, when a component mounts, you will often see code run twice, including side effects like API calls. This happens only in development mode, because React.StrictMode does not run in production.

Click one of the requests to see more information about it. The preview pane within the Network tab shows a formatted version of the response from the server (Figure 8.7).

Figure 8.7 Preview pane

Now that you know your network request is successful, it is time to replace the imported items array with the data from the API.

Use the **useState** hook to add a new state value called items to **App**. Set the initial value to an empty array. When the request is successful, use the setter function to update the state value with the data retrieved from the server. (This code includes some new syntax, such as then and catch. We will explain it in a moment.)

Listing 8.3 Replacing the imported items (App.js)

```
import axios from 'axios';
import { useEffect } from 'react';
import { useEffect, useState } from 'react';
import Header from './components/Header';
import Home from './components/Home';
import { items } from './items';

function App() {
  const [items, setItems] = useState([]);

  useEffect(() => {
    axios.get('/api/items');
    axios.get('/api/items')
      .then((result) => setItems(result.data))
      .catch(console.error);
  }, []);
...
```

Because **console.error** is a function, .catch(console.error) is roughly the same as .catch((error) => console.error(error)).

Now **useEffect** has a dependency that you use within the function: **setItems**. Do you need to add **setItems** to the dependency array? No, because React guarantees that the reference for setter functions will not change throughout renders. This is an exception to the normal pattern of including in the dependency array the values that you define within your component and use inside **useEffect**.

The data from the API is slightly different from the data that was in the local items.js file: now "Drip Coffee" is called "Coffee", and "Chocolate Milk" is just "Milk." Check out your browser to make sure you are seeing the new data (Figure 8.8).

Figure 8.8 Viewing items from the server in the browser

Promises

You have loaded items from the API, taking an important step toward a functional app.

Now, what are then and catch? They are JavaScript constructs for dealing with asynchronous events, such as getting data from the server.

By default, JavaScript is synchronous, executing one operation at a time and not moving to the next operation until the previous operation is complete. When it comes to making network requests, such as the GET request you just made, this presents a problem. Because you make your request to an external resource, you have no control over when the request will be fulfilled. So how can you know when your app has received the items?

One way to handle asynchronous operations, such as requests to an API, is to use *promises*. A promise is a JavaScript object that represents a future value. When the asynchronous operation completes, the promise is considered fulfilled. If there is an error, the promise is considered rejected.

The library you are using to make your network requests, Axios, automatically returns a promise when you make a request. To specify the action that occurs after the promise is fulfilled, you use the promise construct then. Code inside the then block does not execute until the promise is complete. If there is an error, the catch block executes.

How promises work

For many developers, promises are one of the most confusing aspects of JavaScript.

Let's look at an example separate from your project:

```
'use strict';

const getData = () => {
    console.log("getData Running");
    return Promise.resolve("yay!");
};

console.log("top");

getData().then((result) => {
    console.log("result", result);
}).catch((error) => {
    console.error("error", error);
});

console.log("end");
```

Here, `Promise.resolve("yay!");` creates a promise that will be successful and produce the result yay!.

Read through the code. There are seven strings that can print to the console. What do you think will be printed, and in what order?

Ready to find out the answer? This demo code is also in your downloaded resources file, in code-cafe-resources/demos/promiseDemo.js. You can run it using node on your machine. Open a new terminal window, navigate to the demo, and run it:

```
cd YOUR_PATH/resources/code-cafe-resources/demos
node promiseDemo.js
```

Did the output match your expectations?

The first thing that logs is top. Although the **getData** function is defined above `console.log("top")`, the code invokes the log statement first.

Next, the code invokes **getData**, which causes getData Running to log. Then, when it returns `Promise.resolve("yay!")`, it starts a promise. JavaScript does not wait for the call to then to start the promise – the promise starts immediately when you invoke it.

After that, end logs. And finally, result yay! logs.

Why does end log before result yay!? As JavaScript executes, it queues asynchronous work to be done after all available synchronous work is done. `console.log("end");` is synchronous work, so JavaScript does that first. Then, it looks at the task queue, notices that the promise is complete (with `Promise.resolve("yay!")`), and logs the result of the promise.

Feel free to open promiseDemo.js in your editor, make changes, and run the code again with node promiseDemo.js to see the result.

You will have opportunities to practice working with promises and other asynchronous API requests in upcoming chapters. We will also discuss interacting with promises using async/await and try/catch blocks.

Conclusion

Nice work! You have integrated Code Café with the API and made a successful network request to display the available items. In the next chapter, you will add routing to your app to make it more interactive.

For the More Curious: Server Endpoints

Table 8.1 summarizes the Code Café server endpoints that the app can interact with:

Table 8.1 Code Café server endpoints

HTTP verb	Endpoint	Result/Notes
GET	/api/items	Returns all the items for Code Café
GET	/api/employees/ isEmployeeOfTheMonth	With a name as the search query, returns a boolean indicating whether the name belongs to an employee of the month
—	/api/orders	RESTful interface for orders
GET	/api/orders	Returns all submitted orders
POST	/api/orders	Creates an order
DELETE	/api/orders	Deletes all submitted orders
GET	/api/orders/:id	Returns one order
PUT	/api/orders/:id	Updates one order
DELETE	/api/orders/:id	Deletes one order
—	/api/auth	Interface for authenticating users
GET	/api/auth/current-user	Returns the currently logged-in user or {} if no user is logged in
POST	/api/auth/login	With the username and password as the JSON body, logs in a user or returns a 401 status code if the login is invalid
POST	/api/auth/logout	Logs out the currently logged-in user

You will use many of these endpoints as you progress through the book.

For the More Curious: How to Set Up a Proxy in Production

The proxy you set up in package.json affects only local development, when you run npm start. It will not do anything when you run a production build on the server. In production, you need to make sure that the web server – which serves the static files that React builds – is also running a proxy. If your server is running Node.js, one popular package to use for setting up a proxy is http-proxy-middleware. See www.npmjs.com/package/http-proxy-middleware.

For the More Curious: Cross-Origin Resource Sharing (CORS)

CORS occurs when a resource is requested from a domain that does not match the current domain. Although the browser allows scripts and stylesheets to be loaded from other origins, it blocks xhr requests, XMLHttpRequests, and fetch requests made to other origins. (Axios makes XMLHttpRequests internally.)

When a resource request is going to go across origins, the browser sends an OPTIONS request as a preflight check to see whether the server on the other domain will allow the request. One reason to block such requests is to help prevent malicious requests.

You can read more about CORS at developer.mozilla.org/en-US/docs/Web/HTTP/CORS.

For the More Curious: useEffect vs Lifecycle Methods

If you are familiar with class components from previous versions of React, you might remember lifecycle methods, such as **componentDidMount**, **componentDidUpdate**, and **componentWillUnmount**. Those methods are not available for functional components.

Although you can use **useEffect** to perform tasks that those lifecycle events previously triggered – such as fetching data when the component initially renders – there is not a one-to-one substitution. **useEffect** captures the values of the component props and state during each render. This means that it is easy to misuse the **useEffect** hook, resulting in unexpected behavior.

We recommend using the **useEffect** hook only to perform side effects, such as working with external resources (including setting up subscriptions and fetching data from an API) or performing asynchronous behavior.

Silver Challenge: Promise Practice

What if **getData** failed in promiseDemo.js?

Replace return Promise.resolve("yay!"); with return Promise.reject("error!");.

What do you think will happen when you run the code?

Run it and see the result. Make some changes to the code to learn more about promises, and run it again to see what happens.

9

Router

The home page looks great. Visitors to Code Café find a stylish app and can easily see what items are available for purchase.

Unfortunately, clicking a thumbnail does not do anything. Customers have no way to buy or even find out more about the café's tasty treats.

In this chapter, you will take a step toward fixing that. It is time to introduce *routing* to your application.

In React, you use routing to keep the UI in sync as a user navigates through the application. Remember that React is declarative, so you define the UI for a URL, and React will render the elements needed to make it happen.

You will use the popular React Router library to create routes in your application. By the end of this chapter, clicking a `Thumbnail` item will route the user to a new URL and display the item's name (Figure 9.1). Later, you will add the functionality for customers to see details about the item and, finally, order an item from the details page.

Figure 9.1 Item details page

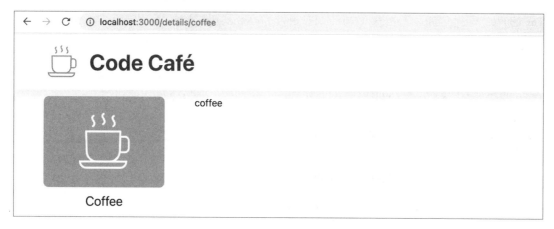

React is not picky about how routing is achieved, and there are multiple ways to add routing. We like React Router because it is a powerful library that lets you tell React which element to render based on a path or URL. React Router also manages the history stack and gives you access to information about the user's location within your app.

React Router is the most popular router to use in combination with Create React App. Other React frameworks, such as Next.js, ship with their own routing libraries.

In a terminal tab or window separate from your development and back-end servers, navigate into your code-cafe directory. Then install the React Router library:

```
npm install --save react-router-dom@6.2.1
```

To enable routing, you add a **Router** component to the top level of your application, in either App.js or index.js. An application can have one **Router** at most, and routing works only in components that are descendants of a **Router**.

Once React Router is installed, add it to App.js.

Listing 9.1 Adding a **BrowserRouter** (App.js)

```
import axios from 'axios';
import { useEffect, useState } from 'react';
import {
  BrowserRouter as Router,
} from 'react-router-dom';
import Header from './components/Header';
import Home from './components/Home';

function App() {
  ...
  return (
    <div>
    <Router>
      <Header />
      <Home items={items} />
    </div>
    </Router>
  );
...
```

The **Router** component in App.js wraps all the content in the application, so all components are its descendants.

Notice the unusual portion of the new import statement: BrowserRouter as Router. This statement uses an *import alias* to import the library's **BrowserRouter** component and rename it **Router** within your app. Renaming **BrowserRouter** to **Router** simplifies future changes to your code.

The React Router library exposes a few different routers you can select from. By design, all the routers have the same interface, so they are interchangeable. The difference is how navigation affects the URL:

- **BrowserRouter** uses the browser's built-in History API, so URLs look like /details/apple.

- **HashRouter** uses the hash portion of the URL: /#/details/apple.

- **MemoryRouter** does not change the URL at all. (**MemoryRouter** is useful for tests or React native applications where there is no URL bar.)

- **StaticRouter** never changes location and is useful for server-side rendering or for tests that do not need to navigate anywhere.

Because you will use **Router** instead of **BrowserRouter** throughout your code, if you change routers in the future, the only line you will need to edit is the import statement. (The most likely reason to change **Router** would be to switch to **HashRouter** to support older browsers.)

Creating Routes

Your browser URL is currently localhost:3000/. Begin implementing routing in your app by adding a route that renders the **Home** component at the index path, using /.

Listing 9.2 Adding a home route (App.js)

```
...
import {
  BrowserRouter as Router,
  Routes,
  Route,
} from 'react-router-dom';
...
function App() {
  ...
  return (
    <Router>
      <Header />
      <Home items={items} />
      <Routes>
        <Route path="/" element={<Home items={items} />} />
      </Routes>
    </Router>
  );
  ...
```

You import two components to set up the route – the **Routes** and **Route** components. Each has a unique job. Let's examine the components that **App** returns, from the inside out.

A **Route** component contains two pieces of information: a path and an element. The path specifies the URL, and the element specifies what should render at the URL. In this case, the path is / and the element is the **Home** component.

You are still passing items to the **Home** component. The element prop accepts valid JSX, so passing props to a component inside a **Route** works the same way as passing props to any other component.

Every **Route** component must be a direct child of a **Routes** component. Though you are starting with just one **Route**, eventually your app will have several.

The **Routes** component contains one or more **Route** components. Most apps have a single **Routes** component, and Code Café will have only one. However, a more complex app might use multiple **Routes** to handle navigation in different sections of the site. The **Routes** component's job is to pick which content to display. It analyzes the paths in all its child **Route** components and picks the one that best matches the URL. The correct element then renders from the matching **Route**.

Previous versions of React Router selected the first matching **Route**. In more recent versions, **Routes** analyzes all the options before selecting the best match, so you do not have to worry about putting the **Route** components in a particular order inside the parent **Routes**.

Recall that routing works only within the context of a **Router**. Though all **Routes** components must be descendants of the **Router** component, they do not need to be direct children. The **Router** and **Routes** do not even have to be in the same component. However, it is common to see them both in App.js.

Save App.js and make sure your browser points to http://localhost:3000/, with nothing after the /. There are no visible changes at this point – you should see the same page content as before.

Now you know what happens when you visit /. Next, try this: Open http://localhost:3000/unknown in your browser.

All you get is a blank page. React Router uses exact matching, and you do not have a **Route** that lists / unknown as a path. When React Router finds no matching **Route**, it renders nothing.

A blank screen is disconcerting to users. It would be better to let them know that a page cannot be found at the URL they entered. But you cannot anticipate all the possible URLs a user might try to enter, so how can you handle this?

In the path that you pass to a **Route**, you can use the * operator as a wildcard to match any string. Add a new **Route** in App.js to catch invalid paths.

Listing 9.3 Adding a catchall route (App.js)

```
...
function App() {
  ...
    <Routes>
      <Route path="/" element={<Home items={items} />} />
      <Route path="*" element={<div>Page Not Found</div>} />
    </Routes>
...
```

The new route matches any URL and acts as a catchall. If the **Routes** component cannot find a better match, the "Page Not Found" <div> element will render.

Navigate again to http://localhost:3000/unknown in your browser. Now you see the words "Page Not Found" (Figure 9.2).

Figure 9.2 Invalid route

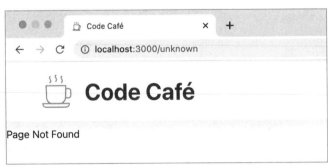

You are about to build several more components for Code Café. To save you some typing and let you focus on learning React, we have supplied the rest of the CSS files you will need for the project. Among them is an updated Header.css file that includes the styles you have already written along with the additional styles you will need as you continue to build Code Café. This updated file will replace the Header.css currently in your project.

In your downloaded resources file, copy all the files from the `stylesheets` directory into your project's `src/components` directory, so that they will be ready to import when you need them. Be sure to replace `Header.css` with the updated version.

Using Link

Now users can see that the URL they tried to visit is invalid. Next, it would be helpful to give them a way to navigate to the home screen.

That would be more work than the **Route** component should do on its own. To keep your code organized, build a new component to render for invalid paths. Then use it to replace the `<div>` that you currently pass to the **Route** component.

Make sure that you have copied the provided stylesheets into your project, so that `NotFound.css` is in your app's `components` folder. Then create a new file (also in your `components` folder) called `NotFound.js`, and build your new component.

Listing 9.4 Building the **NotFound** component (`NotFound.js`)

```
import { Link } from 'react-router-dom';
import './NotFound.css';

function NotFound() {
  return (
    <div className="not-found-component">
      <h2>Page Not Found</h2>
      <Link to="/">Return Home</Link>
    </div>
  );
}

export default NotFound;
```

You import the **Link** component in `NotFound.js` from the React Router library. It renders as an HTML `<a>` tag in the browser. But because you used **BrowserRouter**, React Router adds click event handlers behind the scenes. This means that the **Link** changes the user's location using the HTML5 History API, rather than full-page refreshes.

Now add your new component to the route for the `/*` path.

Listing 9.5 Adding the **NotFound** component to the route (`App.js`)

```
...
import Header from './components/Header';
import Home from './components/Home';
import NotFound from './components/NotFound';

function App() {
  ...
    <Routes>
      <Route path="/" element={<Home items={items} />} />
      <Route path="*" element={<div>Page Not Found</div>} />
      <Route path="*" element={<NotFound />} />
    </Routes>
  ...
```

Save all your files and visit http://localhost:3000/unknown again to see the new 404 page (Figure 9.3).

Figure 9.3 New "Page Not Found"

Click the Return Home link, and you are back at the home page.

Creating the Details Page and Route

So far, so good. In a moment, you will add a third route. This route will display a details page for a single item in Code Café.

But first, you need a details page for the route to display. The details page will have two sections:

- a sidebar containing all the items for sale
- an area displaying the details for the selected item

Begin with the sidebar. You already have the list of available items that you will display there.

Open Home.js and look at how the thumbnails are displayed: The **Home** component uses the array **map** method to iterate through the items and return a list of **Thumbnail**s to display. You will use the same method to create the sidebar.

Make sure that you have copied Details.css from your downloaded resources file into your app's components folder. Then, in Visual Studio Code, create a new components/Details.js file and build your new component.

To build the sidebar, copy the JSX from the **Home** component and paste it into the new file. Update the `className` to access the sidebar styles included in `Details.css`.

For now, add a placeholder for the item detail portion of the screen. You will come back to that soon.

Listing 9.6 Building the **Details** component (`Details.js`)

```
import PropTypes from 'prop-types';
import { itemImages } from '../items';
import ItemType from '../types/item';
import Thumbnail from './Thumbnail';
import './Details.css';

function Details({ items }) {
  return (
    <div className="details-component">
      <div>
        {/* display item */}
      </div>
      <div className="details-component-sidebar">
        {items.map((item) => (
          <Thumbnail
            key={item.itemId}
            image={itemImages[item.imageId]}
            title={item.title}
          />
        ))}
      </div>
    </div>
  );
}

Details.propTypes = {
  items: PropTypes.arrayOf(ItemType).isRequired,
};

export default Details;
```

We said way back in Chapter 2 that reusability is a key benefit of components. Here is a great example – your new sidebar renders the list of items using the **Thumbnail** component you already built.

The placeholder text `{/* display item */}` might look a little strange. This is a JavaScript block comment nested inside JSX. When adding comments inline, you must wrap them in curly braces to ensure they do not render as part of the JSX.

Now add the /details route to App.js.

Listing 9.7 Adding a /details route (App.js)

```
...
import {
  ...
} from 'react-router-dom';
import Details from './components/Details';
import Header from './components/Header';
...
function App() {
  ...
    <Routes>
      <Route path="/details" element={<Details items={items} />} />
      <Route path="/" element={<Home items={items} />} />
      <Route path="*" element={<NotFound />} />
    </Routes>
...
```

In your browser, navigate to http://localhost:3000/details. (Do this manually, not by clicking an item.) Your new **Details** component – or at least its sidebar, styled by the CSS we provided for you – is displayed (Figure 9.4).

Figure 9.4 /details route

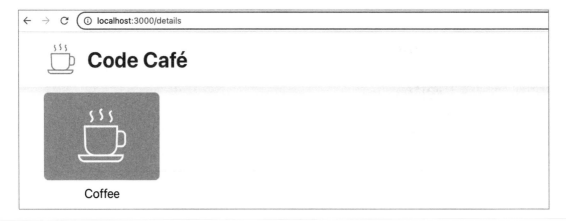

Nesting a route

How can you use routing to insert information about an individual item into the **Details** component? You can nest a route inside the /details route. Do this in App.js:

Listing 9.8 Adding a nested route (App.js)

```
...
function App() {
  ...
    <Routes>
      <Route path="/details" element={<Details items={items} />} />
      <Route path="/details" element={<Details items={items} />}>
        <Route path=":id" element={<div>Detail Item</div>} />
      </Route>
      <Route path="/" element={<Home items={items} />} />
      <Route path="*" element={<NotFound />} />
    </Routes>
...
```

For now, your detail information is just the text "Detail Item."

The full path of the child route is /details/:id. This path looks a little different from the other ones you have seen so far. :id is a dynamic parameter, which we will discuss later in this chapter. For now, what you need to know is that you can use :id to reference the itemId of one of the items. (For a list of all the itemIds available, check out src/items/index.js.)

Save your file and navigate to http://localhost:3000/details/coffee in your browser to try it out (Figure 9.5).

Figure 9.5 Coffee details

Unfortunately, only the sidebar shows up – the "Detail Item" text does not. This is because the new element for the route is not rendering. Fix this by adding a new **Outlet** component from the React Router library to Details.js.

Listing 9.9 Adding the **Outlet** component (Details.js)

```
import PropTypes from 'prop-types';
import { Outlet } from 'react-router-dom';
import { itemImages } from '../items';
import ItemType from '../types/item';
...
function Details({ items }) {
  return (
    <div className="details-component">
      <div>
        {/* display item */}
      </div>
      <Outlet />
      <div className="details-component-sidebar">
...
```

You replace the placeholder in the **Details** component with the React Router component **Outlet**. When there are nested routes, React Router analyzes each child **Route** to find the matching path. The parent component then uses **Outlet** to render the matching child **Route** element.

Save Details.js and try http://localhost:3000/details/coffee again. Now you can see the text "Detail Item" in the browser (Figure 9.6).

Figure 9.6 "Detail Item" text rendering in the browser

Later, you will use the detail area to display the details of an item for sale. Now that you have the details page set up, create a components/DetailItem.js file and refactor **DetailItem** into its own component so it is ready for more development later.

Make sure you have copied DetailItem.css from your downloaded resources file into your app's components directory.

Listing 9.10 Refactoring the **DetailItem** component (DetailItem.js)

```
import './DetailItem.css';

function DetailItem() {
  return (
    <div className="detail-item-component">
      Detail Item
    </div>
  );
}

export default DetailItem;
```

Finally, import and use the new component in App.js.

Listing 9.11 Adding **DetailItem** to the route (App.js)

```
...
import {
  ...
} from 'react-router-dom';
import DetailItem from './components/DetailItem';
import Details from './components/Details';
...
function App() {
  ...
    <Routes>
      <Route path="/details" element={<Details items={items} />}>
        <Route path=":id" element={<div>Detail Item</div>} />
        <Route path=":id" element={<DetailItem />} />
      </Route>
  ...
```

Index route

There is one more nested route to add under /details. It will be an *index* route. When the **Outlet** component is on the parent path (in this case, /details, with no item ID appended), it renders an index route.

Add a nested index route that displays the text "No Item Selected."

Listing 9.12 Adding an index route (App.js)

```
...
function App() {
  ...
      <Route path="/details" element={<Details items={items} />}>
        <Route path=":id" element={<DetailItem />} />
        <Route index element={<div>No Item Selected</div>} />
      </Route>
  ...
```

Here, you use the index keyword, because this index route is a child of another route. But earlier, when you created the home route – which renders the **Home** component at the app's index path – you did not use this keyword. Instead, you specified a path of /. This is because your home route is not a child of another route.

Navigate back to the parent path, http://localhost:3000/details/. Now, instead of a blank screen, it displays "No Item Selected" (Figure 9.7).

Figure 9.7 Displaying the "No Item Selected" index route

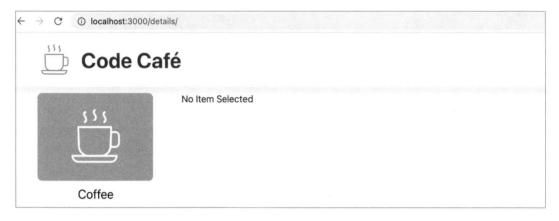

useParams

Let's get back to the detail item's path, /details/:id. The :id in this path is a route parameter. Parameters are dynamic information that you can access inside your component.

A parameter in React Router has two parts:

- the colon, which you use to identify a parameter to React Router
- the parameter name (id, in this case), which follows the colon

How do you get the value of the parameter in your code? React Router provides a hook called **useParams** that returns an object containing all parameters from the current path. (Recall that hooks are JavaScript functions you can use to access state within functional components.)

useParams returns an object containing a key/value pair, with the value passed to it as the key. In this case, because the route is /details/:id, **useParams** returns an object with a key/value pair that has id as the key. Using object destructuring, you can immediately get the value of id with const { id } = useParams();.

Update **DetailItem** to display the ID from the URL.

Listing 9.13 Using the **useParams** hook (DetailItem.js)

```
import { useParams } from 'react-router-dom';
import './DetailItem.css';

function DetailItem() {
  const { id } = useParams();
  return (
    <div className="detail-item-component">
      Detail Item
      {id}
    </div>
  );
}

export default DetailItem;
```

Save your file and navigate once again to http://localhost:3000/details/coffee in your browser. Now it displays the ID of the item specified in the URL (Figure 9.8).

Figure 9.8 Viewing coffee's ID in the browser

In the next chapter, you will update **DetailItem** to show the item's icon and price. For now, you have more navigation to work on.

Navigating Home from the Header

It would be nice if there were an easy way to get back home from the details page – or any other page you might add to your site, for that matter. On many websites, clicking the title or logo in the header sends you back to the home page. Edit the header to add a link that navigates the user back to the home page.

(Can you can implement this change in `components/Header.js` without looking at the code below?)

Listing 9.14 Adding a header link (`Header.js`)

```
import { Link } from 'react-router-dom';
import CoffeeLogo from '../images/logo.svg';
import './Header.css';

function Header() {
  return (
    <header className="header-component">
      <img src={CoffeeLogo} alt="coffee logo" />
      <h1>Code Café</h1>
      <Link to="/">
        <img src={CoffeeLogo} alt="coffee logo" />
        <h1>Code Café</h1>
      </Link>
    </header>
...
```

You use React Router's **Link** component to route the user back to the path /. You wrap both the title and the image in the **Link** component, so the app will redirect the user no matter where they click.

Save your file and test your new navigation in the browser before continuing.

Navigating from Thumbnails to Details

Now let's update the **Thumbnail** component. Clicking a **Thumbnail** should direct the user to the item's details page.

To do this, you will need to pass the itemId prop to the **Thumbnail**. This means you will need to add the prop everywhere that you use the **Thumbnail** component.

Visual Studio Code can help you find all the instances of something throughout your application. Press Command-Shift-F (Ctrl-Shift-F) to access the pane for searching across files. Then enter "<Thumbnail" to find all instances of the **Thumbnail** component (Figure 9.9).

Figure 9.9 Search results

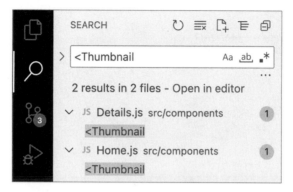

Although the Open in editor link (above the results) opens the list of search results in an editor window, it does not open the listed files. Click the first result to open Details.js for editing, and add itemId as a prop.

Listing 9.15 Adding the itemId prop to **Details** (Details.js)

```
...
function Details({ items }) {
  ...
          <Thumbnail
            key={item.itemId}
            image={itemImages[item.imageId]}
            title={item.title}
            itemId={item.itemId}
          />
...
```

Next, click the second result to add itemId as a prop in Home.js.

Listing 9.16 Adding the itemId prop to **Home** (Home.js)

```
...
function Home({ items }) {
  ...
        <Thumbnail
          key={item.itemId}
          itemId={item.itemId}
          image={itemImages[item.imageId]}
          title={item.title}
        />
...
```

Finally, swap the existing anchor tag for the new **Link** component in Thumbnail.js.

Listing 9.17 Updating the anchor tag to a **Link** (Thumbnail.js)

```
import PropTypes from 'prop-types';
import { Link } from 'react-router-dom';
import './Thumbnail.css';

function Thumbnail({ image, title }) {
function Thumbnail({ itemId, image, title }) {
  return (
    <a
      href="#todo"
    <Link
      className="thumbnail-component"
      to={`/details/${itemId}`}
    >
      <div>
        <img src={image} alt={title} />
      </div>
      <p>{title}</p>
    </a>
    </Link>
  );
}

Thumbnail.propTypes = {
  itemId: PropTypes.string.isRequired,
  image: PropTypes.string.isRequired,
...
```

Because the path for each **Thumbnail** is based on the specific item, you use a template literal, specified by backticks, to compute the correct path from the itemId prop.

Are you wondering why you did not use a **Link** to begin with? **Link** comes from the React Router library and must be a descendant of a **Router** component. You did not have access to it until you added the library and set up your **Router**.

Save your files, then check out your home page and click one of the items. Code Café navigates to the details page for that item. Click the site's title or icon in the header to go back home, or click another item in the sidebar to see its details page. All your navigation should be running smoothly.

Conclusion

Routing allows users to interact with your app and enhances the overall user experience. Using React Router, React works to keep the UI in sync; new information displays onscreen when a user navigates to a new URL.

Now each of your thumbnails is clickable and takes users to a new page where they can learn more about an item. You also added links to help your users navigate back to the home page and to keep them from getting stuck.

In the next chapter, you will learn about another useful feature of React, conditional rendering, as you build out the item details page.

Silver Challenge: More Routes

Code Café is adding a loyalty program! Customers can learn about each tier at /rewards/:tier – for example, /rewards/gold for the gold tier.

Add a /rewards/:tier route that displays the name of the tier from the route parameter. For example, a user visiting /rewards/gold should see "gold" as the content of the page.

10

Conditional Rendering

In the last chapter, you implemented routing in Code Café using the React Router library. Routing is useful because it gives you, the developer, control over which elements will render based on the user's location in your app.

Sometimes, you need to exert a similar kind of control over individual components depending on the app state. For example, you might want to render only part of a component.

Conditional rendering lets you specify which parts of a component should render based on the state of your app. This keeps the UI and the application state in sync. Because components are JavaScript functions, you implement conditional rendering using JavaScript conditional syntax.

In this chapter, you will continue building the **DetailItem** component, using conditional rendering to display all the information a user needs about the items for sale (Figure 10.1).

Figure 10.1 Completed **DetailItem**

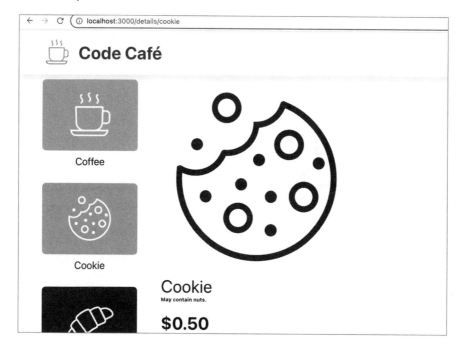

Getting Additional Item Info

In the **DetailItem** component, you use the **useParams** hook to find and display the dynamic itemId for a particular item. Now it is time to use the itemId to display more information to your users.

You will need access to the items array, so pass it as a prop to the **DetailItem** component in App.js.

Listing 10.1 Adding the items prop (App.js)

```
...
function App() {
  ...
        <Route path="/details" element={<Details items={items} />}>
          <Route path=":id" element={<DetailItem />} />
          <Route path=":id" element={<DetailItem items={items} />} />
          <Route index element={<div>No Item Selected</div>} />
        </Route>
...
```

Now, with access to the items array in **DetailItem**, you can find the specified item and display its title, image, and price. Add this item information to your **DetailItem** component.

(During this step, you might run into an error in your browser. In the next step, you will learn what is causing the error and how to fix it.)

Listing 10.2 Displaying all item info (DetailItem.js)

```
import { useParams } from 'react-router-dom';
import PropTypes from 'prop-types';
import { itemImages } from '../items';
import ItemType from '../types/item';
import './DetailItem.css';

function DetailItem() {
function DetailItem({ items }) {
  const { id } = useParams();
  const detailItem = items.find((item) => item.itemId === id);

  return (
    <div className="detail-item-component">
      {id}
      <img
        className="details-image"
        src={itemImages[detailItem.imageId]}
        alt={detailItem.title}
      />
      <h2>{detailItem.title}</h2>
      <div>
        $
        {detailItem.price.toFixed(2)}
      </div>
    </div>
  );
}

DetailItem.propTypes = {
  items: PropTypes.arrayOf(ItemType).isRequired,
};

export default DetailItem;
```

You use the JavaScript array method **find** to iterate through the list of items and find one with an itemId that matches the ID from the parameters.

When displaying the item price, you call detailItem.price.toFixed(2) so that the price always displays two decimal places. **toFixed** is a JavaScript method that you can call on a number; it returns a string with the specified number of decimal places. It addresses two potential problems when working with prices. First, when you convert a decimal that ends in zero to a string, the final zero is removed, so 7.50 becomes 7.5. And second, because of rounding errors, sometimes a number such as 7.50 ends up displaying as 7.4999999999998.

Using **toFixed** takes care of both problems by rounding and making sure the result has exactly the specified number of decimal places. The return value is a string because numbers cannot store an exact number of decimal places and are subject to internal rounding errors.

Save your files. From Code Café's home screen, click the coffee thumbnail to navigate to http://localhost:3000/details/coffee (Figure 10.2).

Figure 10.2 Coffee details

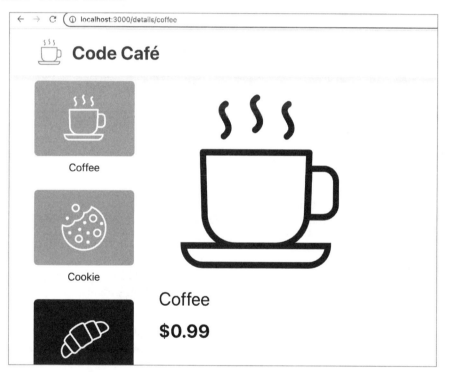

Undefined Items

You might have run into an error in your browser if you tried to go directly to http://localhost:3000/details/coffee instead of clicking the coffee thumbnail.

If you have not encountered the error, trigger it now by manually navigating to http://localhost:3000/details/coffee or by refreshing your browser.

Oops! The app crashes, and the browser displays a blank screen.

Why? What is going on?

The browser console is often the best place to start investigating when you run into a problem with your application. Open the Console tab in the DevTools.

There is a red error message that begins with Uncaught TypeError: Cannot read properties of undefined (reading 'imageId') (Figure 10.3).

Figure 10.3 Console error

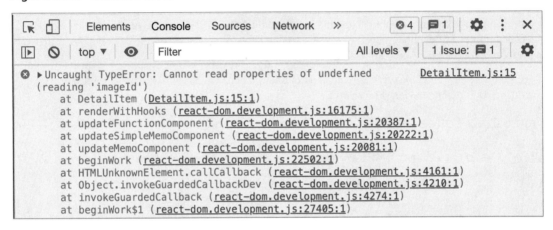

In the first line that begins with "at," the error message points to the file and line that the error occurred in: DetailItem.js:15:1.

Open DetailItem.js and check out line 15:

```
src={itemImages[detailItem.imageId]}
```

The error message indicates a problem with trying to read the value for imageId, which is associated with the **DetailItem** variable. You created **DetailItem** earlier in the component, using the array method **find** to find an item whose itemId matches the URL parameter id. When there is no matching item, the **find** method returns undefined.

DetailItem relies on the items array from the **App** component to find and display the item onscreen. When the browser refreshes, **App** has to refetch items from the server. Until the server request is complete, **DetailItem** will be undefined.

So when you refresh the browser through manual navigation, **DetailItem** is initially undefined. This is why **DetailItem** throws an error when it tries to access detailItem.imageId. This error propagates up through **Details** to **App**, which means the app crashes and the page is blank.

A page crashing is not a good user experience. You cannot control how long it takes until **DetailItem** has a defined value. But instead of crashing, you can show a loading message while the items request is completing.

if Statements

One way to implement conditional rendering in React is with a JavaScript if statement. Add some conditional logic in App.js:

Listing 10.3 Adding conditional loading (App.js)

```
...
function App() {
  ...
  useEffect(() => {
    ...
  }, []);

  if (items.length === 0) {
    return <div>Loading...</div>;
  }

  return (
...
```

This is a regular JavaScript if statement, which returns different JSX if items.length is 0.

Save your file. From the details page, refresh your browser again. The app no longer crashes while the items are loading. Instead, you briefly see the new loading screen before the coffee details appear (Figure 10.4).

Figure 10.4 "Loading..." rendered

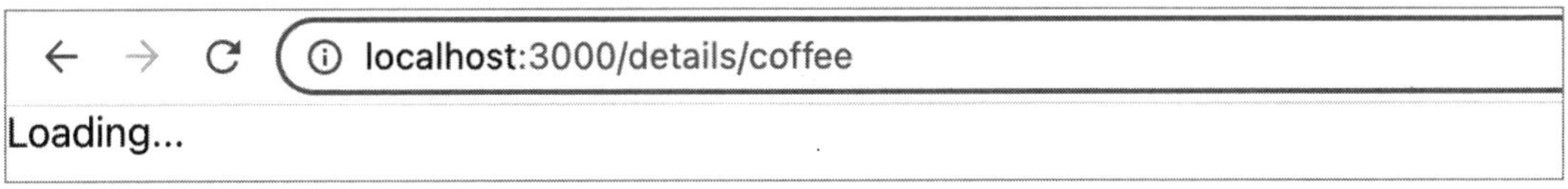

Recall that you used **useState** to set the initial value of items to an empty array, which has a length of 0. Therefore, items.length === 0 is initially true, so JavaScript returns the JSX from inside the if block, and React renders "Loading..." to the page.

Once the server responds with items and the contents of the array update in **useState**, the page re-renders. Because items.length is no longer 0, JavaScript skips the if block and continues to the return statement, which contains the full application.

Inline Logical Operators

if blocks are a great way to tell React what to render when there are multiple possibilities. But in a complex component, the extra return statements from if blocks can make it difficult to tell at a glance what is rendering. A single return statement that covers all the possibilities can help keep your code cleaner and easier to read.

Recall that JSX – such as **App**'s return statement – can contain JavaScript, as long as you wrap it in curly braces ({}). React uses the result from evaluating the code inside curly braces. Because if blocks do not return values inline, you cannot use them directly inside curly braces. However, JavaScript has other inline operators you can use directly inside curly braces to conditionally render elements.

For example, a *ternary* allows you to express the logic of an if statement in a single inline statement.

Besides keeping your code cleaner and easier to maintain, inline operators also allow you to reuse parent elements if needed. Refactor your loading message in App.js to use a ternary inside the parent <div>, which will allow the header to show while the items are loading. (You will need to indent the <Routes> element and its contents.)

Listing 10.4 Using a ternary to display the loading message (App.js)

```
...
function App() {
  ...
  useEffect(() => {
    ...
  }, []);

  if (items.length === 0) {
    return <div>Loading...</div>;
  }

  return (
    <Router>
      <Header />
      {items.length === 0
        ? <div>Loading...</div>
        : (
          <Routes>
            ...
          </Routes>
        )}
    </Router>
  );
}

export default App;
```

A ternary has three parts, separated by the ? and : operators (Figure 10.5). The first part is the *predicate*, the condition that will be evaluated, followed by ?. The second is the code that executes if the predicate is *truthy*, followed by :. And the third is the code that executes if the predicate is *falsy*.

In JavaScript, values that evaluate to true in a Boolean context are considered truthy. Falsy values are any values that evaluate to false when cast to a boolean. Falsy values include false, null, undefined, NaN, 0, and '' (an empty string).

Figure 10.5 Parts of a ternary

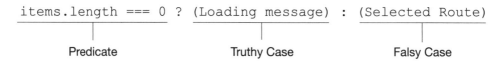

If `items.length` is equal to 0, the predicate has a truthy value, and React renders the loading message (the code after the `?` operator). Otherwise, React renders the **Routes** component and all its children (the code after the `:` operator).

Save your file and check out the app again in your browser. Because the loading message is now nested inside the parent `<div>`, the app header always displays (Figure 10.6). And as a bonus, your code is clean and easy to read.

Figure 10.6 "Loading..." rendered with the header

Fragments

Although you fixed the error that occurs when `items` is not yet available, unfortunately there is still a bug in your code. What happens if `items` is available but the item is still not found?

Visit http://localhost:3000/details/unknown to find out.

Similar to before, the app crashes and shows a blank screen. The error in the console is the same, pointing to **DetailItem** being undefined (Figure 10.7).

Figure 10.7 Undefined item console error

There are at least two states your component can be in after loading is complete:

- the happy state, where **DetailItem** is a valid item object
- the error state, where **DetailItem** is undefined

Code Café must be able to handle both states.

Similar to what you did in **App** above, use a ternary in **DetailItem** to display the item details or a message reading "Unknown Item," depending on the validity of **DetailItem**. This code will contain some new syntax, which we will explain shortly. (Once again, you will need to indent the existing code that you are embedding in the new ternary.)

Listing 10.5 Using a ternary in **DetailItem** (DetailItem.js)

```
...
function DetailItem({ items }) {
  ...
  return (
    <div className="detail-item-component">
      {detailItem ? (
        <>
          <img
            ...
          />
          <h2>{detailItem.title}</h2>
          <div>
            ...
          </div>
        </>
      ) : <h2>Unknown Item</h2>}
    </div>
  );
}

DetailItem.propTypes = {
  items: PropTypes.arrayOf(ItemType).isRequired,
};

export default DetailItem;
```

Save your file and refresh your browser to see the new "Unknown Item" message (Figure 10.8).

Figure 10.8 Unknown Item

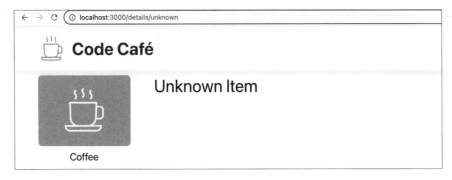

You use some new tags in **DetailItem**: <> and </>. These empty tags create a JSX *fragment*. You will likely run into fragments when working with conditional rendering.

When React evaluates a ternary statement or other conditional operator, the returned value is a JSX expression. Each JSX expression can contain only one element as a direct child.

In **DetailItem**, there are three sibling elements to render if the ternary's predicate is truthy: <img>, <h2>, and <div>. Because JSX requires a single direct child element in the expression, these three elements need a parent to contain them.

One option is to wrap the elements with a <div>. Although this would work, it would introduce unnecessary complexity to your app and could have unintended effects on styling, among other things. The only reason to use a <div> would be if you need it for applying styles.

Fragments behave differently from <div>s or other JSX elements. To see this, navigate to the details page of a known item, such as /coffee for coffee. Right-click the coffee image and choose Inspect Element to find the element in the DevTools Elements tab (Figure 10.9).

Figure 10.9 Inspecting the fragment

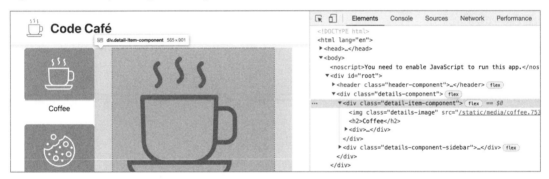

The <img>, <h2>, and price <div> are all direct children of <div class="detail-item-component">. The empty element is nowhere to be seen.

Fragments do not render in the browser, which means they do not create extra nodes in the DOM. This is the difference between using a fragment to group elements in JSX and using an element such as a <div>.

Incidentally, you can also write a fragment as <React.Fragment>. But usually, developers just represent fragments with the empty tags <> and </>.

More Logical Operators

You can use other logical operators to conditionally render React elements, combining operators as needed. Next you will refine your item details page by using logical AND and OR operators to get different information for different items.

To begin, check out the list of items from the server in the DevTools Network tab (Figure 10.10). (Click items in the list of requests to open the preview pane.)

Figure 10.10 items in the Network tab

Expand items 0 and 1 (coffee and cookie) to see all of their fields:

```
{
    itemId: 'coffee',
    imageId: 'coffee',
    title: 'Coffee',
    price: 0.99,
    description: '',
    salePrice: 0,
},
{
    itemId: 'cookie',
    imageId: 'cookie',
    title: 'Cookie',
    price: 1,
    description: 'May contain nuts.',
    salePrice: 0.50,
}
```

These items have two fields that the other items do not: description and salePrice. (You can expand the other items to check this.)

The description and salePrice information does not yet display in the **DetailItem** component. Because only some of the items have these data fields, you will use conditional rendering to display this information only when it is available from the selected item.

The && operator

Before rendering the item description, you will check whether the field exists on the selected item using the logical AND.

Listing 10.6 Using the logical AND operator (`DetailItem.js`)

```
...
function DetailItem({ items }) {
  ...
        <h2>{detailItem.title}</h2>
        {detailItem.description && <h6>{detailItem.description}</h6>}
        <div>
...
```

JavaScript represents the logical AND operator with &&. This operator returns either the first falsy value it encounters or, if all values are truthy, the last value of the statement.

Let's see the results of this statement, starting with the cookie item.

The cookie object's `detailItem.description` (the first value in the logical AND statement) is a string. Non-empty strings are truthy, so the code returns the last item of the statement, which is the JSX to render the description to the screen.

Save your file and look at your browser to see the new description field for the cookie item (Figure 10.11).

Figure 10.11 Conditionally rendering the cookie description

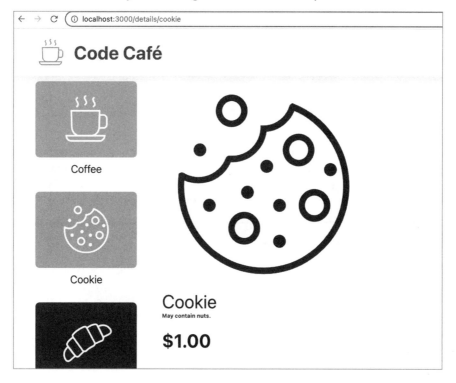

Now click the coffee thumbnail to check out its details (Figure 10.12).

Figure 10.12 Conditionally rendering the coffee description

The description for coffee is an empty string, which is considered a falsy value. When the logical AND statement returns a falsy value, React ignores the statement (in most cases – more on that in just a moment). Here, React skips the JSX that renders the description.

Click one of the other item thumbnails, such as the croissant. Because it has no description field, detailItem.description is undefined, which is falsy. React skips the statement, and no description renders.

We said that React ignores the statement when the logical AND returns a falsy value "in most cases." The exceptions to this rule are the values 0 and NaN (or "not a number"). When the logical AND operator returns either of these values, React does not ignore the statement. If the variable you are evaluating might be one of these values, you can convert it to a boolean using !! (*double NOT*) or **Boolean** to avoid this problem.

You can use the double NOT operator like this:

```
{!!detailItem.description && <h6>{detailItem.description}</h6>}
```

And the equivalent **Boolean** function like this:

```
{Boolean(detailItem.description) && <h6>{detailItem.description}</h6>}
```

The || operator

`coffee` and `cookie` also have fields called `salePrice`. When an item has a sale price assigned, the sale price should override the regular price. Use the JavaScript logical OR operator, represented by ||, to display the sale price or the regular price.

Listing 10.7 Using the logical OR operator (`DetailItem.js`)

```
...
function DetailItem({ items }) {
  ...
        <div>
          $
          {detailItem.price.toFixed(2)}
          {(detailItem.salePrice || detailItem.price).toFixed(2)}
        </div>
...
```

Save your file and navigate once again to the `cookie` item in your browser. Now cookies are on sale for $0.50 instead of $1.00 (Figure 10.13).

Figure 10.13 Cookie sale price

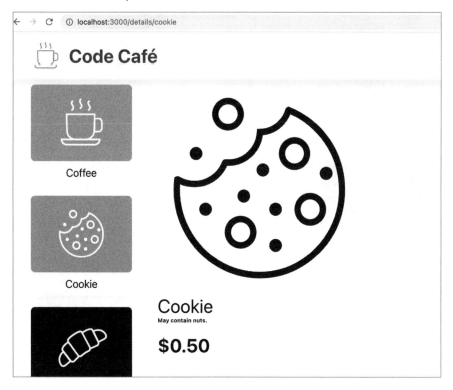

As with the && operator, React renders the result from the JavaScript expression. If the code preceding || evaluates to a truthy value, JavaScript returns that value, and React ignores the rest of the statement. If the code evaluates to a falsy value, JavaScript returns the code following ||, and React renders its value.

Because cookie.salePrice is a truthy value, that value renders. For items with no sale price, the value of detailItem.salePrice is undefined, and React renders the second value of the statement, the price.

What happens when the first value is 0, as it is for the coffee item? Click the coffee thumbnail to find out (Figure 10.14).

Figure 10.14 Coffee is not on sale

The sale price of 0 does not render. This is because the OR operator evaluates all falsy values, including 0, as false, so it returns the right side of the statement instead.

Suppose you really want to offer coffee for free. You will need a different solution.

The ?? operator

The JavaScript *nullish coalescing* operator, represented by ??, works very similarly to the OR operator. The difference is in how they handle falsy values: Unlike the OR operator, the nullish coalescing operator returns *any* left-side value from the statement except null or undefined. This means the ?? operator considers 0 valid and will return it. It also considers false, NaN, and '' valid.

Try it out by refactoring **DetailItem** to use the nullish coalescing operator in place of the OR operator.

Listing 10.8 Using the ?? operator (DetailItem.js)

```
...
function DetailItem({ items }) {
  ...
        <div>
          $
          {(detailItem.salePrice || detailItem.price).toFixed(2)}
          {(detailItem.salePrice ?? detailItem.price).toFixed(2)}
        </div>
...
```

Save your file and check your browser to see what happened (Figure 10.15).

Figure 10.15 Free coffee!

Now the sale price for coffee is showing. If you look at another item that does not have a sale price, the default price still renders.

Boolean Type Conversion

In this chapter, you used logical operators based on truthy and falsy values and learned that the !! operator converts any falsy or truthy value to its respective boolean. You also saw that some values, such as 0, require special consideration.

If you ever need to verify your assumptions about logical statements, you can do that in the DevTools Console tab.

Open the Console tab and place the cursor next to the blue arrow (Figure 10.16).

Figure 10.16 Console tab arrow

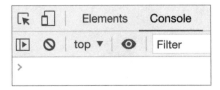

Then type out what you want to test, such as !!0 to see if 0 is truthy or falsy. You will see a preview of the result in light colors. Press Return to execute the line, and the result will darken.

Enter a few more tests, such as !!'' to check whether an empty string is truthy or falsy. You can also test statements such as 0 || 1 and 0 ?? 1 and compare the results (Figure 10.17).

Figure 10.17 Testing values in the console

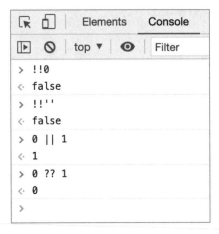

The console is a great place to experiment with logical statements and verify your assumptions.

Conclusion

Conditional rendering is an important tool to keep the UI in sync with the component and application states, prevent errors, and provide a positive user experience. JavaScript conditional statements and the conditional operators in ternary statements let you declare which parts of the component should render at which time.

And you can use fragments when you need to group elements together but want to avoid unnecessary nesting and complexity.

You are making great progress with Code Café. In the next chapter, you will learn about a new hook, `useReducer`, as you build out a cart for users to add items to.

For the More Curious: Truthy and Falsy Values

For more examples of truthy and falsy values, check out

- developer.mozilla.org/en-US/docs/Glossary/truthy
- developer.mozilla.org/en-US/docs/Glossary/falsy

Silver Challenge: Promote Sale Items

To promote sale items, add `<div>On Sale!</div>` above the image if an item has a sale price.

Remember that `salePrice` can be `0`, which is falsy, so you will want your conditional to be more specific than just a truthy/falsy check.

11

useReducer

In Chapter 4, you used the **useState** hook to access a component's state. In this chapter, you will explore another React hook: **useReducer**, which lets you set, modify, and access a state variable within a component.

You will take advantage of **useReducer** to add a shopping cart to Code Café and manage its ongoing value.

If you have previously used Redux, a third-party library for managing state, some of the patterns you see in this chapter might be familiar. However, you do not need any prior knowledge of or experience with Redux to use the **useReducer** hook.

By the end of this chapter, users will be able to add items to a cart, and a new cart icon in the header will display the number of items in the cart (Figure 11.1).

Figure 11.1 Code Café's header at the end of the chapter

useReducer vs useState

In a moment, you will use the **useReducer** hook to add a new piece of state, called `cart`.

Why use **useReducer** instead of **useState**? The short answer is that **useState** is better for simple state management, while **useReducer** is better for complex state management.

Users expect several functions from a shopping cart, such as adding an item, removing an item, and emptying the cart.

With the **useState** hook, you have access to one method to update the value of the state. Each time you use that method, you overwrite the entire state value. When you need to interact with the state in multiple ways, such as for different cart actions, things can get messy.

Unlike **useState**, **useReducer** allows you to write your own *reducer function*, which can contain a variety of actions to perform on the state value. This way, the reducer handles all the logic needed for the cart actions in one place.

useReducer is also useful when the next state depends on the previous state, such as when you want to update the quantity of an existing item in the cart.

It is OK if this does not all make sense right now. This chapter will walk you through the **useReducer** hook and give you some practice so you can see how it works.

Implementing useReducer

The **useReducer** hook accepts two arguments: a reducer function and an initial state value. To keep your code organized, you will create these in a separate reducer directory and file.

Add a new folder in the src directory called reducers, then create a reducers/cartReducer.js file to export the two variables you will need: initialCartState and the **cartReducer** function.

Listing 11.1 Creating the cart reducer variables (cartReducer.js)

```
export const initialCartState = [];

export const cartReducer = (state, action) => {
  switch (action.type) {
    case 'add':
      return [
        ...state,
        { itemId: action.itemId, quantity: 1 },
      ];
    default:
      throw new Error(`Invalid action type ${action.type}`);
  }
};
```

The first variable is initialCartState. The cart state will be an array of item objects, where the key is the itemId and the value is the quantity of that item in the cart. The initial state is an empty array, because there are no items in the cart yet.

The second variable is **cartReducer**. Do not worry about understanding what the **cartReducer** function is doing yet. You will explore this in more detail shortly.

Now that you have these two values, add the **useReducer** hook to your application.

Listing 11.2 Adding **useReducer** (App.js)

```
import axios from 'axios';
import { useEffect, useState } from 'react';
import { useEffect, useReducer, useState } from 'react';
...
import NotFound from './components/NotFound';
import { cartReducer, initialCartState } from './reducers/cartReducer';

function App() {
  const [items, setItems] = useState([]);
  // eslint-disable-next-line no-unused-vars
  const [cart, dispatch] = useReducer(cartReducer, initialCartState);

  useEffect(() => {
...
```

174

You pass the **useReducer** hook the two values you just created – the reducer function and the initial state value. **useReducer** returns an array with two values, which you access using array destructuring.

As with **useState**, the first value of the returned array is the current state value. Here, you name the state cart.

The second value in the returned array is the **dispatch** function. This is a special function that **useReducer** creates. To update the state value, you will call the **dispatch** function and pass it an action object.

Because you are not using the values of cart and **dispatch** yet, you add eslint-disable-next-line no-unused-vars in a comment above the line where you define them. This will stop ESLint from applying the no-unused-vars rule and complaining about these unused variables until you make use of them.

The Reducer Function

Now let's take a closer look at the **cartReducer** function you created in cartReducer.js.

The reducer function receives two arguments: state and action. state is the current state of your hook. action – the same object given to the **dispatch** function – contains the type of action that you want your reducer to perform.

You define actions using the cases in **cartReducer**'s switch statement. Right now, the reducer supports only one action type, add.

The reducer also handles a default case. You use this to ensure that the code throws an error if there is no matching action type. This will alert you or other developers using the reducer that there is a mismatch between the supported actions and the action type passed to the **dispatch** function.

Check out the return statement of the add action type:

```
return [
    ...state,
    { id: action.itemId, quantity: 1 },
];
```

JavaScript spread syntax creates a shallow copy of state, and the item being added is appended to the new array.

Reducers should never mutate state directly. This is because React uses reference equality to determine when to re-render, instead of looking deeply into objects. Although mutating the initial state value might seem to work as expected, it usually causes hard-to-debug issues down the road.

Instead, use spread or similar syntax to create a new state object. This will create a new reference and trigger React to re-render when state changes.

Updating the Quantity

The action type add inserts the itemId in the array and sets the quantity to 1. But what happens if the item is already in the cart? In that case, add should update the quantity of the existing item instead.

Update the reducer function to handle the second case using a conditional expression.

Listing 11.3 Updating **cartReducer** (cartReducer.js)

```
export const initialCartState = [];

const findItem = (cart, itemId) => cart.find((item) => item.itemId === itemId);

export const cartReducer = (state, action) => {
  switch (action.type) {
    case 'add':
      if (findItem(state, action.itemId)) {
        return state.map((item) => (item.itemId === action.itemId
          ? { ...item, quantity: item.quantity + 1 }
          : item));
      }
      return [
...
```

In your if statement, you use the **findItem** method to check whether the item already exists in the cart. If the item is present, you create a new, updated array of items using **map**. Within the **map**, the ternary increments the quantity of the matching item and leaves all the other items as they are. And you avoid mutating the state directly by using spread syntax again for the state change.

Now the add action is ready to go.

Before adding more actions to **cartReducer**, make your code easier to maintain by refactoring the reducer to use variables for action types instead of strings.

Listing 11.4 Using action variables (cartReducer.js)

```
export const initialCartState = [];

export const CartTypes = {
  ADD: 'ADD',
};

const findItem = (cart, itemId) => cart.find((item) => item.itemId === itemId);

export const cartReducer = (state, action) => {
  switch (action.type) {
    case 'add':
    case CartTypes.ADD:
      if (findItem(state, action.itemId)) {
...
```

Now you can use the exported CartTypes variable in the reducer and in the **dispatch** function.

Replacing strings with variables allows you to take advantage of your editor's code completion tools, which will greatly reduce the likelihood of spelling or syntax errors. It also provides documentation for the available reducer actions.

Displaying Information in the Header

Now Code Café has a cart, and the cart can hold items – these are big steps. But at the moment, the user gets no feedback to let them know that items are in the cart. For that matter, they have no way to select items to add to the cart.

Next you will add a shopping cart icon to the header, along with the number of items in the cart. This will let you easily see when an item has been added to the cart, without having to use the DevTools. When that is complete, you will add the functionality to actually put items in the cart.

You should already have `cart.svg` under `src/images`. If you do not, copy it from your downloaded resources file.

Now, to access the current value of the `cart` state object, pass `cart` to **Header** as a prop.

Listing 11.5 Passing `cart` as a prop (`App.js`)

```
...
function App() {
  ...
  return (
    <Router>
      <Header />
      <Header cart={cart} />
      {items.length === 0
...
```

Add the cart icon and badge to **Header**, using the class names defined in Header.css. The cart icon will also link to a separate cart page, which you will build out soon.

Listing 11.6 Adding the cart icon to the header (Header.js)

```
import { Link } from 'react-router-dom';
import PropTypes from 'prop-types';
import CoffeeLogo from '../images/logo.svg';
import CartIcon from '../images/cart.svg';
import './Header.css';

function Header() {
function Header({ cart }) {
  const cartQuantity = cart.reduce((acc, item) => acc + item.quantity, 0);
  return (
    <header className="header-component">
      <Link to="/">
        <img src={CoffeeLogo} alt="coffee logo" />
        <h1>Code Café</h1>
      </Link>
      <div className="menu">
        <Link to="#todo">
          <img src={CartIcon} alt="Cart" />
          <div className="badge">{cartQuantity}</div>
        </Link>
      </div>
    </header>
  );
}

Header.propTypes = {
  cart: PropTypes.arrayOf(PropTypes.shape({
    itemId: PropTypes.string.isRequired,
    quantity: PropTypes.number.isRequired,
  })).isRequired,
};

export default Header;
```

You use the **Array.reduce** method to evaluate the quantity of items in the cart for the cartQuantity variable. Although its name is similar, this method is not related to the **useReducer** hook or its associated reducer function. The **reduce** method allows you to reduce the data in an array to a single value – in this case, the total number of items in the cart.

Save your files and take a look at your browser. You have a shiny new cart icon and badge (Figure 11.2)!

Figure 11.2 Cart icon

This will give users instant feedback when they add items to the cart, which is the functionality you will add next.

Adding Items to the Cart

The user should be able to add items to the cart from a button on each item's details page. For this to happen, **DetailItem** needs access to the **dispatch** function.

Pass **dispatch** as a prop to the **DetailItem** component in App.js. Also, now that you are using both of the values from **useReducer**, you no longer need to disable the ESLint warning about unused variables.

Listing 11.7 Passing **dispatch** as a prop (App.js)

```
...
function App() {
  const [items, setItems] = useState([]);
  // eslint-disable-next-line no-unused-vars
  const [cart, dispatch] = useReducer(cartReducer, initialCartState);
  ...
  return (
            <Route path="/details" element={<Details items={items} />}>
              <Route path=":id" element={<DetailItem items={items} />} />
              <Route
                path=":id"
                element={<DetailItem items={items} dispatch={dispatch} />}
              />
              <Route index element={<div>No Item Selected</div>} />
  ...
```

Next, open DetailItem.js. Add the **dispatch** function to the component props. Then add a new Add to Cart button that calls the **dispatch** function when clicked.

Listing 11.8 Adding an Add to Cart button (DetailItem.js)

```
...
import './DetailItem.css';
import { CartTypes } from '../reducers/cartReducer';

function DetailItem({ items }) {
function DetailItem({ dispatch, items }) {
  const { id } = useParams();
  const detailItem = items.find((item) => item.itemId === id);

  const addItemToCart = () => {
    dispatch({ type: CartTypes.ADD, itemId: detailItem.itemId });
  };

  return (
    ...
        <div>
          $
          {(detailItem.salePrice ?? detailItem.price).toFixed(2)}
        </div>
        <button
          type="button"
          onClick={addItemToCart}
        >
          Add to Cart
        </button>
      </>
...
DetailItem.propTypes = {
  dispatch: PropTypes.func.isRequired,
  items: PropTypes.arrayOf(ItemType).isRequired,
...
```

You saw the **onClick** attribute in Ottergram; it is how you instruct React to listen for click events. When the user clicks the Add to Cart button, React calls the **dispatch** function with an object containing the action type and the itemId.

Internally, **useReducer** then calls **cartReducer**, passing it the current state of the reducer as the first argument and the object passed to **dispatch** as the second argument. Finally, the value that **cartReducer** returns becomes the new state of your reducer (Figure 11.3).

Figure 11.3 Reducer flow

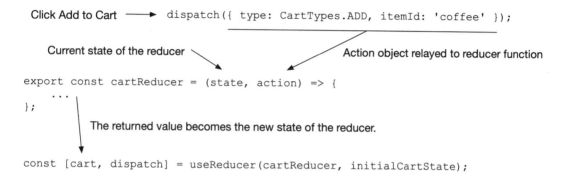

It is time to take your newly functional cart out for a spin. Save your files and head to your browser. On the details page for any item, click Add to Cart, and you will see the cart badge change from 0 to 1. Click Add to Cart again, and you will see the badge update to 2 (Figure 11.4).

Figure 11.4 Working cart badge

Action Creators

One disadvantage of **dispatch** is that it is hard to know what other properties need to be in the action object besides the type. For example, although the ADD action requires the itemId, another developer might not know this.

Action creators are a pattern you can use with **useReducer** to help solve this issue. They also help reduce coupling between the reducer and the component using the reducer.

Action creators are essentially helper functions that call the **dispatch** function with a specific action and the other necessary properties. Instead of calling **dispatch** directly, a component instead calls the action creator.

Refactor `App.js` to include an action creator for adding an item to the cart. Pass the new function to **DetailItem** as a prop, instead of passing **dispatch**. This will decouple **DetailItem** from the cart reducer and make it clear that adding an item to the cart requires an `itemId`.

Listing 11.9 Adding an action creator (`App.js`)

```
...
import NotFound from './components/NotFound';
import { cartReducer, initialCartState } from './reducers/cartReducer';
import { cartReducer, CartTypes, initialCartState } from './reducers/cartReducer';

function App() {
  const [items, setItems] = useState([]);
  const [cart, dispatch] = useReducer(cartReducer, initialCartState);
  const addToCart = (itemId) => dispatch({ type: CartTypes.ADD, itemId });
  ...
  return (
    ...
            <Route
              path=":id"
              element={<DetailItem items={items} dispatch={dispatch} />}
              element={<DetailItem items={items} addToCart={addToCart} />}
            />
    ...
```

The **addToCart** helper function allows components to add items to the cart without needing to know about the reducer. This decouples the components from the implementation of the reducer.

Now update the Add to Cart button's **onClick** handler to call the **addToCart** function instead of **dispatch**.

Listing 11.10 Using the action creator in **DetailItem** (`DetailItem.js`)

```
...
import './DetailItem.css';
import { CartTypes } from '../reducers/cartReducer';

function DetailItem({ dispatch, items }) {
function DetailItem({ addToCart, items }) {
  ...
  const addItemToCart = () => {
    dispatch({ type: CartTypes.ADD, itemId: detailItem.itemId });
    addToCart(detailItem.itemId);
  };
  ...
DetailItem.propTypes = {
  dispatch: PropTypes.func.isRequired,
  addToCart: PropTypes.func.isRequired,
  items: PropTypes.arrayOf(ItemType).isRequired,
  ...
```

Save your files. In the browser, try adding items to the cart again. After refactoring, your code should work as before.

Action creators are optional, so you can decide if they make sense for your app. Generally, action creators are most useful for avoiding coupling between a component and the reducer and for documenting the required properties for a given action. Action creators are less helpful when you have a component that uses many actions from a reducer, because the component is naturally more coupled to the reducer.

Conclusion

React provides the **useState** and **useReducer** hooks for managing state inside your components. Each hook has its own use case: You generally use **useState** to manage relatively simple state and **useReducer** to manage more complex state.

In this chapter, you used the **useReducer** hook and your own reducer function to set up a cart for Code Café that users can add items to. In the next chapter, you will allow users to view and edit the cart.

12

Editing the Cart

Developing Code Café has given you experience with building functional components. You have also added state to keep track of the user's `cart` and are using the **useReducer** hook to manage that state.

In this chapter, you will create a route for users to view and edit the cart. This chapter uses concepts you already know, giving you the opportunity to practice your skills as you expand your app.

Try to write each new piece of code without first looking at the snippets we provide. When you finish, compare your code with ours. You might do some things differently from how we do them – that is fine, as long as your app behaves as expected. But we do recommend that you edit your code to match ours before moving forward to make sure you do not run into compatibility issues later.

Figure 12.1 shows what your cart page will look like at the end of the chapter:

Figure 12.1 Completed cart

Creating the Cart Page

Your first task is to add the new page, complete with a header. The route for this page should be /cart.

Create a new **Cart** component in your components directory. Begin with a simple component that returns a header with the text "Your Cart." If you have not already done so, copy the Cart.css stylesheet from your downloaded resources file into your components directory. Then import it in the **Cart** component.

Finally, display the **Cart** component when the user visits the route /cart. See if you can do this without looking at the solution below.

Listing 12.1 Creating the **Cart** component (Cart.js)

```
import './Cart.css';

function Cart() {
  return (
    <div className="cart-component">
      <h2>Your Cart</h2>
    </div>
  );
}

export default Cart;
```

Now add the new route in App.js.

Listing 12.2 Adding the /cart route (App.js)

```
...
import DetailItem from './components/DetailItem';
import Cart from './components/Cart';
import Details from './components/Details';
...
function App() {
  ...
        <Routes>
          <Route path="/cart" element={<Cart />} />
          <Route path="/details" element={<Details items={items} />}>
...
```

Save your files and visit http://localhost:3000/cart in your browser to see your new cart page (Figure 12.2).

Figure 12.2 Cart page

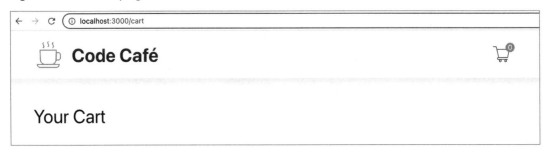

Linking to the cart page

Now users need an intuitive way to get to the new page. Update the cart icon in **Header** by replacing the **Link**'s #todo destination attribute with the new /cart route.

Listing 12.3 Updating the **Link** for the cart icon (Header.js)

```
...
function Header({ cart }) {
  ...
    <div className="menu">
      <Link to="#todo">
      <Link to="/cart">
        <img src={CartIcon} alt="Cart" />
...
```

Save your file. In your browser, click Code Café in the header to navigate home, then click the cart icon in the header to return to the cart page.

Viewing the Cart's Contents

Now that users can access the cart page, you need to display the cart's contents. To do this, you must share the cart state with the **Cart** component.

The cart state that the **useReducer** hook manages is stored in the **App** component. Should you move the cart state to **Cart**?

You should not, because you need access to the cart state in all of the following:

- **Header**, to set the value in the icon badge
- **DetailItem**, so the **dispatch** function can add items to the cart
- **Cart**, to display the contents of the cart

useReducer does not inherently create global state. To share cart and its related **dispatch** function with all three of these components, you must create the state in a parent of the components. In Code Café, the closest parent component is **App**.

Before you add the cart state to the **Cart** component, let's explore how the state behaves in your current code.

In your browser, open the DevTools. In the Components tab, select the **App** component (Figure 12.3).

Figure 12.3 **App** component in the DevTools

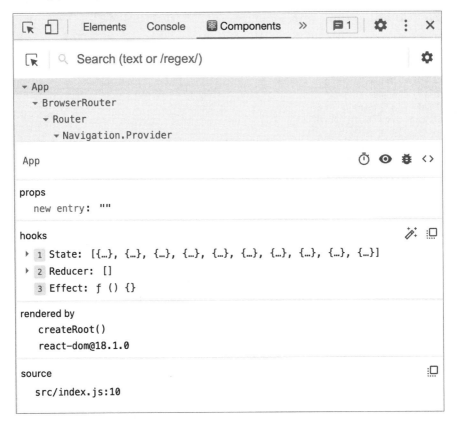

In the hooks section, you can see a list of the hooks you used in **App** – **useState**, **useReducer**, and **useEffect** – ordered as they appear in the component. (They are listed as State, Reducer, and Effect, without the use prefix.)

The value for Reducer is an empty array. **App** calls **useReducer** one time, to create the cart state and the **dispatch** function, so the Reducer you see in the Components tab represents the cart state.

If your app used multiple reducer hooks, the Components tab would show each one. To get the most benefit from the DevTools information, you need to know which instance of a hook you want to explore.

Click the magic wand icon to the right of the hooks (Figure 12.4).

Figure 12.4 Parsing the hook names

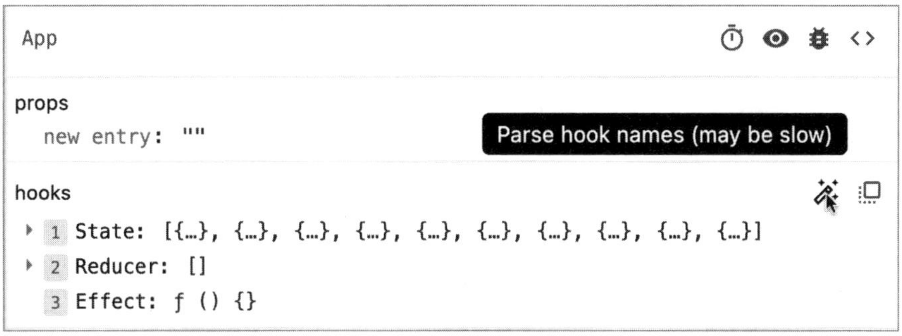

The DevTools add hook names to each hook displayed. This can be valuable when you have multiple hooks and want to quickly differentiate them (Figure 12.5).

Figure 12.5 Displaying the hook names

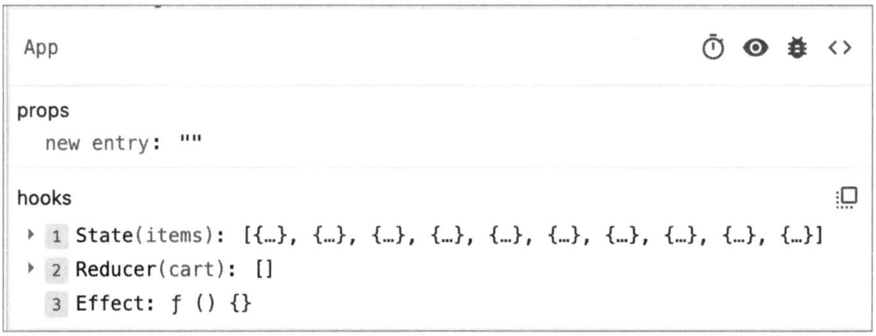

Now you can see that the name of the reducer value is cart.

Next, add items to the cart by clicking the **Add to Cart** button on your site. Watch the state change in the DevTools as the items are added to cart (Figure 12.6).

Figure 12.6 Displaying the hook state

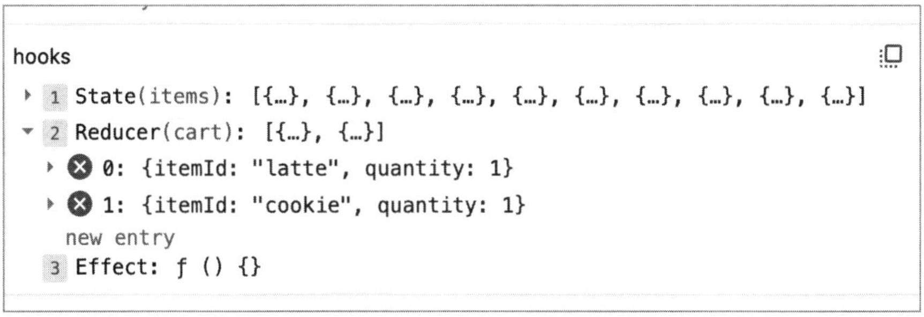

Now refresh your browser. The state value returns to an empty array.

React state does not persist across refreshes. To add persistence, you can use browser storage, which you will implement in Chapter 14.

Being able to see the current state in the DevTools is useful for making sure the app behaves as expected during development and for debugging the app if it does not.

Now it is time to provide the **Cart** component with updated state information.

Displaying the Cart Contents

Get started by passing the cart prop to the **Cart** component.

Listing 12.4 Passing the cart prop (App.js)

```
...
function App() {
  ...
        <Routes>
          <Route path="/cart" element={<Cart />} />
          <Route path="/cart" element={<Cart cart={cart} />} />
          <Route path="/details" element={<Details items={items} />}>
  ...
```

See if you can make the next changes without looking at the code. You need to import the cart prop into the **Cart** component and add the corresponding propTypes. (Remember that the cart prop is an array. Each element in the array is an object with the keys itemId and quantity.)

You can use table elements to display data in React, just like in HTML. Use a table to display the **Cart** data in rows, with the item quantity in the first column and the item ID in the second column.

Listing 12.5 Building the cart contents display (Cart.js)

```
import PropTypes from 'prop-types';
import './Cart.css';

function Cart() {
function Cart({ cart }) {
  return (
    <div className="cart-component">
      <h2>Your Cart</h2>
      <table>
        <thead>
          <tr>
            <th>Quantity</th>
            <th>Item</th>
          </tr>
        </thead>
        <tbody>
          {cart.map((item) => (
            <tr key={item.itemId}>
              <td>{item.quantity}</td>
              <td>{item.itemId}</td>
            </tr>
          ))}
        </tbody>
      </table>
    </div>
  );
}

Cart.propTypes = {
  cart: PropTypes.arrayOf(PropTypes.shape({
    itemId: PropTypes.string.isRequired,
    quantity: PropTypes.number.isRequired,
  })).isRequired,
};

export default Cart;
```

Save your file.

In the browser, add some items to the cart. Then click the cart icon to navigate to the cart page and see its contents (Figure 12.7).

Figure 12.7 Displaying the cart contents

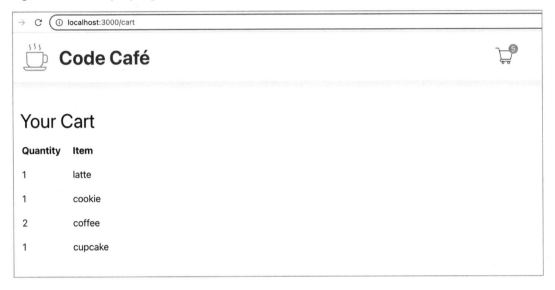

Displaying the item title and price

It would be better to display the item `title` instead of the `itemId`. You should also show the item `price`.

Right now, the `cart` object stores only the `itemId` of each item. Should you store `title` and `price` in `cart` as well? Actually, no.

An item's price and even its name might change periodically. If you store only the `itemId` – and find the title and price later, when the user visits the cart page – you do not have to worry about updating every user's cart with the latest title and price when they change.

So next, you need to pass `items` to the cart as a prop.

Listing 12.6 Passing `items` as a prop (`App.js`)

```
...
function App() {
    ...
        <Routes>
            <Route path="/cart" element={<Cart cart={cart} />} />
            <Route path="/cart" element={<Cart cart={cart} items={items} />} />
            <Route path="/details" element={<Details items={items} />}>
    ...
```

Now add `items` and the corresponding prop types to the **Cart** component, using the `ItemType` you created in Chapter 6. Use the array **find** method to display the `title` instead of the `itemId` of each item in the cart.

Listing 12.7 Displaying the item title (`Cart.js`)

```
import PropTypes from 'prop-types';
import ItemType from '../types/item';
import './Cart.css';

function Cart({ cart }) {
function Cart({ cart, items }) {
  return (
    ...
        {cart.map((item) => (
          <tr key={item.itemId}>
            <td>{item.quantity}</td>
            <td>{item.itemId}</td>
            <td>{items.find((i) => i.itemId === item.itemId).title}</td>
          </tr>
...
Cart.propTypes = {
  cart: PropTypes.arrayOf(PropTypes.shape({
    ...
  })).isRequired,
  items: PropTypes.arrayOf(ItemType).isRequired,
};
...
```

Save your file and take a look at the changes in your browser (Figure 12.8).

Figure 12.8 Item titles in the cart

193

Next you will add the item's price to a third column in the table. The price shown should be the total price, taking into account the quantity of the item in the cart. Also, recall that some items have a salePrice field that takes precedence over the regular price field.

One option for handling the price column is to call the **find** method again to find the item's price, just like you did with the title. This approach would work fine for this application, because of the small number of items in the items array.

But imagine if there were hundreds or thousands of possible items – which could easily be the case in a production app. Calling **find** multiple times to iterate through so many items, every time the component rendered or re-rendered, would be an expensive task.

You need a new variable to save the matching item. Though you can create new variables within **cart.map**, it adds complexity to the JSX, making it harder to understand. Instead of creating new inline variables, it is a better idea to create a new component.

You will create a new **CartRow** component to represent a row of data in the cart. This component will take two props: a cartItem and the items array.

Create a new file called CartRow.js and build the new component.

Listing 12.8 Building the **CartRow** component (CartRow.js)

```
import PropTypes from 'prop-types';
import ItemType from '../types/item';

function CartRow({ cartItem, items }) {
  const item = items.find((i) => i.itemId === cartItem.itemId);

  return (
    <tr>
      <td>{cartItem.quantity}</td>
      <td>{item.title}</td>
      <td>
        $
        {((item.salePrice ?? item.price) * cartItem.quantity).toFixed(2)}
      </td>
    </tr>
  );
}

CartRow.propTypes = {
  cartItem: PropTypes.shape({
    itemId: PropTypes.string.isRequired,
    quantity: PropTypes.number.isRequired,
  }).isRequired,
  items: PropTypes.arrayOf(ItemType).isRequired,
};

export default CartRow;
```

Now refactor your table in **Cart** so that **map** returns the new component with the needed props. Remember to keep the key attribute for the child components of **map**.

Listing 12.9 Refactoring the cart table (`Cart.js`)

```
import PropTypes from 'prop-types';
import ItemType from '../types/item';
import CartRow from './CartRow';
import './Cart.css';

function Cart({ cart, items }) {
  ...
            <th>Item</th>
            <th>Price</th>
          </tr>
        </thead>
        <tbody>
          {cart.map((item) => (
            <tr key={item.itemId}>
              <td>{item.quantity}</td>
              <td>{items.find((i) => i.itemId === item.itemId).title}</td>
            </tr>
            <CartRow key={item.itemId} cartItem={item} items={items} />
          ))}
  ...
```

Check out the browser to see the table (Figure 12.9).

Figure 12.9 Displaying the cart contents with prices

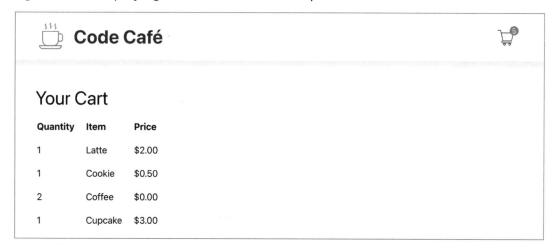

Removing Items from the Cart

The user should be able to remove items from their cart if they change their mind. You will add a button to each row of the cart table to let the user delete that row's item.

The first step is to update the cart reducer to support a new REMOVE action type. This action type removes an item from the cart by removing it from the array in state.

Listing 12.10 Adding a REMOVE action to the reducer (`cartReducer.js`)

```
...
export const CartTypes = {
  ADD: 'ADD',
  REMOVE: 'REMOVE',
};
...
export const cartReducer = (state, action) => {
  ...
    return [
      ...
    ];
    case CartTypes.REMOVE:
      return state.filter((item) => item.itemId !== action.itemId);
    default:
...
```

Remember from Chapter 11 that reducer functions should be pure – they should never mutate state directly. For example, the **Array.splice** method operates on arrays in place, so if you were to use it, you would first need to clone the array to avoid mutating the incoming state.

Array.filter returns a *new* array with only the elements that passed the test (in other words, those that returned **true**). Though using **filter** is not the only way to accomplish this task, it is a good single-line solution that avoids mutating state.

Passing dispatch as a prop

The button to remove an item will be in the **CartRow** component. When the button is clicked, it will call the **dispatch** function with the REMOVE action type you just created.

The **dispatch** function lives in App.js, and it needs to get to **CartRow**, which is the child of **Cart**. You can pass props from a component only to its direct children, so you will need to pass **dispatch** as a prop first from **App** to **Cart**, then from **Cart** to **CartRow**.

Pass the **dispatch** function from **App** to **Cart** as a prop.

Listing 12.11 Passing **dispatch** from **App** to **Cart** (App.js)

```
...
function App() {
  ...
        <Routes>
          <Route path="/cart" element={<Cart cart={cart} items={items} />} />
          <Route
            path="/cart"
            element={<Cart cart={cart} dispatch={dispatch} items={items} />}
          />
          <Route path="/details" element={<Details items={items} />}>
  ...
```

Why not create an action creator for the REMOVE action?

You can. But the **Cart** component is strongly coupled to the cart reducer by the shape of the data and will eventually use several reducer actions. Passing the **dispatch** function as a prop eliminates the need to pass each action creator as a separate prop. However, if you prefer the style of action creators, it is perfectly valid to use one here.

Now add **dispatch** to the prop signature for **Cart**. Finally, pass it as a prop to **CartRow**.

Listing 12.12 Passing **dispatch** from **Cart** to **CartRow** (Cart.js)

```
...
function Cart({ cart, items }) {
function Cart({ cart, dispatch, items }) {
  ...
        <tbody>
          {cart.map((item) => (
            <CartRow key={item.itemId} cartItem={item} items={items} />
            <CartRow
              key={item.itemId}
              cartItem={item}
              items={items}
              dispatch={dispatch}
            />
          ))}
        </tbody>
...
Cart.propTypes = {
  cart: PropTypes.arrayOf(PropTypes.shape({
    ...
  })).isRequired,
  dispatch: PropTypes.func.isRequired,
  items: PropTypes.arrayOf(ItemType).isRequired,
...
```

Now **CartRow** has access to the **dispatch** function, and you can add the button that will depend on **dispatch**.

Setting up the remove button

In the cart table, add a fourth column containing a button to remove the given item from the cart. The button should call **dispatch** when clicked.

Listing 12.13 Adding a button to remove items (`CartRow.js`)

```
import PropTypes from 'prop-types';
import ItemType from '../types/item';
import { CartTypes } from '../reducers/cartReducer';

function CartRow({ cartItem, items }) {
function CartRow({ cartItem, dispatch, items }) {
  const item = items.find((i) => i.itemId === cartItem.itemId);

  const removeItemFromCart = () => {
    dispatch({ type: CartTypes.REMOVE, itemId: item.itemId });
  };

  return (
    ...
      </td>
      <td>
        <button
          type="button"
          onClick={removeItemFromCart}
        >
          X
        </button>
      </td>
    </tr>
  );
}

CartRow.propTypes = {
  cartItem: PropTypes.shape({
    ...
  }).isRequired,
  dispatch: PropTypes.func.isRequired,
  items: PropTypes.arrayOf(ItemType).isRequired,
...
```

Rather than creating a variable, you could call **dispatch** inline in **onClick**. In that case, you would need to use an anonymous arrow function, like () => dispatch(...). This is because React evaluates the content inside curly braces on render, so onClick={dispatch(...)} would invoke the **dispatch** function on render and immediately remove all the items from the cart.

Save all your files and check out your work in the browser (Figure 12.10).

Figure 12.10 Removing items from the cart

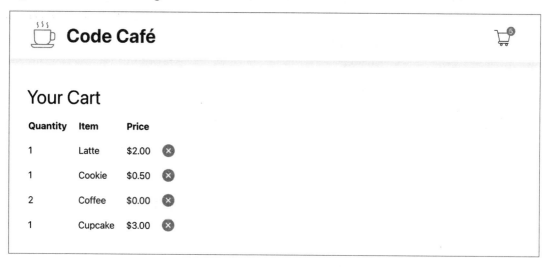

Add some items to your cart. Then visit the cart page and use the remove button to remove them. Success!

Emptying the Cart

Remove all the items from your cart. You are left with an empty table (Figure 12.11).

Figure 12.11 Displaying an empty table

This is also what you see when you visit the page before adding any items to the cart. A better user experience would be to show a message letting the user know that the cart is empty.

Refactor the cart, using conditional rendering to show the user a message instead of the table when the cart is empty. (You will need to reindent the `<table>` opening and closing tags and everything in between. You can use ESLint's auto-fix feature to take care of the indentation for you once you add the new code.)

Listing 12.14 Adding the empty cart message (`Cart.js`)

```
...
function Cart({ cart, dispatch, items }) {
  return (
    <div className="cart-component">
      <h2>Your Cart</h2>
      {cart.length === 0 ? (
        <div>Your cart is empty.</div>
      ) : (
        <table>
          ...
        </table>
      )}
    </div>
  );
...
```

Save your file and visit your cart in the browser. As long as it is empty, you should see your new message (Figure 12.12).

Figure 12.12 Empty cart

Displaying the Subtotal

You have one last task for this chapter – displaying the subtotal below the table. To accomplish this, you will need to do the following:

- Compute the subtotal for the cart. For each item, multiply its price by its quantity, then sum all the calculated values. (Remember that an item might have a `salePrice` that you should use in place of `price`.)

- Display the subtotal in a `<div>` below the table, making sure that it always has exactly two digits after the decimal point. (You will need a way to have two child elements. How did you do this before?)

Make the changes in **Cart**. (Again, you will need to reindent the newly nested elements.)

Listing 12.15 Adding the subtotal (Cart.js)

```
...
function Cart({ cart, dispatch, items }) {
  const subTotal = cart.reduce((acc, item) => {
    const detailItem = items.find((i) => i.itemId === item.itemId);
    const itemPrice = detailItem.salePrice ?? detailItem.price;
    return item.quantity * itemPrice + acc;
  }, 0);

  return (
    <div className="cart-component">
      <h2>Your Cart</h2>
      {cart.length === 0 ? (
        <div>Your cart is empty.</div>
      ) : (
        <>
          <table>
            ...
          </table>
          <div>
            Subtotal: $
            {subTotal.toFixed(2)}
          </div>
        </>
      )}
...
```

The JavaScript array **reduce** function provides a nice way to get the subtotal from all the cart items. But again, there are many ways to compute the subtotal.

The ternary statement returns a JSX expression, which must have one parent element. This code uses a React fragment to wrap the <table> and <div> elements so that only one root element returns from either side of the ternary.

Save your file, add some items to your cart, and check out the subtotal (Figure 12.13).

Figure 12.13 Drinks for two

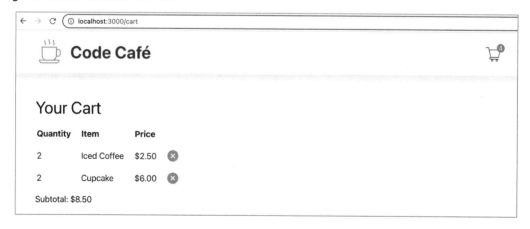

$8.50 for drinks and snacks for two? Not bad!

Conclusion

In this chapter, your React skills got a workout as you added functionality and a better user experience to your app.

In the next chapter, you will learn more about forms and input elements in React. You will add a form to the cart page so users can check out and place their orders.

Bronze Challenge: Increasing the Quantity

What happens if a user gets to the cart and remembers that they wanted to add a second coffee for a friend? Right now, they have to go back home, click the coffee thumbnail, and click Add to Cart again.

Add a + (plus) button so the user can increase the quantity of an item by 1. You can use the existing ADD action type with the **dispatch** function.

Silver Challenge: Decreasing the Quantity

What happens if a user accidentally orders two coffees instead of one?

Right now, they have to click the remove button, which removes both coffees. Then, they have to go back to the coffee details page to add one coffee again. This is not ideal.

Add a - (minus) button so the user can decrease the quantity of an item by 1. You will need to add a new DECREASE reducer type, which has a special case: If the user has only 1 of the item in the cart, decreasing the quantity should remove it from the cart, rather than leaving it in the cart with a quantity of 0.

13

Forms

Code Café's users can add tasty treats to the cart and update it to have exactly the items they want. Next, they need to be able to submit their orders.

When the user places an order, you need to collect certain information, such as the customer's name. To do this, you will add a form to the cart page.

Forms allow users to input and submit information. If you are familiar with HTML forms, you will probably recognize the basic elements used to build forms in React. Because these elements are interactive and used to capture input, there are some caveats to working with them in React. This chapter will explore ways to implement form elements in your application, including managing state.

When the user is ready to place an order, they will need to enter their name and their ZIP code (to compute tax). They will also have the option to enter a phone number. To keep things simple, you will add the checkout form right on the cart page, rather than creating a new route (Figure 13.1).

Figure 13.1 Completed checkout form

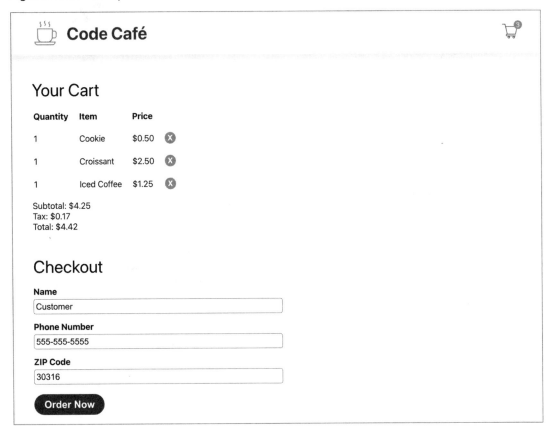

Building the Form

Let's get started by adding a form with just one input, for the user to enter their name.

Listing 13.1 Building the checkout form (`Cart.js`)

```
...
function Cart({ cart, dispatch, items }) {
  ...
        <div>
          Subtotal: $
          {subTotal.toFixed(2)}
        </div>
        <h2>Checkout</h2>
        <form>
          <label htmlFor="name">
            Name
            <input
              id="name"
              type="text"
            />
          </label>
        </form>
      </>
...
```

You wrap the `<input>` element in a `<label>`. Labels provide information about their associated elements and are important for accessibility. They also provide a nice UI benefit: When you click a label, the focus automatically moves to the associated `<input>` element.

There are two ways to bind a label and an element together in React.

One way is to use the `htmlFor` attribute. In HTML, you use the `for` attribute to associate labels with elements. Because `for` is a reserved word in JavaScript, JSX uses `htmlFor` instead. The label is bound to the input using the input's `id`.

The other way is to nest the bound element in the label.

You use both nesting and `htmlFor` to bind the label and the input. This helps ensure that accessibility features, such as screen readers, will work across all browsers. Also, the ESLint rules you are using require you to use both methods to bind labels and elements.

Save your file. To see the form in your browser, add at least one item to the cart (Figure 13.2).

Figure 13.2 New checkout form

It is looking great so far.

Next, take a look at the form elements in the DevTools Elements tab (Figure 13.3).

Figure 13.3 Inspecting the form elements

```
Elements   Console   Sources   »                      1

<!DOCTYPE html>
<html lang="en">
 ▶<head>…</head>
 ▼<body>
    <noscript>You need to enable JavaScript to run this app.</noscript>
  ▼<div id="root" data-ol-has-click-handler>
    ▶<header class="header-component">…</header>  flex
    ▼<div class="cart-component">
       <h2>Your Cart</h2>
     ▶<table>…</table>
     ▶<div>…</div>
       <h2>Checkout</h2>
···    ▼<form> == $0
       ▼<label for="name">
          "Name"
          <input id="name" type="text">
       </label>
       </form>
     </div>
   </div>
```

The htmlFor attribute renders as for on each label.

Add two more inputs with labels to the form, one for the phone number and one for the ZIP code, following the pattern you just used for the name input.

Listing 13.2 Adding phone and ZIP code inputs (Cart.js)

```
...
function Cart({ cart, dispatch, items }) {
  ...
            <label htmlFor="name">
              ...
            </label>
            <label htmlFor="phone">
              Phone Number
              <input
                id="phone"
                type="tel"
              />
            </label>
            <label htmlFor="zipcode">
              ZIP Code
              <input
                id="zipcode"
                type="text"
                maxLength="5"
                inputMode="numeric"
              />
            </label>
          </form>
...
```

There are several attributes you can add to JSX elements, just like HTML elements.

In addition to the id attribute, each input also has a type attribute. This attribute defines the input behavior. The tel type indicates an input for a phone number. It does not add phone number formatting, such as dashes – you will add that yourself later in this chapter. But it cues the browser to offer to autofill the field if the user has phone numbers stored in their profile, and on mobile browsers it triggers the numeric keyboard.

In both HTML and JSX, the default type value is text, which you use for the name and zipcode inputs. Because it is the default, you could have left the type specification out. However, it is a best practice to include the type for all inputs to keep your code clear.

The extra attributes that you added to zipcode are inputMode and maxLength. Though inputMode does not restrict the type of characters that the user can enter into an input, it does specify which keyboard a browser should use. maxLength restricts the length of the input, to five characters in this case.

Now, add the last piece of the form: a button to place the order. A button does not need a label, so you do not need to worry about binding it to one.

Listing 13.3 Adding a submit button (`Cart.js`)

```
...
function Cart({ cart, dispatch, items }) {
  ...
            <label htmlFor="zipcode">
              ...
            </label>
            <button type="submit">
              Order Now
            </button>
          </form>
...
```

The button has the type `submit`. This is the default type for buttons associated with a form in HTML and JSX. When the user clicks the button, the form's **onSubmit** event is triggered.

Save your file and take another look at the cart page (Figure 13.4). (If the cart is empty, add an item to it.)

Figure 13.4 Cart with checkout form

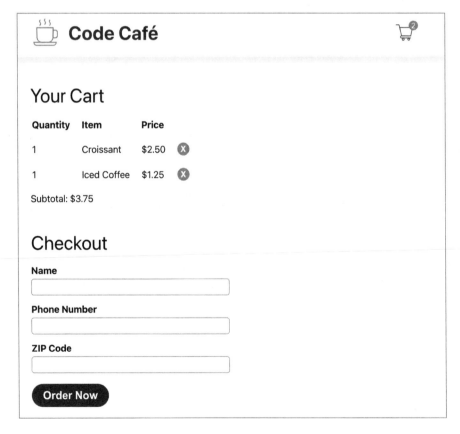

onSubmit

You have not yet added any user event handlers to the form. So what will happen if you click the Order Now button? Try it and see (Figure 13.5).

Figure 13.5 After submitting

The cart is empty and the URL ends in a ?. This is due to the browser's native form submission. By default, the browser submits the form values as a new GET request to the current URL, then displays the result. (Because your form fields do not have name properties, the values do not show in the URL.)

In most scenarios, you will implement your own behavior for form submission. React allows you to listen for form submission events with a form's **onSubmit** prop. You pass the event as the first argument to the **onSubmit** callback function. (This is similar to the **onClick** attribute you used for buttons in Ottergram.)

Add an **onSubmit** handler to the form. In the function, call **preventDefault** on the event to prevent the browser's native form submission behavior. To ensure the function is firing as expected, add console.log(event) to the function.

Listing 13.4 Adding **onSubmit** (Cart.js)

```
...
function Cart({ cart, dispatch, items }) {
  const subTotal = cart.reduce((acc, item) => {
    ...
  }, 0);

  const submitOrder = (event) => {
    event.preventDefault();
    console.log(event);
  };

  return (
    ...
        <div>
          Subtotal: $
          {subTotal.toFixed(2)}
        </div>
        <h2>Checkout</h2>
        <form>
        <form onSubmit={submitOrder}>
          <label htmlFor="name">
  ...
```

Save your file. Back in the browser, add items to your cart and navigate to the cart page. Try clicking the Order Now button again. The page no longer reloads, because you are preventing the default behavior.

Value from Inputs

In the DevTools, open the console to see the output from the event handler function. Look for the **SyntheticBaseEvent** entry and expand its contents (Figure 13.6).

Figure 13.6 **SyntheticBaseEvent** in the console log

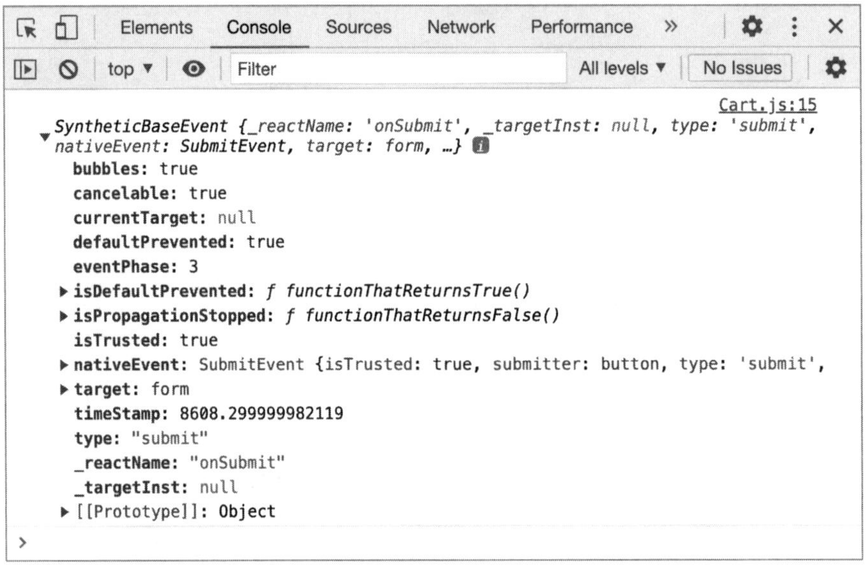

You looked briefly at **SyntheticBaseEvent** in Chapter 3: It is a wrapper that React puts around native events to ensure that events work the same across all browsers.

Here, the **SyntheticBaseEvent** object allows you to access the current internal state of the form. Information about the event itself is stored in properties on the **SyntheticBaseEvent** instance. For example, you can access the underlying native event through the nativeEvent property. (However, it is unlikely that you will ever need it.)

Expand the contents of the `target` property (Figure 13.7).

Figure 13.7 Event `target`

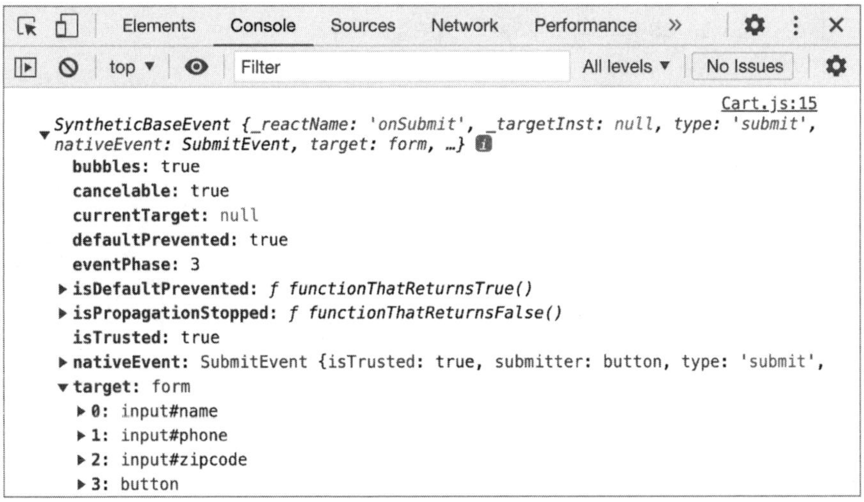

```
⌕  ⧉  │  Elements   Console   Sources   Network   Performance   »   │  ⚙  ⋮  ✕
▶  ⊘  │  top ▼  ◉  │  Filter                        All levels ▼   No Issues   ⚙
                                                                    Cart.js:15
  ▼ SyntheticBaseEvent {_reactName: 'onSubmit', _targetInst: null, type: 'submit',
    nativeEvent: SubmitEvent, target: form, …} ⓘ
      bubbles: true
      cancelable: true
      currentTarget: null
      defaultPrevented: true
      eventPhase: 3
    ▶ isDefaultPrevented: ƒ functionThatReturnsTrue()
    ▶ isPropagationStopped: ƒ functionThatReturnsFalse()
      isTrusted: true
    ▶ nativeEvent: SubmitEvent {isTrusted: true, submitter: button, type: 'submit',
    ▼ target: form
      ▶ 0: input#name
      ▶ 1: input#phone
      ▶ 2: input#zipcode
      ▶ 3: button
```

Each input is listed along with its input ID.

Let's update the `console.log` in the `onSubmit` handler to print the value of each input using the id.

Listing 13.5 Targeting individual inputs (`Cart.js`)

```
...
function Cart({ cart, dispatch, items }) {
  ...
  const submitOrder = (event) => {
    event.preventDefault();
    console.log(event);
    console.log('name: ', event.target.name.value);
    console.log('phone: ', event.target.phone.value);
    console.log('zipcode: ', event.target.zipcode.value);
  };
  ...
```

Save your file and return to the browser. Fill in values for each of the form fields and click the Order Now button. Check the end of the console output to ensure that the values are printing as expected (Figure 13.8).

Figure 13.8 Input values in the console log

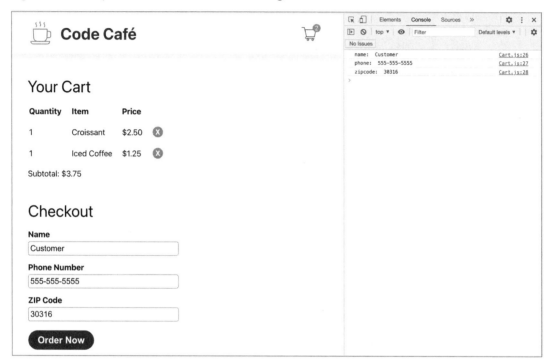

Now you have a working form that can take in information from a user and submit that information. In Chapter 15, you will work more on what happens with the information once it is submitted. But first, you will add a number of refinements to the form.

The input elements you have been using so far are *uncontrolled* components. The DOM controls the components' values, which are accessible through the DOM element or the event. As the developer, you have little or no way to manipulate them.

In simple forms, such as the one you have here, this might be sufficient. But what if you wanted to add behavior such as text formatting or validation? Although you could do that, it would be tricky and would involve plain JavaScript – not an ideal solution.

It is worth stating again: React is declarative. The UI that React renders should exactly match the current state of the component. With uncontrolled components, it can be difficult to know what that state is – and even more difficult to assert control over it when needed.

React gives us a better way.

Controlled Components

Unlike uncontrolled components, *controlled components* allow you to control the value of a form element using React tools.

To experiment with this, add the `value` attribute to the `name` input element and set it to `"M. Mouse"`.

Listing 13.6 Setting name's value to "M. Mouse" (`Cart.js`)

```
...
function Cart({ cart, dispatch, items }) {
  ...
            <label htmlFor="name">
              Name
              <input
                id="name"
                type="text"
                value="M. Mouse"
              />
...
```

Save your file, head back to the cart page, and try to edit the value in the Name field. Even though the input is not `readonly` or `disabled`, you cannot edit it.

This is because React uses one-way data binding. React ensures that the value returned from the component matches what renders. When you try to change the value, React notices the change and immediately reverts it to match the value from the component. The result is that the UI is the same, because the value that the component returns, `"M. Mouse"`, does not change.

So how do you tell React to update the value when the user makes a change?

Open the console to see a helpful warning from React, as shown in Figure 13.9:

Figure 13.9 Input error

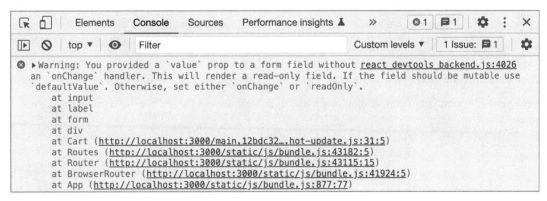

(If you see a different warning message, try refreshing the page and adding an item to the cart so the component reloads.)

The error gives you helpful information on how to make this form editable again: You can add an **onChange** handler to an individual form element. In the **onChange** handler, you tell React what to do when the user edits the input value.

onChange

The first thing you need is a state value to keep track of the name input. Add this using the **useState** hook.

In the name input element, use the **onChange** attribute to update the state value each time the user makes an edit. Replace the hardcoded value with the new state value.

Listing 13.7 Adding **useState** (Cart.js)

```
import PropTypes from 'prop-types';
import { useState } from 'react';
import ItemType from '../types/item';
...
function Cart({ cart, dispatch, items }) {
  const [name, setName] = useState('');

  const subTotal = cart.reduce((acc, item) => {
    ...
            <label htmlFor="name">
              Name
              <input
                id="name"
                type="text"
                value="M. Mouse"
                value={name}
                onChange={(event) => setName(event.target.value)}
              />
...
```

Why **useState** instead of **useReducer**? Recall that **useReducer** is usually better for complex data management. Because the value of name is a single string that changes all at once and does not depend on previous state, the **useState** hook is sufficient.

onChange (like **onClick** or **onSubmit**) passes the event to the event handler (the arrow function you defined). The event contains the input's new value in event.target.value. You use that to update the state, which React passes as the value to the element.

Each time the state name updates, React re-renders the component with the new value.

Save your file, visit your form, and enter a name in the Name field. Nice – the field is editable again.

Now open the Components tab in the DevTools and select the **Cart** component. Under hooks, you can see the current value for the name state (Figure 13.10).

Figure 13.10 name state in the DevTools

Next, follow the same pattern to store the values for the phone number and ZIP code in state, as phone and zipCode.

See if you can make these changes without first looking at the solution below.

Listing 13.8 Adding state for the phone number and ZIP code (Cart.js)

```
...
function Cart({ cart, dispatch, items }) {
  const [name, setName] = useState('');
  const [phone, setPhone] = useState('');
  const [zipCode, setZipCode] = useState('');

  const subTotal = cart.reduce((acc, item) => {
    ...
            <label htmlFor="phone">
              Phone Number
              <input
                id="phone"
                type="tel"
                value={phone}
                onChange={(event) => setPhone(event.target.value)}
              />
            </label>
            <label htmlFor="zipcode">
              ZIP Code
              <input
                ...
                inputMode="numeric"
                value={zipCode}
                onChange={(event) => setZipCode(event.target.value)}
              />
...
```

Save your file and confirm that you can enter a name, phone number, and ZIP code and see all three state values in the DevTools.

Now you have local state variables that you can access and manage. This gives you much more control over what information the form eventually submits.

Because of React's declarative design approach, you need the loop of interaction between **onChange** and value to give you control over editable values. Although the declarative approach requires more typing than some other front-end frameworks, the benefits outweigh this inconvenience.

Next, update the **onSubmit** handler to log the new state values in the console when the form is submitted.

Listing 13.9 Updating **onSubmit** (Cart.js)

```
...
function Cart({ cart, dispatch, items }) {
  ...
  const submitOrder = (event) => {
    event.preventDefault();
    console.log('name: ', event.target.name.value);
    console.log('name: ', name);
    console.log('phone: ', event.target.phone.value);
    console.log('phone: ', phone);
    console.log('zipcode: ', event.target.zipcode.value);
    console.log('zipcode: ', zipCode);
  };
  ...
```

Calculating the Tax

Because you store your form's values in state, now you can use those values in other areas. Having easy-to-access values is a benefit of using controlled components.

To compute the total for the order, you need to add tax. For simplicity, assume that the tax rate is the first digit of the ZIP code plus 1. Then compute and display the tax.

Listing 13.10 Computing the tax (`Cart.js`)

```
...
function Cart({ cart, dispatch, items }) {
  ...
  const subTotal = cart.reduce((acc, item) => {
    ...
  }, 0);

  const taxPercentage = parseInt(zipCode.substring(0, 1) || '0', 10) + 1;
  const taxRate = taxPercentage / 100;
  const tax = subTotal * taxRate;

  const submitOrder = (event) => {
    ...
  };

  return (
    ...
          <div>
            Subtotal: $
            {subTotal.toFixed(2)}
          </div>
          <div>
            Tax: $
            {tax.toFixed(2)}
          </div>
          <h2>Checkout</h2>
...
```

Save your file. Back on the cart page, fill in a ZIP code, and you will see the tax display (Figure 13.11).

Figure 13.11 Cart page with tax

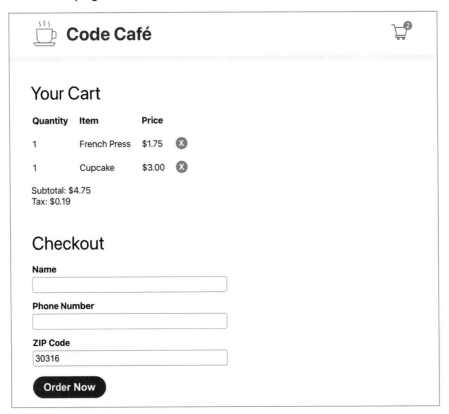

Now you can use the subtotal and tax to compute the total cost of the order.

Calculating the Total

The total should be the sum of the subtotal and the tax. Add it to your cart page below the tax.

Listing 13.11 Computing the total (`Cart.js`)

```
...
function Cart({ cart, dispatch, items }) {
  ...
  const tax = subTotal * taxRate;
  const total = subTotal + tax;

  const submitOrder = (event) => {
    ...
  };

  return (
    ...
        <div>
          Tax: $
          {tax.toFixed(2)}
        </div>
        <div>
          Total: $
          { total.toFixed(2) }
        </div>
        <h2>Checkout</h2>
...
```

Save your file and check out your browser to view the total (Figure 13.12).

Figure 13.12 Displaying the total

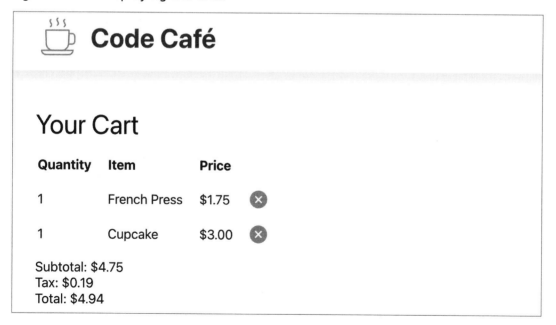

No surprise fees for your users.

Displaying the total conditionally

There is another UI state you must handle. To see it, clear out the ZIP code field.

When no ZIP code is entered – such as when the user first visits the cart page – the tax and total displayed are based on a 1% tax rate. Since the tax rate is actually unknown, the page should not show the tax or total until the user enters their ZIP code.

Use the local state value for `zipCode` to determine whether the tax and total should render. If the user has entered a five-digit ZIP code, they should see the tax and the total. If the ZIP code is missing or incomplete, the cart should display a message telling the user what they need to do (enter their ZIP code) to see the total.

You will need to reindent the `<div>`s for the tax and the total.

Listing 13.12 Displaying the total conditionally (`Cart.js`)

```
...
function Cart({ cart, dispatch, items }) {
  ...
          <div>
            Subtotal: $
            {subTotal.toFixed(2)}
          </div>
          { zipCode.length === 5
            ? (
              <>
                <div>
                  Tax: $
                  {tax.toFixed(2)}
                </div>
                <div>
                  Total: $
                  { total.toFixed(2) }
                </div>
              </>
            ) : (
              <div className="warning">Enter ZIP Code to get total</div>
            )}
          <h2>Checkout</h2>
  ...
```

Save your file and test your changes in the browser (Figure 13.13).

Figure 13.13 ZIP code error

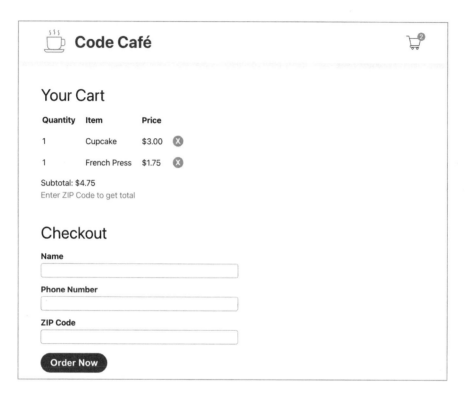

Now you see the tax and total only after entering a five-digit ZIP code.

Formatting Input

Another benefit of using controlled components is having control over how you set the input value in state. You can use functions to format the value for the user.

Start by formatting the phone number with dashes, like 555-555-5555.

Listing 13.13 Formatting the phone number (`Cart.js`)

```
...
function Cart({ cart, dispatch, items }) {
  ...
  const submitOrder = (event) => {
    ...
  };

  const setFormattedPhone = (newNumber) => {
    const digits = newNumber.replace(/\D/g, '');
    let formatted = digits.substring(0, 3);
    if (digits.length === 3 && newNumber[3] === '-') {
      formatted = `${formatted}-`;
    } else if (digits.length > 3) {
      formatted = `${formatted}-${digits.substring(3, 6)}`;
    }
    if (digits.length === 6 && newNumber[7] === '-') {
      formatted = `${formatted}-`;
    } else if (digits.length > 6) {
      formatted = `${formatted}-${digits.substring(6, 10)}`;
    }
    setPhone(formatted);
  };

  return (
    ...
            <input
              id="phone"
              type="tel"
              value={phone}
              onChange={(event) => setPhone(event.target.value)}
              onChange={(event) => setFormattedPhone(event.target.value)}
            />
...
```

Now the **onChange** function calls the helper function **setFormattedPhone**. This helper function performs the logic to format the phone number and then calls **setPhone** to update the state value with the newly formatted number. This logic is more complicated, so the helper function exists outside the JSX.

Type in a phone number without dashes. The form will automatically insert the dashes for you (Figure 13.14).

Figure 13.14 Formatted phone number

Name

Customer

Phone Number

555-555-5555

This is great! But it is not perfect: Try editing the middle of the phone number. Your cursor will continually jump to the end of the input.

Although React and JavaScript allow you to work with the exact cursor position, it is complicated. There are npm packages that can help you apply formatting and deal with the cursor position. At the end of this chapter, there is a challenge to add a package for handling this issue.

Form Validation

For Code Café to process an order, the shop needs the user's name (for identification) and ZIP code (for tax). The Order Now button should be enabled only if the user has supplied the required information. On the other hand, the phone number is not required, so the button should not depend on whether the user has entered a phone number.

You can use the `required` HTML attribute with React form elements. Go ahead and mark both the `name` and `zipcode` inputs as `required`.

Listing 13.14 Marking elements as `required` (Cart.js)

```
...
function Cart({ cart, dispatch, items }) {
  ...
              <input
                id="name"
                type="text"
                value={name}
                onChange={(event) => setName(event.target.value)}
                required
              />
            </label>
            <label htmlFor="phone">
              ...
            </label>
            <label htmlFor="zipcode">
              ZIP Code
              <input
                ...
                onChange={(event) => setZipCode(event.target.value)}
                required
              />
  ...
```

React allows you to bind Boolean values to the HTML attributes. If the value is truthy, React adds the attribute to the element. If it is falsy, React does not add the attribute.

When you do not give a value, React assumes the value is `true`. So you could also have written

```
required={true}
```

However, the Airbnb ESLint rule set requires that you omit `true` values.

Save your file and try to submit the form with one or both of the required fields blank. The **onSubmit** handler does not fire. Instead, you get an alert to fill out the empty field (Figure 13.15).

Figure 13.15 Required field alert

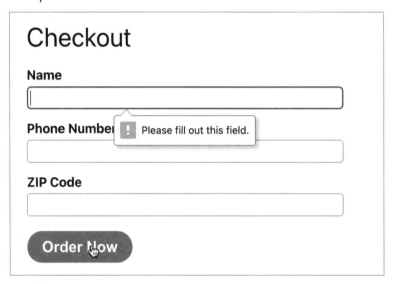

Another useful HTML attribute is `disabled`. Create a new variable called `formValid` that is truthy if the form is valid and falsy if not. Then use the value to determine whether the `submit` button should be disabled.

Listing 13.15 Disabling the button (`Cart.js`)

```
...
function Cart({ cart, dispatch, items }) {
  ...
  const tax = subTotal * taxRate;
  const total = subTotal + tax;
  const isFormValid = zipCode.length === 5 && name.trim();

  const submitOrder = (event) => {
    ...
  };
  ...
            <label htmlFor="zipcode">
              ...
            </label>
            <button type="submit">
            <button type="submit" disabled={!isFormValid}>
              Order Now
  ...
```

Save your file, visit the browser again, and confirm that the Order Now button is disabled until you enter a name and ZIP code (Figure 13.16).

Figure 13.16 Disabled Order Now button

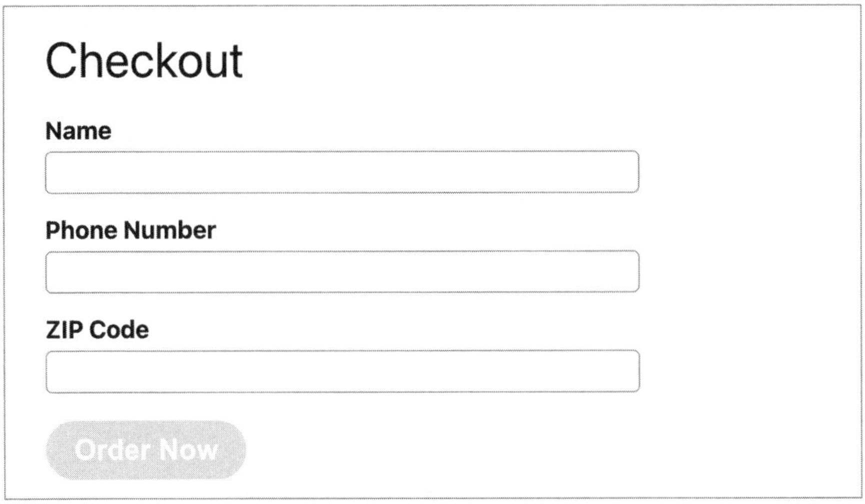

Conclusion

Forms can be tricky, because they have their own internal state and default behavior. Using controlled components allows you to access and work with that state to provide a better user experience and to ensure your application stays in sync.

Think about how far Code Café has come. Now users can add items to their cart, see all the items in their cart, and review the total cost, including tax. And as a React developer, you have built multiple components and used two hooks for managing state: `useState` and `useReducer`.

In Chapter 15, you will allow users to submit their orders.

But first, you will learn about another hook often used with form elements and much more: `useRef`. You will also get more practice working with form data.

Silver Challenge: Coupon Code

Add a coupon code field to the checkout form.

Code Café's coupon codes are all uppercase. If the user types lowercase characters, reformat them appropriately.

Gold Challenge: Maintaining the Cursor Position in the Phone Number

Advanced number formatting and patterns, such as the ability to edit the middle of a phone number, can require complex code. Most front-end developers reach for a package that takes care of formatting for them.

Take a look at the documentation for the popular `react-number-format` package (www.npmjs.com/package/react-number-format). Use this package to spiff up your phone number input field by allowing users to edit the number in a more intuitive way.

You will need to install this new package with `npm install --save react-number-format` and then replace the phone number `<input>` with `<PatternFormat>`. Follow the link from the `react-number-format` page to its full documentation. There, read the Pattern Format section to see how to specify the input pattern. Also, look at the Props section. Instead of **onChange**, `react-number-format` uses **onValueChange** and provides you with an object, rather than the event, as the first parameter.

Gold Challenge: Setting the Quantity

There are other available form elements that you have not used in building the checkout form. One of these is the `<select>` element.

Though the plus and minus buttons from the previous chapter's challenge are nice, you could also offer the user a way to set the quantity directly. Instead of an `<input>` element (which has additional complexity when it is blank), use a `<select>` element that lets the user choose their desired quantity.

You will need to add a new `SET_QUANTITY` reducer type.

For an added challenge, remove the item when the quantity entered is 0.

14

Local Storage and useRef

In the last chapter, you built a form for users to input their information and submit it. You also used controlled components to manage the state of each form element.

In this chapter, you will use local storage to persist the values in the cart in case the user closes or refreshes the browser. You will also use the form you created to learn about another React hook: **useRef**.

The **useRef** hook creates and stores a mutable JavaScript object that persists through re-renders. This means you can use **useRef** to store values that are not intended to trigger a re-render of the component, such as a reference to a timer. A more common use case for this hook is storing a reference to a React element, giving you direct access to the DOM node that the element creates. This chapter will show you examples of both.

useRef is a specialized hook, so most production applications use it only in a couple of places. This chapter will help you understand when to reach for **useRef** and when you might want **useState** instead.

But before diving into **useRef**, you will work on persisting cart values across browser refreshes.

Local Storage

Right now, items in the cart disappear when you refresh the browser because the application stores them only in local state. During development, this is frustrating because you must return to the home screen and re-add items. And your users certainly will not want to lose all their items if they refresh the browser.

Browsers can persist information using the Web Storage API. This API has mechanisms for both local storage and session storage. Though both types of storage use key/value pairs and persist through refreshes, local storage persists even if the browser closes and reopens, so it will work best for storing Code Café's cart.

There are several methods for interacting with local storage, including a setter method for storing a value and a getter method for accessing it.

Open App.js and use the setter **localStorage.setItem** to store the cart value each time it updates.

Listing 14.1 Setting local storage (App.js)

```
...
import { cartReducer, CartTypes, initialCartState } from './reducers/cartReducer';

const storageKey = 'cart';

function App() {
  const [items, setItems] = useState([]);
  const [cart, dispatch] = useReducer(cartReducer, initialCartState);
  const addToCart = (itemId) => dispatch({ type: CartTypes.ADD, itemId });

  useEffect(() => {
    localStorage.setItem(storageKey, JSON.stringify(cart));
  }, [cart]);

  useEffect(() => {
...
```

Recall from Chapter 8 that you use the **useEffect** hook to perform side effects during the render cycle. Updating the application state, such as the value of cart, causes **App** to re-render. React then evaluates **useEffect**'s dependency array to determine whether it should execute the effect. If the values in the dependency array have changed, the code in **useEffect** runs.

Here, you add **useEffect** with one value, cart, in its dependency array. Each time **App** re-renders, React determines whether the value of cart has changed. If so, it runs the code inside **useEffect** to set the cart value in local storage.

localStorage.setItem takes two arguments. The first is the key that identifies the data you are storing. The second is the value you are storing. Because you can save only strings in local storage, you use the **JSON.stringify** method to convert the value to a string before passing it to **setItem**.

Save your file, then test the new code by adding several items to your cart. Open the DevTools. In the Application tab, double-click Local Storage in the left pane to expand it. You will see the current domain, http://localhost:3000. Select the domain to see the stored cart value (Figure 14.1).

Figure 14.1 cart in local storage

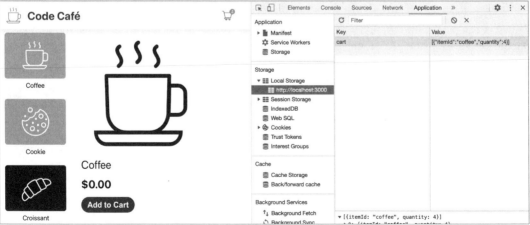

The next step is to use the getter method to access the local storage value and use it as the initial value for **useReducer**.

useReducer gives you two ways to set the initial value. You have already seen one way: passing the initial value as the second argument to **useReducer**. You can also pass a function as the third argument to lazily create the initial state. Creating initial state lazily lets you avoid running expensive calculations – such as reading and parsing local storage – on every render cycle.

Pass a function to **useReducer** that fetches the value of cart from local storage using **localStorage.getItem**, and set that value as the hook's initial value.

Listing 14.2 Getting local storage (App.js)

```
...
function App() {
  const [items, setItems] = useState([]);
  const [cart, dispatch] = useReducer(cartReducer, initialCartState);
  const [cart, dispatch] = useReducer(
    cartReducer,
    initialCartState,
    (initialState) => {
      try {
        const storedCart = JSON.parse(localStorage.getItem(storageKey));
        return storedCart || initialState;
      } catch (error) {
        console.log('Error parsing cart', error);
        return initialState;
      }
    },
  );
  const addToCart = (itemId) => dispatch({ type: CartTypes.ADD, itemId });
...
```

You use the new function as **useReducer**'s third argument to lazily initialize the state value. But then what is the second argument, initialCartState, doing?

In **useReducer**, the function – which you pass as the third argument – automatically has access to the initial state value – which you pass as the second argument. To use the initial state value inside the function, you add a parameter (here called initialState) to the function definition. The parameter's name does not matter; its value is always **useReducer**'s second argument. Here, the second argument is the variable initialCartState, whose value is an empty array, so initialState is an empty array.

Earlier, you used **JSON.stringify** to ensure you were sending the cart value to local storage as a string. Here, you use **JSON.parse** to read the stored cart value, parsing it as a JavaScript array or object. Then you use the OR operator (| |) to check whether this parsed value is truthy. If it is, you return it. Otherwise, you return the initialState.

Wrapping the code in a try/catch block provides a fallback: In case of an error, the code returns initialState. This prevents the application from crashing if there is a problem reading or parsing the value from local storage.

Save your file. In the browser, make sure there are some items in your cart. In the DevTools' Application tab, make sure you can see the cart value in the Local Storage section. Now refresh the browser and navigate to the cart page. All your items are still in the cart.

useRef vs useState

Now that the cart data persists even if the browser closes, it is time to look at **useRef**. Let's start by exploring how **useRef** differs from **useState**.

Each time the state updates, the component re-renders to keep the UI in sync with the state. Try this exercise to see these re-renders in action: In the **Cart** component, add a new state variable that increases by 1 each time the user clicks the Order Now button. Add a <div> below the checkout form that displays the new state. While you are updating **submitOrder**, go ahead and remove the **console.log** calls – you do not need them anymore.

Every time the state changes, the variable will update onscreen, so you will know the component has re-rendered.

Listing 14.3 Tracking component renders using state (`Cart.js`)

```
...
function Cart({ cart, dispatch, items }) {
  const [name, setName] = useState('');
  const [phone, setPhone] = useState('');
  const [zipCode, setZipCode] = useState('');
  const [renderCounter, setRenderCounter] = useState(0);

  const subTotal = cart.reduce((acc, item) => {
    ...
  }, 0);
  ...
  const submitOrder = (event) => {
    event.preventDefault();
    console.log('name: ', name);
    console.log('phone: ', phone);
    console.log('zipcode: ', zipCode);
    setRenderCounter(renderCounter + 1);
  };
  ...
  return (
    ...
            <button type="submit" disabled={!isFormValid}>
              Order Now
            </button>
          </form>
          <div>
            RenderCounter:
            {renderCounter}
          </div>
        </>
  ...
```

Save your file. In the browser, add items to your cart and navigate to the cart page. Fill in the name and ZIP code to enable the Order Now button.

Click the button several times to see what happens (Figure 14.2).

Figure 14.2 Testing component re-renders with **useState**

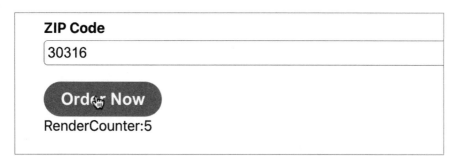

As expected, each time the **onSubmit** handler updates renderCounter, the component re-renders so that the UI matches the new value.

Now refactor the experiment to use the **useRef** hook instead of **useState**.

One difference between **useState** and **useRef** is right in the names: **useState** uses a *state*, and **useRef** uses a *ref*. Refs are objects that allow you to reference a value such as a DOM node or another piece of data.

Add a **console.log** statement that logs the current value of the ref, using the ref's current property.

Listing 14.4 Tracking component renders using a ref (Cart.js)

```
import PropTypes from 'prop-types';
import { useState } from 'react';
import { useRef, useState } from 'react';
import ItemType from '../types/item';
...
function Cart({ cart, dispatch, items }) {
  const [name, setName] = useState('');
  const [phone, setPhone] = useState('');
  const [zipCode, setZipCode] = useState('');
  const [renderCounter, setRenderCounter] = useState(0);
  const renderCounter = useRef(0);

  const subTotal = cart.reduce((acc, item) => {
    ...
  }, 0);
  ...
  const submitOrder = (event) => {
    event.preventDefault();
    setRenderCounter(renderCounter + 1);
    console.log('RenderCounter: ', renderCounter.current);
    renderCounter.current += 1;
  };
  ...
  return (
    ...
        <div>
          RenderCounter:
          {renderCounter}
          {renderCounter.current}
        </div>
  ...
```

The **useRef** hook returns a ref object.

You access the ref object's current value by using its current property. Because objects are passed by reference in JavaScript, ref.current always reflects the current value of the reference, even if ref is from an old render cycle. Therefore, you should never destructure a ref or otherwise cache ref.current in a variable.

Unlike **useState**, the **useRef** hook does not return a setter for updating the relevant value. Instead, React updates the renderCounter.current value directly, adding 1 each time you click the button.

Save your file. In the browser, open the DevTools' Console tab, then test your new code by clicking the Order Now button several times.

Each time you click the button, the ref value updates, and the new value prints in the console. But the updated value does not trigger the component to re-render. As a result, the RenderCounter value on the page stays at 0 (Figure 14.3).

Figure 14.3 Testing component re-renders with **useRef**

Remove the code changes you made for this experiment, replacing the **console.log** call in **submitOrder** with a TODO. You will add the order submission functionality in the next chapter.

Listing 14.5 Removing experimental code (`Cart.js`)

```
import PropTypes from 'prop-types';
import { useRef, useState } from 'react';
import { useState } from 'react';
import ItemType from '../types/item';
...
function Cart({ cart, dispatch, items }) {
  const [name, setName] = useState('');
  const [phone, setPhone] = useState('');
  const [zipCode, setZipCode] = useState('');
  const renderCounter = useRef(0);

  const subTotal = cart.reduce((acc, item) => {
    ...
  }, 0);
  ...
  const submitOrder = (event) => {
    event.preventDefault();
    console.log('RenderCounter: ', renderCounter.current);
    renderCounter.current += 1;
    // TODO
  };
  ...
  return (
    ...
            <button type="submit" disabled={!isFormValid}>
              Order Now
            </button>
          </form>
        <div>
          RenderCounter:
          {renderCounter.current}
        </div>
      </>
...
```

The **useRef** hook is a powerful tool that you should use only sparingly. In most cases, you should store values in state to ensure that the component re-renders as needed and the UI stays in sync with the data. However, refs are useful for keeping up with references to timeouts you might need to clear or API calls you might need to cancel.

Using setTimeout with useRef

Each month, Code Café recognizes two employees for their hard work and gives them free orders. To determine who is eligible, the API provides the endpoint /api/employees/isEmployeeOfTheMonth, which takes a name as the query string. The endpoint checks this name against a list of the current employees of the month and returns an object that looks like { isEmployeeOfTheMonth: boolean }.

Loren and Ashley are the current employees of the month for Code Café, so their names will return { isEmployeeOfTheMonth: true }. All other strings will return { isEmployeeOfTheMonth: false }.

Create a function to handle change events for the Name field. As the user types their name in the Name field, make a GET request to the endpoint to determine whether the name belongs to an eligible employee. Set the result in a new piece of state. If the result is `true`, change the cart subtotal to 0.

Listing 14.6 Determining eligible employees (`Cart.js`)

```
import axios from 'axios';
import PropTypes from 'prop-types';
...
function Cart({ cart, dispatch, items }) {
  const [name, setName] = useState('');
  const [phone, setPhone] = useState('');
  const [zipCode, setZipCode] = useState('');
  const [isEmployeeOfTheMonth, setIsEmployeeOfTheMonth] = useState(false);

  const subTotal = cart.reduce((acc, item) => {
  const subTotal = isEmployeeOfTheMonth ? 0 : cart.reduce((acc, item) => {
    ...
  }, 0);
  ...
  const setFormattedPhone = (newNumber) => {
    ...
  };

  const onNameChange = (newName) => {
    setName(newName);
    axios
      .get(`/api/employees/isEmployeeOfTheMonth?name=${newName}`)
      .then((response) => setIsEmployeeOfTheMonth(
        response?.data?.isEmployeeOfTheMonth,
      ))
      .catch(console.error);
  };

  return (
    ...
              <input
                id="name"
                type="text"
                value={name}
                onChange={(event) => setName(event.target.value)}
                onChange={(event) => onNameChange(event.target.value)}
                required
  ...
```

The new **onNameChange** function allows you to trigger events when the user is typing, just like you did when formatting the phone number before storing it in state. In this case, the additional event is a network call to /api/employees/isEmployeeOfTheMonth. The query string ?name=${newValue} is appended to the end of the request.

Save your file and return to your browser. In the DevTools, navigate to the Network tab. Begin typing in the Name field. Each time you make a change to the string, the app makes a new network request with the new string (Figure 14.4).

Figure 14.4 Network requests made while typing

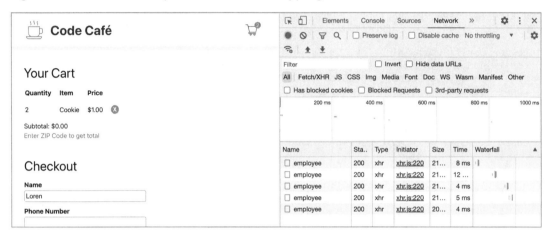

When you type the name Loren, as in the example above, the app makes five requests. The first four requests are superfluous, because you are still typing. Only the last request returns true, because only the full name matches that of an eligible employee. That is a lot of unnecessary requests.

What if the app makes the request only when the user takes a short break from typing? This is called *debouncing* and is often how search inputs work. Debouncing actions can dramatically reduce the number of network calls your app makes.

To begin implementing debouncing, use **setTimeout** to delay the request by 300 milliseconds, giving the user time to type their full name. (You will need to reindent the code within the function that you pass to **setTimeout**.)

Listing 14.7 Adding **setTimeout** (Cart.js)

```
...
function Cart({ cart, dispatch, items }) {
  ...
  const onNameChange = (newName) => {
    setName(newName);
    setTimeout(() => {
      axios
        .get(`/api/employees/isEmployeeOfTheMonth?name=${newName}`)
        .then((response) => setIsEmployeeOfTheMonth(
          response?.data?.isEmployeeOfTheMonth,
        ))
        .catch(console.error);
    }, 300);
  };
  ...
```

Save the file. In the browser, type a name into the checkout form. Watch the results in the DevTools.

Although the requests are being delayed, each input change still triggers a new request. What is going on?

setTimeout is a global JavaScript function. To use it, you pass it a function to execute and a delay in milliseconds, as you do here. **setTimeout** creates a timer for the delay and executes the provided function only when the timer has expired. In this case, each call to **onNameChange** creates a new timer – so the provided function runs once for each timer that expires.

To get debouncing working properly, you need to clear any previous timers before creating the next one.

setTimeout returns a value that identifies the current timer. Using another global JavaScript function called **clearTimeout**, you can use this value to stop the timer.

This is where **useRef** comes in handy. You can store the value of the **setTimeout** function in **useRef**, because updating that value should not trigger any re-renders in the application.

Try it out by adding a new ref. When the name value changes, check the ref's current value to see if a previous timer already exists. If it does, clear the timer using **clearTimeout**. Then set the ref equal to a new **setTimeout** timer.

Listing 14.8 Using **clearTimeout** (Cart.js)

```
import axios from 'axios';
import PropTypes from 'prop-types';
import { useState } from 'react';
import { useRef, useState } from 'react';
import ItemType from '../types/item';
...
function Cart({ cart, dispatch, items }) {
  ...
  const [isEmployeeOfTheMonth, setIsEmployeeOfTheMonth] = useState(false);
  const debounceRef = useRef(null);
  ...
  const onNameChange = (newName) => {
    setName(newName);
    setTimeout(() => {
    if (debounceRef.current) {
      clearTimeout(debounceRef.current);
    }
    debounceRef.current = setTimeout(() => {
      axios
...
```

After saving your file, clear the network requests by clicking the ⊘ button in the Network tab's menu bar. Then type in the Name field again. Now only one network request occurs, when you finish typing. (If you pause and begin typing again, you will see multiple requests.)

If you entered the name of an eligible employee, the subtotal and subsequent calculations will all show as $0.00 (Figure 14.5).

Figure 14.5 Free orders for an employee of the month

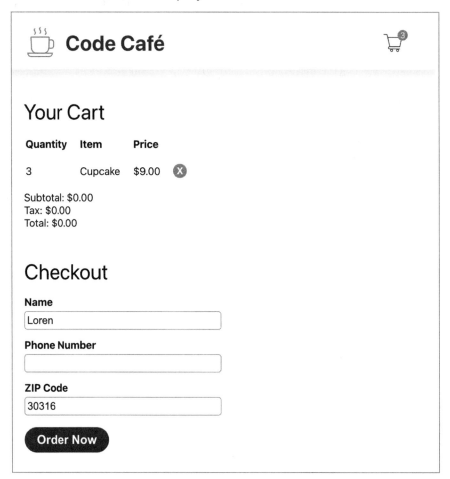

Accessing DOM Elements

Next, you will explore the other use case for **useRef**: directly accessing DOM elements. **useRef**'s persistence through re-renders allows you to create a consistent reference to a DOM node.

Take a look at the checkout form you built. Since a phone number has a fixed number of digits, it would be nice if the user's cursor automatically moved from the phone number input to the ZIP code input once they have entered the last digit of the phone number.

To advance the focus to the ZIP code input, you will need to call **focus** on the related DOM node. To access the DOM node, you will use **useRef**.

Each element has a ref prop to which you can pass the ref object that **useRef** returns. Create a ref for the zipCode input:

Listing 14.9 Creating a ZIP code ref (Cart.js)

```
...
function Cart({ cart, dispatch, items }) {
  ...
  const debounceRef = useRef(null);
  const zipRef = useRef(null);
  ...
  return (
    ...
              <input
                id="zipcode"
                ...
                onChange={(event) => setZipCode(event.target.value)}
                required
                ref={zipRef}
              />
...
```

Since zipRef is a ref object, React sets the object's current property to the relevant DOM node when the component renders. This allows you to access the DOM node using zipRef.current.

In the **setFormattedPhone** function, check whether the phone number has the required number of digits. If it does, call the **focus** method on the ZIP code input, using the current value of the ref object.

Listing 14.10 Advancing the focus to zipRef's DOM node (Cart.js)

```
...
function Cart({ cart, dispatch, items }) {
  ...
  const setFormattedPhone = (newNumber) => {
    ...
    } else if (digits.length > 6) {
      formatted = `${formatted}-${digits.substring(6, 10)}`;
    }

    if (digits.length === 10) {
      zipRef.current.focus();
    }
    setPhone(formatted);
...
```

Save your file and test the changes in your browser.

In the checkout form, enter 10 digits in the phone number input. As you enter the 10th digit, the focus will advance to the ZIP code input, highlighting the input and moving your cursor (Figure 14.6).

Figure 14.6 ZIP code input with focus

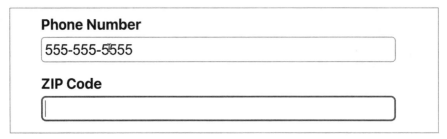

Accessibility Considerations

Manipulating DOM elements like this can interfere with important accessibility features such as screen readers. Be careful when making any assumptions about how the user will interact with the screen.

To make Code Café more accessible, add instructions to let the user know exactly what will happen when the phone number is complete.

Listing 14.11 Adding accessibility instructions (Cart.js)

```
...
function Cart({ cart, dispatch, items }) {
  ...
  return (
    ...
              <input
                id="phone"
                ...
                onChange={(event) => setFormattedPhone(event.target.value)}
                aria-label="Enter your phone number.
                After a phone number is entered,
                you will automatically be moved to the next field."
              />
...
```

The aria-label gives accessibility information to screen readers. Now users know they should expect the focus to change after they enter the phone number.

Conclusion

useRef is an important tool that gives you added control over the behavior of your components. It allows you to keep track of a value without triggering component re-renders and lets you directly access DOM elements.

In the next chapter, you will integrate your form with the server so that users can submit their orders. If you feel like you need more practice with **useRef** before moving on, check out the challenge below.

Silver Challenge: Returning Focus to the Name Input

You programmatically advance focus when the user finishes entering their phone number. Now, do the same with the ZIP code, but only if the user has neglected to enter their name: When the user finishes inputting the five-digit ZIP code, check whether the name is blank. If so, move focus to the name input. Otherwise, leave the focus alone.

(Why not move focus to the Order Now button? Pressing Return in any form field submits the form, so many browsers will not move focus to a **submit** button.)

Hint: You will likely want to create a separate function to handle the **onChange** event for the ZIP code, as the logic will be difficult to fit in **onClick**.

15

Submitting Orders

Although Code Café's users can build an order, they cannot actually send it to the café.

By the end of this chapter, you will store orders on the server, ready for the café staff to fulfill (Figure 15.1).

Figure 15.1 Orders submitted to the server

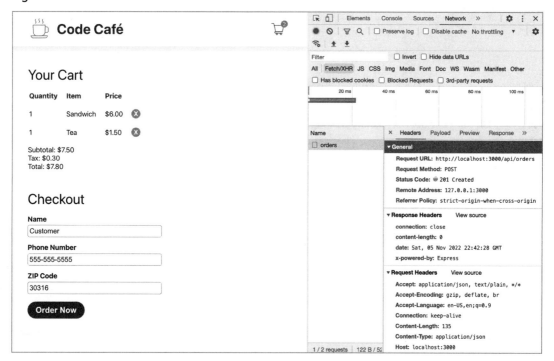

Submitting a Form

Back in Chapter 8, you made your first request to the API to fetch items. You wrapped the request in the **useEffect** hook to ensure that it would send when the component initially rendered:

```
useEffect(() => {
  axios.get('/api/items')
    .then((result) => setItems(result.data))
    .catch(console.error);
}, []);
```

The request you will make to submit the form will be different, because its trigger will be a direct user action: clicking the Order Now button.

Start by updating the form's **onSubmit** handler. Use Axios to make a POST request to the API that includes the order items and the user details.

Listing 15.1 Adding a POST request (`Cart.js`)

```
...
function Cart({ cart, dispatch, items }) {
  ...
  const submitOrder = (event) => {
    event.preventDefault();
    // TODO
    axios.post('/api/orders', {
      items: cart,
      name,
      phone,
      zipCode,
    });
  };
...
```

items, name, and zipCode are required fields. Ensure that the POST body includes these fields, as shown here.

Save your file. In your browser, open the DevTools to the Network tab. Add an item to your cart and navigate to the cart page. Enter user information in the checkout form and click the Order Now button.

(Do not use the ZIP code 99999 when checking out. It intentionally causes an error, which you will handle later in this chapter.)

You should see a network request to `orders` in your DevTools. Click it and check out the headers pane to see information about the request, including the 201 status code that indicates the order was created (Figure 15.2).

Figure 15.2 Viewing the created order in the Network tab

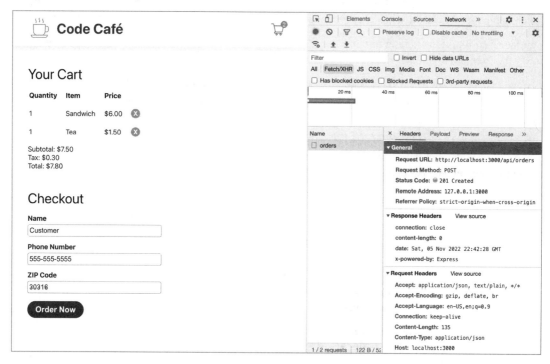

You can also confirm that the order was created by viewing the list of orders from the server at http://localhost:3030/api/orders in your browser (Figure 15.3).

Figure 15.3 Viewing the list of orders

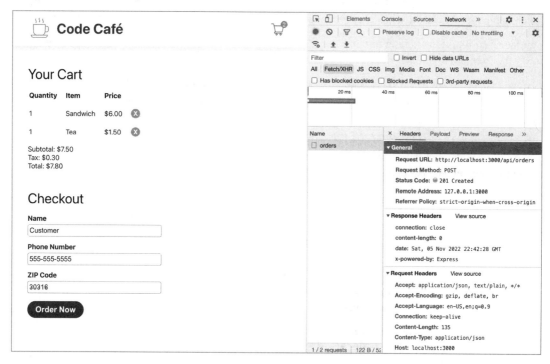

The server does not use persistent storage, so each time you restart your server, you lose all the orders. Restart the server only if your computer restarts or if you are taking a long break; otherwise, leave it running.

async/await

Now you have successfully submitted an order to the API. The next step is to provide a nice user experience by letting the user know that their order was created (or that there was an error).

Recall that when you were fetching items from the server, you used the promise constructs then and catch, which let you know when the server returned the items, so you could save them into state.

You face a similar issue here: Your app needs to wait until the network request completes before it can notify the user about whether their order submission was successful.

You will use promises again. This time, instead of then and catch, you will use the async/await syntax to get the result. This syntax allows you to write code that looks synchronous while still handling asynchronous behavior.

Label your **submitOrder** function as async, then await the Axios request. After the wait, add a **console.log** statement indicating that the order was submitted. (You will replace this with a user-facing message in the next chapter.)

Listing 15.2 Adding a success message (Cart.js)

```
...
function Cart({ cart, dispatch, items }) {
  ...
  const isFormValid = zipCode.length === 5 && name.trim();

  const submitOrder = (event) => {
  const submitOrder = async (event) => {
    event.preventDefault();
    axios.post('/api/orders', {
    await axios.post('/api/orders', {
      items: cart,
      name,
      phone,
      zipCode,
    });
    console.log('Order Submitted');
  };
```

Save your file. Back in your browser, switch your DevTools to the Console tab, then click the Order Now button again. Your new success message prints to your console (Figure 15.4).

Figure 15.4 Success message in the console

Recall that making a request with Axios automatically returns a promise. The await keyword signals JavaScript to wait for the promise to complete before executing any subsequent code in the function.

Frequently, you will see code that saves the data resulting from the promise into a variable, like this: `const result = await axios.post(...);`. However, when you submit an order, the server returns only a 201 status code, indicating that the request was created. In this case, there is no resulting data to save. You know the order is successful if your code makes it to the next line, the call to **console.log**.

How do you know if the promise with `await` failed? The code throws an error. You can catch this error using a `try/catch` block. Add this to your code so you can log an error message when needed. (You will need to reindent the lines you embed in the `try` block.)

Listing 15.3 Adding an error message (`Cart.js`)

```
...
function Cart({ cart, dispatch, items }) {
  ...
  const submitOrder = async (event) => {
    event.preventDefault();
    try {
      await axios.post('/api/orders', {
        ...
      });
      console.log('Order Submitted');
    } catch (error) {
      console.error('Error submitting the order', error);
    }
  };
};
```

Save your file and return to your browser. Change the ZIP code to 99999 and click Order Now. Because the API is written so that it returns a 400 status error for this ZIP code, the error message prints to the console (Figure 15.5).

Figure 15.5 Error message in the console

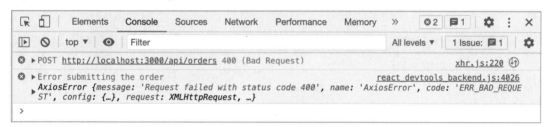

Open the Network tab to see the failed `orders` request highlighted in red. Click the failed request, then open the response pane to see the error message from the server (Figure 15.6).

Figure 15.6 Error message in the Network tab

You will work with this error message in the next chapter.

Comparing async/await and then/catch

Let's look at a short demo on async/await and compare it with the promise demo you saw in Chapter 8. This demo file is also in your downloaded resources file, at code-cafe-resources/demos/asyncAwait.mjs. Though it is similar to the promiseDemo.js demo file that you looked at before, instead of using then and catch, this demo uses await inside a try/catch block.

Note: The .mjs extension allows you to use await at the top level of a file. In your React application, you do not need this extension because you will use functions with the async keyword instead.

Here is the function:

```
'use strict';

const getData = () => {
    console.log("getData Running");
    return Promise.resolve("yay!");
};

console.log("top");

try {
    const result = await getData();
    console.log("result", result);
} catch (error) {
    console.error("error", error);
}

console.log("end");
```

There are several differences between this file and promiseDemo.js. First, instead of using getData().then, this code uses await getData(). Second, a try block wraps the await. And third, the error-handling code uses a catch block.

In Chapter 8, you saw the then/catch code in promiseDemo.js output the following result:

```
% node promiseDemo.js
top
getData Running
end
result yay!
```

In what order will the logs in asyncAwait.mjs print? Will it be the same order as in promiseDemo.js, or will the order change?

Run the code with

```
cd YOUR_PATH/resources/code-cafe-resources/demos
node asyncAwait.mjs
```

Did the output match your expectations?

```
% node asyncAwait.mjs
top
getData Running
result yay!
end
```

The first thing that logs is top. As before, this is because the code has not yet invoked the **getData** function.

Next, the code invokes **getData**, which causes getData Running to log. As before, JavaScript does not wait for the await result to start the promise; the promise starts immediately when you invoke it.

Then, result yay! logs. Finally, end logs.

Why does result yay! log before end now? Unlike then, the await keyword pauses execution of the script and waits for the result to come back before continuing to evaluate code. Frequently, this behavior is more aligned with what developers expect.

On the other hand, there is a downside to pausing execution when you need to execute several asynchronous things at once: await can cause them to run sequentially instead of in parallel. To avoid this, you can group several promises with **Promise.all** and await that result.

Before closing your demo, consider one more question: If you replace return Promise.resolve("yay!"); with return Promise.reject("error!");, what will happen? Check your answer before moving on.

Preventing Inadvertent Submissions

The delay between when the user clicks Order Now and when the request completes is an issue not only for you and your code base. It can be an issue for your users too: A user clicking the Order Now button multiple times could end up inadvertently creating extra orders – especially if their network connection is slow and the request takes a while to complete.

Right now, every part of the app runs locally on your machine, so everything loads quickly. The DevTools let you test what would happen over a slow connection, so you can see what the user might experience.

In the Network tab's menu bar, click No Throttling and select Slow 3G in the dropdown (Figure 15.7).

Figure 15.7 Modeling a slow network

When you select Slow 3G, the Network tab shows an exclamation point to remind you that you have altered your internet access (Figure 15.8).

Figure 15.8 Altered network status indicator

Click Order Now and watch the Status column in the Network tab to see how long it takes for the request to complete. Initially, the status shows as (pending). Once the request completes, the status code shows as 201. If the user clicks the button repeatedly while the status is pending, they can create a lot of orders.

To prevent the user from accidentally submitting duplicate orders, add a new state value called isSubmitting that is true while the request is completing. During this state, disable the Order Now button to prevent additional orders.

Listing 15.4 Adding the isSubmitting state (`Cart.js`)

```
...
function Cart({ cart, dispatch, items }) {
  ...
  const [isEmployeeOfTheMonth, setIsEmployeeOfTheMonth] = useState(false);
  const [isSubmitting, setIsSubmitting] = useState(false);
  const debounceRef = useRef(null);
  ...
  const submitOrder = async (event) => {
    event.preventDefault();
    setIsSubmitting(true);
    try {
      ...
    } catch (error) {
      console.error('Error submitting the order', error);
    } finally {
      setIsSubmitting(false);
    }
  ...
  return (
    ...
          <label htmlFor="zipcode">
            ...
          </label>
          <button type="submit" disabled={!isFormValid}>
          <button type="submit" disabled={!isFormValid || isSubmitting}>
            Order Now
...
```

When you first initiate the request, you set isSubmitting to true. JavaScript does not execute the remaining code in the function until the code following the await keyword has completed. Finally, once the request is complete (or there is an error), you set isSubmitting back to false.

You use the || operator to specify that the Order Now button should be disabled if the form is invalid *or* if isSubmitting is true.

Save your file, then submit an order in the browser again.

Now the Order Now button is disabled while the order is submitting (Figure 15.9).

Figure 15.9 Disabled Order Now button

Before moving on, restore your model network to its full speed. In the Network tab's menu bar, click Slow 3G and select No Throttling in the dropdown.

Conclusion

Now users can submit orders to the API after adding items to the cart. You handle the asynchronous behavior in React using the async/await syntax, and you have implemented a new state to prevent users from unintentionally submitting extra orders.

In the next chapter, you will add an alert to let users know whether their order was successful or had an error.

Bronze Challenge: Reset the Cart State

After the user successfully submits an order, reset the state values for the name, phone number, and ZIP code fields. If the order submission fails, leave the values in place.

Silver Challenge: How Many Orders Are in the Queue?

After submitting the order, users might like to know how many orders are ahead of theirs.

Update **submitOrder** so that after submitting the orders, it makes a GET request to /api/orders. Remember, you can make this request with axios.get("/api/orders"). However, instead of using then and catch, await the request.

The result will be an array of orders. Save the result into a variable, like in the demo code above. The number of orders in the array will be the user's place in line. Log this value to the console.

16

Component Composition

In this chapter, you will use *component composition* to build a reusable alert component. Component composition allows you to pass child components as props to another component, giving you flexible control over what renders. Component composition is a dynamic, powerful React tool that developers frequently use in component libraries.

You will use the alert component to display messages in two scenarios:

- When the order submission is successful, you will display a thank-you message.
- When the order submission fails, you will display an error message.

By the end of this chapter, your cart page will be complete (Figure 16.1).

Figure 16.1 Completed cart page

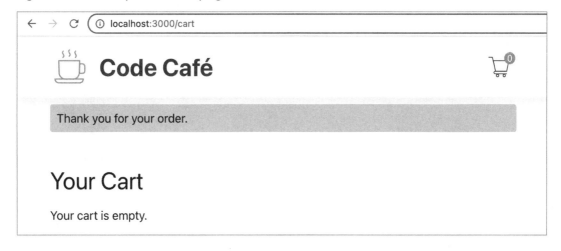

Alert

Right now, you can use the DevTools to see the order submissions and whether they succeeded or failed. But users do not open the DevTools to see console statements or network requests. You need another way to show them the status of their orders.

As we did for other components, we have provided the stylesheet for the **Alert** component you are about to create. If you have not done so already, copy **Alert.css** from your downloaded resources file into **src/components**.

Create a new **Alert** component that can display status messages. Remember to import Alert.css. This component is different from previous components you have built, because it relies on the children prop.

Listing 16.1 Building the **Alert** component (Alert.js)

```
import PropTypes from 'prop-types';
import './Alert.css';

function Alert({
  children,
}) {
  return (
    <div
      className="alert-component visible"
    >
      {children}
    </div>
  );
}

Alert.propTypes = {
  children: PropTypes.node.isRequired,
};

export default Alert;
```

children is a reserved word in React. You use it to represent any elements that render between the opening and closing tags of a component. Every component has a children prop you can access.

To see how this works, add the **Alert** component to Cart.js. Put it above the cart header so it is nice and visible to the user. For now, set it to display a thank-you message.

Listing 16.2 Adding an alert (Cart.js)

```
...
import './Cart.css';
import Alert from './Alert';

function Cart({ cart, dispatch, items }) {
  ...
  return (
    <div className="cart-component">
      <Alert>Thank you for your order.</Alert>
      <h2>Your Cart</h2>
...
```

You place the string Thank you for your order. between the opening and closing tags of the **Alert** component. This means that the string will render as the children prop of **Alert**.

Now the alert displays at the top of the cart page, below the application header (Figure 16.2).

Figure 16.2 Alert displayed on the cart page

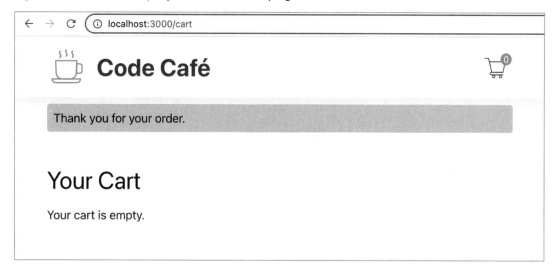

You will add some controls in a moment so that the message appears only when the user has submitted an order.

But first, open the Elements tab in the DevTools to inspect the elements. **Alert**'s child string renders as a child of the nested <div> (Figure 16.3).

Figure 16.3 Element hierarchy in the DevTools

```
▼<body>
    <noscript>You need to enable JavaScript to run this app.</noscript>
  ▼<div id="root">
    ▶<header class="header-component">…</header>  flex
    ▼<div class="cart-component">
...    ▼<div class="alert-component"> == $0
         <div>Thank you for your order.</div>
       </div>
       <h2>Your Cart</h2>
     ▶<table>…</table>
```

Being able to access and control how a component's children render is extremely powerful. It makes your components much more flexible and reusable. You are likely to use this tool often in React, especially when working with reusable UI components.

Conditionally Showing an Alert

Let's update the success alert so it is visible to the user only when their order submission is successful.

You currently apply styles from two CSS classes to the component: alert-component and visible. (Remember that in JSX, you apply styles from CSS classes using the keyword className.) By default, the alert-component class hides the component from view using CSS style rules. The visible class overrides those style rules to display the component onscreen.

The visible class should apply only when the component should display. Add a visible prop to the component. Then conditionally add the visible class name if the prop value is true.

Listing 16.3 Adding the `visible` prop (`Alert.js`)

```
...
function Alert({
  children,
  visible,
}) {
  return (
    <div
      className="alert-component visible"
      className={`alert-component ${visible && 'visible'}`}
      role="alert"
      hidden={!visible}
    >
      ...
Alert.propTypes = {
  children: PropTypes.node.isRequired,
  visible: PropTypes.bool.isRequired,
};
...
```

Now, when visible is true, both the alert-component and visible classes apply, so the component displays to the user. When visible is false, only the alert-component class applies, and the alert component does not display.

You also added the role of "alert" to the component. This role alerts accessibility tools when the component changes and is visible onscreen. For example, screen readers will read the contents of the component when it becomes visible. Adding the attribute hidden also ensures that screen readers will skip the component when it is not visible.

In the **Cart** component, add state for controlling when the success **Alert** is visible. The initial state value will be false, and it will update to true only when the POST request is successful.

Listing 16.4 Showing alerts based on state (`Cart.js`)

```
...
function Cart({ cart, dispatch, items }) {
  ...
  const [isEmployeeOfTheMonth, setIsEmployeeOfTheMonth] = useState(false);
  const [isSubmitting, setIsSubmitting] = useState(false);
  const [showSuccessAlert, setShowSuccessAlert] = useState(false);
  const debounceRef = useRef(null);
  ...
  const submitOrder = async (event) => {
    event.preventDefault();
    setIsSubmitting(true);
    try {
      ...
      });
      console.log('Order Submitted');
      setShowSuccessAlert(true);
    } catch (error) {
      ...
  return (
    <div className="cart-component">
      <Alert>Thank you for your order.</Alert>
      <Alert visible={showSuccessAlert}>
        Thank you for your order.
      </Alert>
      <h2>Your Cart</h2>
....
```

Save your file and try your new **Alert** in the browser. When you click Order Now, the new alert appears at the top of the page (Figure 16.4).

Figure 16.4 Success alert in the browser

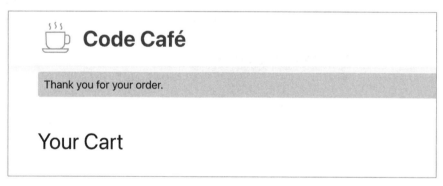

Component Composition with Props

It is valid JSX to pass child elements inline using the `children` prop instead of nesting them between the component's opening and closing tags:

```
<Alert visible={showSuccessAlert} children="Thank you for your order." />
```

And if you wanted to use JSX with `children`, you would need to use curly braces like this:

```
<Alert visible={showSuccessAlert} children={<p>Thank you for your order.</p>} />
```

But React recommends that you always pass child elements by nesting them within the component's opening and closing tags, so there is a React ESLint rule against passing them inline using the `children` prop.

However, the `children` prop is just one case. There is another case in which you compose components directly as props, and you are already using it.

The **Route** component accepts an `element` to display:

```
<Route path="/" element={<Home items={items} />} />
```

Why does **Route** use `element` instead of just making **Home** a child element? **Route** is already using child elements to specify child routes. Look at the nested routes for /details:

```
<Route path="/details" element={<Details items={items} />}>
  <Route
    path=":id"
    element={<DetailItem items={items} addToCart={addToCart} />}
  />
  <Route index element={<div>No Item Selected</div>} />
</Route>
```

The :id and index routes are children of the /details route, and `element` specifies what to display on each route. Other front-end frameworks such as Vue and Angular have a concept called *slots* that lets you pass multiple sets of child elements and specify different purposes for them. Although React does not have this concept, it does allow you to pass JSX as a prop, which accomplishes a similar task.

When composing components, reach for actual children first, to keep your code easy to read. Then, if you need multiple sets of child components, add a prop.

Reusing Alert

With only a small adjustment, you can reuse the **Alert** component to let the user know when an error occurs.

Add a type prop to the **Alert** component and use it to add an inline backgroundColor style.

Listing 16.5 Adding an inline style (`Alert.js`)

```
import PropTypes from 'prop-types';
import './Alert.css';

const BACKGROUND_COLORS = {
  success: '#adc6a8',
  error: '#f5c6cb',
};

function Alert({
  children,
  visible,
  type,
}) {
  return (
    <div
      className={`alert-component ${visible && 'visible'}`}
      role="alert"
      hidden={!visible}
      style={{ backgroundColor: BACKGROUND_COLORS[type] }}
    >
      ...
Alert.propTypes = {
  children: PropTypes.node.isRequired,
  visible: PropTypes.bool.isRequired,
  type: PropTypes.oneOf(['success', 'error']).isRequired,
};
...
```

You define the possible background colors in a new object, BACKGROUND_COLORS, which you then reference in the object passed inline to the style attribute. You reference the background-color property as backgroundColor because the names of inline style properties are camelCase.

In Cart.js, set the **Alert**'s type prop to "success".

Listing 16.6 Using the type prop (`Cart.js`)

```
...
function Cart({ cart, dispatch, items }) {
  ...
  return (
    <div className="cart-component">
      <Alert visible={showSuccessAlert}>
      <Alert visible={showSuccessAlert} type="success">
        Thank you for your order.
...
```

Now create a new error alert. Similar to the success alert, this alert should be visible only after an error has occurred with the order submission.

This time, instead of using a Boolean to set the visibility state, use the error message that the server returns. (Recall that in the last chapter, you looked at an error message in the Network tab of your DevTools.) This way, you can provide the user with the information they need to correct the error instead of showing a generic error message.

Listing 16.7 Adding an error alert (`Cart.js`)

```
...
function Cart({ cart, dispatch, items }) {
  ...
  const [isSubmitting, setIsSubmitting] = useState(false);
  const [showSuccessAlert, setShowSuccessAlert] = useState(false);
  const [apiError, setApiError] = useState('');
  const debounceRef = useRef(null);
  ...
  const submitOrder = async (event) => {
    ...
    } catch (error) {
      console.error('Error submitting the order', error);
      setApiError(error?.response?.data?.error || 'Unknown Error');
    } finally {
    ...
  return (
    <div className="cart-component">
      <Alert visible={showSuccessAlert} type="success">
        Thank you for your order.
      </Alert>
      <Alert visible={!!apiError} type="error">
        <p>There was an error submitting your order.</p>
        <p>{apiError}</p>
        <p>Please try again.</p>
      </Alert>
      <h2>Your Cart</h2>
...
```

When setting the API error, you use optional chaining to avoid problems with getting the error message from the server. If there is no error message, you use the generic message "Unknown Error" instead.

Recall that the `!!` operator converts any falsy or truthy value to its respective `boolean`. An empty string is `false`; any other string value is `true`. (Also, remember that you can check the result of using operators like this in the console.)

Save your file, return to your browser, and try to place an order with the ZIP code 99999. Now the error alert appears at the top of the screen (Figure 16.5).

Figure 16.5 Error alert

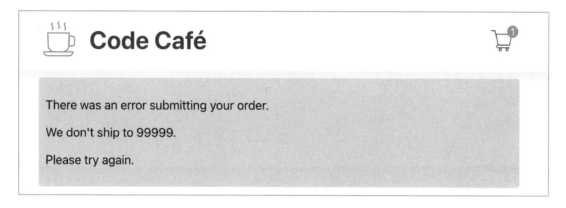

This time the **Alert** component has multiple children, which all render as expected.

There is one problem. Once the error is visible onscreen, it does not go away – even if you subsequently make a successful request. (Try it for yourself.)

Add logic to reset apiError to an empty string when the user initiates a new request.

Listing 16.8 Resetting state (`Cart.js`)

```
...
function Cart({ cart, dispatch, items }) {
  ...
  const submitOrder = async (event) => {
    event.preventDefault();
    setIsSubmitting(true);
    setApiError('');
    try {
      ...
```

Save your file, submit an order with the 99999 ZIP code, and then resubmit using any other ZIP code. The success alert replaces the error alert.

Emptying the Cart

One final consideration: It would be nice to empty the cart after a successful order submission, so that the user can start their next order afresh.

Start by creating a new action in **cartReducer** called EMPTY to empty the cart.

Listing 16.9 Adding the EMPTY action to **cartReducer** (cartReducer.js)

```
export const initialCartState = [];

export const CartTypes = {
  ADD: 'ADD',
  EMPTY: 'EMPTY',
  REMOVE: 'REMOVE',
};
...
export const cartReducer = (state, action) => {
  ...
      return [
        ...
      ];
    case CartTypes.EMPTY:
      return [];
    case CartTypes.REMOVE:
...
```

Now **dispatch** that action in the **Cart** component's **submitOrder** function, after the Axios request completes.

Listing 16.10 Dispatching the EMPTY action (Cart.js)

```
...
import './Cart.css';
import Alert from './Alert';
import { CartTypes } from '../reducers/cartReducer';

function Cart({ cart, dispatch, items }) {
  ...
  const submitOrder = async (event) => {
    event.preventDefault();
    setIsSubmitting(true);
    try {
      ...
      });
      dispatch({ type: CartTypes.EMPTY });
      setShowSuccessAlert(true);
...
```

Save your files and test the new functionality in your browser. After you successfully submit an order, your cart is empty (Figure 16.6).

Figure 16.6 Empty cart after submitting order

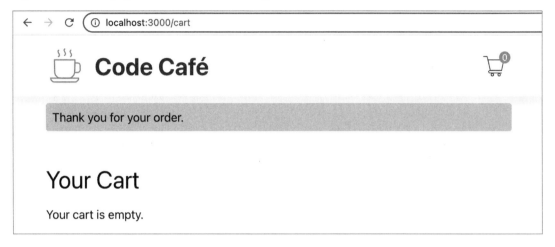

Conclusion

Congratulations! Your cart page is fully functional. After adding items to the cart, the user can now submit their order to the API and see a message about whether their request was successful.

In the next chapter, you will learn about another hook called **useContext** as you add functionality for users to log in to Code Café.

Gold Challenge: Closeable Alert

It would be nice if users could close the error alert once they have read the message. Currently, they have to submit a successful order to make it go away. Because you might eventually want multiple closeable alerts, add this functionality in a new component.

Create a **CloseableAlert** component. To practice the component composition skills you learned in this chapter, use the **Alert** component in the rendering of **CloseableAlert**.

CloseableAlert should

- take in content via `children`
- accept an **onClose** function as a prop
- accept `visible` and `type` props and pass them to **Alert**
- render a button with the text Close, in addition to rendering the `children`
- call **onClose** when you click the Close button

In **Cart**, the **onClose** function should set `apiError` back to an empty string. This will make the alert no longer visible.

17

Context

In this chapter, you will explore React *context*. Context provides a way for components to access information stored higher in the component tree without needing to pass props.

To see how context works, you will set up the logic to allow Code Café's users to log in. You will store user information at a high level in the app, since multiple components will need to access it. And you will use context to access the user information in your components.

The server API for Code Café already has login functionality, so all you need to do is build the UI to enable it. You will build a new route, /login, that displays a form where the user will enter a username and password.

You will also add a new section to the header, next to the cart icon, that shows either the username and a button to log out or, if no user is logged in, a link to the login page (Figure 17.1).

Figure 17.1 Code Café at the end of this chapter

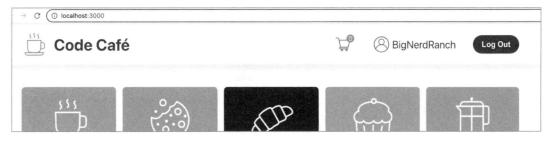

As you work through this chapter, try to write the code without looking at the solution first, then compare what you have written with the solution provided.

Getting the Logged-In User

Although the user data is stored on the server, it needs to be available if the user refreshes the page while visiting Code Café. The first step is to add state for holding information about the currently logged-in user, if there is one.

The API endpoint /api/auth/current-user returns the current user if one is logged in or an empty object if not. From **App**, make a request to this endpoint and save the results into a new state variable called currentUser.

Because you are not using currentUser yet, disable the lint rule about unused variables with

```
// eslint-disable-next-line no-unused-vars
```

Listing 17.1 Getting current user information (App.js)

```
...
function App() {
  const [items, setItems] = useState([]);
  // eslint-disable-next-line no-unused-vars
  const [currentUser, setCurrentUser] = useState({});
  const [cart, dispatch] = useReducer(
    ...
  useEffect(() => {
    axios.get('/api/items')
      .then((result) => setItems(result.data))
      .catch(console.error);
  }, []);

  useEffect(() => {
    axios.get('/api/auth/current-user')
      .then((result) => setCurrentUser(result.data))
      .catch(console.error);
  }, []);

  return (
...
```

Although you could write this request using async/await syntax, it would require some extra work. The main function for the **useEffect** hook has to be synchronous, not asynchronous. So you would need to refactor the request into its own function and then call it from within the hook.

That is why we prefer to use promises with then and catch for simple data fetching. But this is a style choice; in your own code, you might prefer async/await instead.

You might be wondering why you do not just add to your existing **useEffect** that fetches items from the server. Though you can, it would be harder to adjust later if the dependencies for one API call change or if you need to move one of the API calls to another component.

Hooks are designed to help separate concerns so that you can contain unrelated logic in separate methods. Therefore, it is best to put each unrelated API call in its own **useEffect** block.

Save your file and, in the browser, make sure the Network tab is open in the DevTools. Click one of the current-user requests and check out the response pane. It shows that the initial state for currentUser is an empty object: {} (Figure 17.2).

Figure 17.2 Current user request

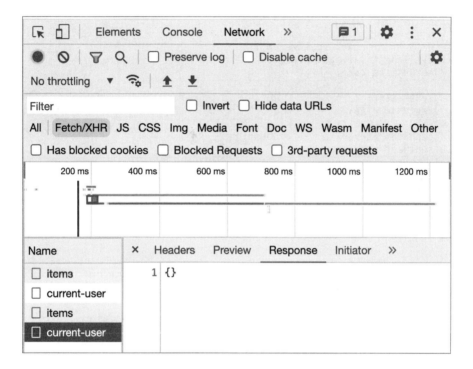

This is expected: Because there is no user logged in, the server returns an empty object.

Login Button

Next, you will create a new **UserDetails** component to display either the user's username or a login link. If you have not already done so, copy the UserDetails.css stylesheet from your downloaded resources file into your components directory. Then import it in your component to enable the provided styles.

Listing 17.2 Building **UserDetails** (UserDetails.js)

```
import { Link } from 'react-router-dom';
import Profile from '../images/profile.svg';
import './UserDetails.css';

function UserDetails() {
  const currentUser = {};
  return (
    <div className="user-details-component">
      { currentUser.username
        ? (
          <div>
            <img src={Profile} alt="profile" />
            <p>{currentUser.username}</p>
          </div>
        ) : <Link to="/login">Log In</Link> }
    </div>
  );
}

export default UserDetails;
```

You use a ternary to conditionally render the profile icon and username if a user is logged in, or the login link if not.

For now, you stub out currentUser as an empty object. You will update this value soon.

Next, add the new component to **Header**.

Listing 17.3 Adding **UserDetails** to **Header** (Header.js)

```
...
import CartIcon from '../images/cart.svg';
import UserDetails from './UserDetails';
import './Header.css';

function Header({ cart }) {
  const cartQuantity = cart.reduce((acc, item) => acc + item.quantity, 0);
  return (
    ...
        <Link to="/cart">
          <img src={CartIcon} alt="Cart" />
          <div className="badge">{cartQuantity}</div>
        </Link>
        <UserDetails />
      </div>
...
```

Save your files and take a look at your new and improved header in the browser (Figure 17.3).

(The login link currently leads to your Page Not Found route. You will fix this when you build the login page later in this chapter.)

Figure 17.3 Login link in header

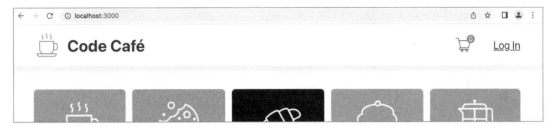

Avoiding Prop Drilling

The **UserDetails** component needs the value of the currentUser state from **App**. But **UserDetails** is a child of **Header**, not **App**, and **Header** does not care about the user details.

You could pass currentUser as a prop from **App** to **Header**, and then from **Header** to **UserDetails**. React developers have a name for this kind of pattern, where you pass a prop through components that do not need it to get to a component that does: *prop drilling*.

Prop drilling is problematic: It clutters your components with props they do not need, and it makes your code harder to reason about and maintain. Thankfully, React provides a few ways to avoid prop drilling.

In the previous chapter, you learned about component composition when you built the **Alert** component. Component composition allows you to pass children to a component, so you can pass **UserDetails** to **Header** as a child, like this:

```
<Header cart={cart}>
  <UserDetails currentUser={currentUser} />
</Header>
```

Doing this supplies the currentUser prop directly to **UserDetails**, so **Header** does not need to be concerned with currentUser. It only needs to render its children at the correct place.

While this approach works for this particular scenario, component composition allows you to bypass only a single level, so it does not work for a structure more than two levels deep. Also, it adds more complexity to the parent component.

Component composition is a great tool when you only need to skip one level and share something in a few places. But as Code Café expands, many components at various levels will need currentUser. It will be better if **App** can share it one time for all of its descendants.

The React tool that you need this time is context.

Think of context like a river. You provide the context value upstream, and it flows downstream, so any component below the context can access it if needed. Context avoids prop drilling by allowing components to *subscribe* to the context only if they need it.

Passing currentUser with Context

Create a new directory called `src/contexts` and a new file in it called `CurrentUserContext.js`.

In your new file, create your first context.

Listing 17.4 Creating a context (`CurrentUserContext.js`)

```
import { createContext } from 'react';

const CurrentUserContext = createContext();

export default CurrentUserContext;
```

The React method **createContext** returns a context object that contains a **Provider** and a **Consumer**. Continuing the river metaphor, the **Provider** is the component that pours the context value into the river to make it available downstream, and the **Consumer** is the component that accesses that value.

Although it is possible to pass a default value to **createContext**, you usually need that only for testing or if the **Consumer** is outside of the **Provider**. In Code Café, currentUser is stored in **App**, so that is where the **Provider** component will be.

Add the context provider to **App** by embedding the <Header> and <Routes> elements in a new <CurrentUserContext.Provider> element, as shown below. (You will need to reindent the newly nested code. You can add the provider's opening and closing tags and use ESLint's auto-fix to indent the other lines.)

Listing 17.5 Adding the context provider (`App.js`)

```
...
import NotFound from './components/NotFound';
import { cartReducer, CartTypes, initialCartState } from './reducers/cartReducer';
import CurrentUserContext from './contexts/CurrentUserContext';

const storageKey = 'cart';

function App() {
  const [items, setItems] = useState([]);
  // eslint-disable-next-line no-unused-vars
  const [currentUser, setCurrentUser] = useState({});
  ...
  return (
    <Router>
      <CurrentUserContext.Provider
        value={currentUser}
      >
        <Header cart={cart} />
        ...
          </Routes>
        )}
      </CurrentUserContext.Provider>
    </Router>
...
```

Why did you not place the provider around <Router>? The **Router** component is actually also a context provider, which is how the route parameters make it into your components. Though it would have worked to place <Router> below your provider, by convention, you place <Router> as high as possible.

Save your files and head over to the browser. Open the DevTools Components tab. There is a new component called **Context.Provider**. (You might need to refresh your browser to see it.)

Click the **Context.Provider** component to see information about it below the component tree (Figure 17.4).

Figure 17.4 Viewing the context in the DevTools

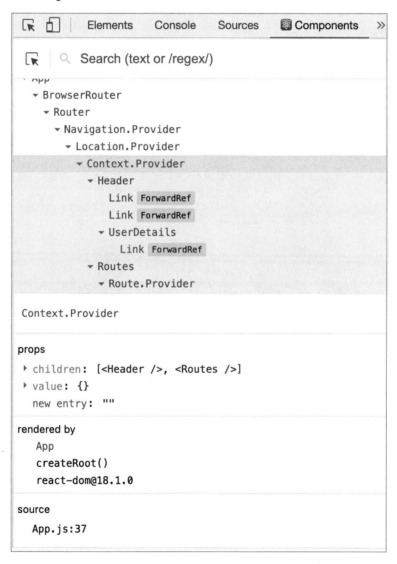

As with other components, the props of the **Provider** component show in the bottom panel. **App** passes currentUser as the value prop, and **Provider** also has a children prop.

It would be nice if the component's name showed in the DevTools as **CurrentUserContext.Provider**, instead of the generic **Context.Provider**. Often, you will have multiple contexts and providers, and it is helpful to be able to differentiate them.

In most cases, React automatically infers the name of the component from the name of the function defining the component. In this case, that was not possible because you used `createContext` to create the component. But React also provides a way to specify the component name: You can edit the `displayName` property, like how you can edit the `propTypes` property to specify prop types.

Add a display name to the context in your code.

Listing 17.6 Adding a context display name (`CurrentUserContext.js`)

```
import { createContext } from 'react';

const CurrentUserContext = createContext();

CurrentUserContext.displayName = 'CurrentUserContext';

export default CurrentUserContext;
```

Save your file and check the DevTools again to see your new display name (Figure 17.5).

Figure 17.5 Context display name in the DevTools

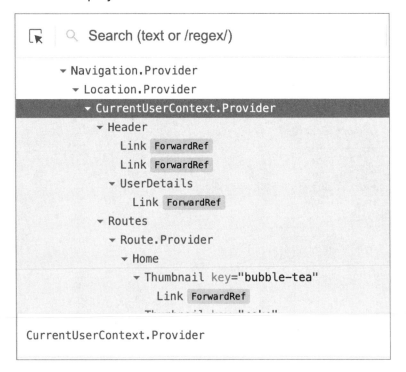

Much better. Now you can easily identify your context.

useMemo

Currently, you pass only the `currentUser` object to context. However, it is common for a context provider to have both a value and a function for updating that value available.

Update the value of **CurrentUserContext.Provider** to be an object containing both currentUser and **setCurrentUser**.

Listing 17.7 Passing **setCurrentUser** (App.js)

```
...
function App() {
  ...
  useEffect(() => {
    axios.get('/api/auth/current-user')
      .then((result) => setCurrentUser(result.data))
      .catch(console.error);
  }, []);

  const currentUserContextValue = { currentUser, setCurrentUser };

  return (
    <Router>
      <CurrentUserContext.Provider
        value={currentUser}
        value={currentUserContextValue}
      >
...
```

Right away, ESLint highlights a problem (Figure 17.6).

Figure 17.6 Constructed context error

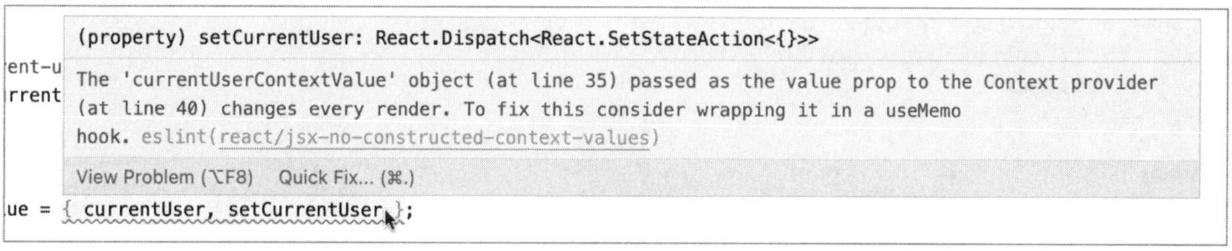

Each time the value of the context provider changes, it triggers all the subscribed children to re-render. This is often what you want, because the goal is to keep the onscreen components in sync with the current data.

However, when you updated value, you created the currentUserContextValue object to hold both currentUser and **setCurrentUser**. This object is created within the **App** function, so it will be re-created each time **App** renders.

We have mentioned before that React uses reference equality to determine when to re-render. When **App** re-renders, the object is re-created, creating a new object identity (even if the contents of the object are the same). Because the identity has changed, the provider believes value has changed and re-renders all subscribed components. And because a single provider can have many subscribers, this can have performance implications.

The ESLint warning gives a clue as to how to fix the problem: Use the **useMemo** hook to create a *memoized* version of this object. A memo is like a cache, holding on to a value until it needs to change. In Chapter 19, you will learn about using memos for values that are expensive to calculate. In this chapter, you will use a memo to hold on to an object so its identity does not change unnecessarily.

273

Like the **useEffect** hook, **useMemo** takes in two arguments:

- a callback function
- a dependency array

useMemo executes the callback function and returns a memoized value. React uses this value until the callback function executes again. During each render cycle, React compares the contents of the dependency array and reruns the callback function if there are changes.

Add **useMemo** to **App**, including `currentUser` in the dependency array so that React reruns the callback function only if `currentUser` updates.

Listing 17.8 Adding **useMemo** (App.js)

```
import axios from 'axios';
import { useEffect, useReducer, useState } from 'react';
import {
  useEffect, useMemo, useReducer, useState,
} from 'react';
import {
...
function App() {
  ...
  useEffect(() => {
    ...
  }, []);

  const currentUserContextValue = { currentUser, setCurrentUser };
  const currentUserContextValue = useMemo(
    () => ({ currentUser, setCurrentUser }),
    [currentUser],
  );

  return (
...
```

Passing the memoized `currentUserContextValue` object to the context provider ensures that it is only re-created when `currentUser` updates.

(At least, this is generally the case. Although React uses memos to improve efficiency, it does not *guarantee* that it will execute the callback function only when the values change. It is possible for React to clean out some memory or perform another operation that requires rerunning the function.)

You will learn more about **useMemo** in Chapter 19.

Check the DevTools to see the updated values of the context (Figure 17.7).

Figure 17.7 Context values

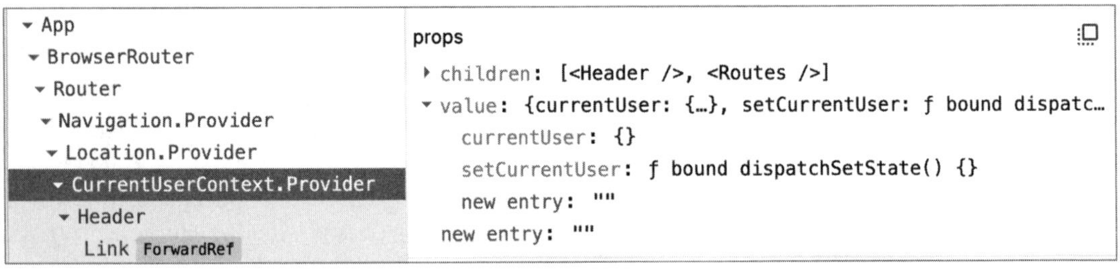

useContext

Now it is time to subscribe to the context.

Use the **useContext** hook to connect **UserDetails** to the `CurrentUserContext`.

Listing 17.9 Subscribing to `CurrentUserContext` (`UserDetails.js`)

```
import { useContext } from 'react';
import { Link } from 'react-router-dom';
import CurrentUserContext from '../contexts/CurrentUserContext';
import Profile from '../images/profile.svg';
import './UserDetails.css';

function UserDetails() {
  const currentUser = {};
  const { currentUser } = useContext(CurrentUserContext);

  return (
...
```

The **useContext** hook takes one argument: the context object you are referencing. The hook returns the value from the nearest matching context provider. You use object destructuring to target the specific context values the component needs.

Currently, **UserDetails** does not update the user information, so it does not need access to the setter function. (That will change later in this chapter.)

Now, **UserDetails** has access to `currentUser`. Its parent, **Header**, does not. This is just what you want.

Save your file and check the DevTools Components tab. Select the **UserDetails** component in the tree, then expand the hooks section in the bottom pane. You can see the value of `currentUser`, showing that the component does indeed have access to the context object (Figure 17.8).

Figure 17.8 Context values in the DevTools

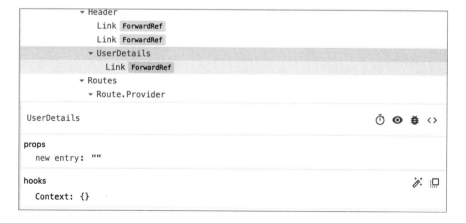

Login Component

Now you are ready to build the **Login** component in a new components/Login.js file. Copy the Login.css stylesheet from your downloaded resources file into your components directory, if you have not already done so, and import it in the component. Then create a form that requests a username and password and stores the user's input in state. Do not worry about handling the form's **onSubmit** event yet.

Listing 17.10 Building the **Login** component (Login.js)

```
import { useState } from 'react';
import './Login.css';

function Login() {
  const [username, setUsername] = useState('');
  const [password, setPassword] = useState('');

  return (
    <div className="login-component">
      <h2>Log In</h2>
      <form>
        <div>
          <label htmlFor="username">
            Username
            <input
              type="text"
              id="username"
              value={username}
              autoComplete="username"
              onChange={(event) => setUsername(event.target.value)}
              required
            />
          </label>
        </div>
        <div>
          <label htmlFor="password">
            Password
            <input
              type="password"
              id="password"
              value={password}
              autoComplete="current-password"
              onChange={(event) => setPassword(event.target.value)}
              required
            />
          </label>
        </div>
        <button type="submit">Log In</button>
      </form>
    </div>
  );
}

export default Login;
```

The autoComplete prop that you pass to the JSX input elements will render in HTML as the autocomplete attribute, which cues password managers to insert the appropriate values.

Next, add the new component as a new route on **App** for the `/login` path.

Listing 17.11 Adding the login route (`App.js`)

```
...
import { cartReducer, CartTypes, initialCartState } from './reducers/cartReducer';
import CurrentUserContext from './contexts/CurrentUserContext';
import Login from './components/Login';

const storageKey = 'cart';

function App() {
  ...
  return (
    ...
            </Route>
            <Route path="/" element={<Home items={items} />} />
            <Route path="/login" element={<Login />} />
            <Route path="*" element={<NotFound />} />
...
```

Save your files. In the browser, navigate to the new route by clicking the Log In link in the header (Figure 17.9).

Figure 17.9 New login page

Although you can fill in a username and password, you cannot log in until you handle the `submit` event.

When the user submits the form, make a POST request to /api/auth/login with the data { username, password }.

On success, call **setCurrentUser**, which you can get from context, and pass it result.data. (This is similar to the request for /api/auth/current-user.) In the error case, log to the console. Later, you will replace this behavior using the **Alert** component.

Listing 17.12 Handling the submit event (Login.js)

```
import { useState } from 'react';
import { useContext, useState } from 'react';
import axios from 'axios';
import CurrentUserContext from '../contexts/CurrentUserContext';
import './Login.css';

function Login() {
  const { setCurrentUser } = useContext(CurrentUserContext);
  const [username, setUsername] = useState('');
  const [password, setPassword] = useState('');

  const login = async (event) => {
    event.preventDefault();
    try {
      const result = await axios.post('/api/auth/login', {
        username,
        password,
      });
      setCurrentUser(result.data);
    } catch (error) {
      console.error(error);
    }
  };

  return (
    <div className="login-component">
      <h2>Log In</h2>
      <form>
      <form onSubmit={login}>
        <div>
...
```

Now you are ready to test logging in.

Though the API accepts any username, the only valid password is *pass*.

First, try logging in with any username and an invalid password (such as *invalid*). Open the console in the DevTools to see the error (Figure 17.10).

Figure 17.10 Login error

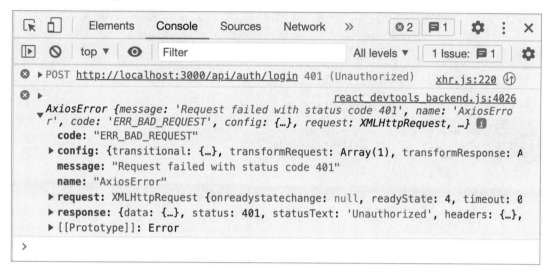

Now, log in with a valid username and password (such as *BigNerdRanch* and *pass*). The header displays the username you entered instead of the Log In link (Figure 17.11).

Figure 17.11 Logged-in user

Because the server uses a cookie for the login, you will stay logged in even if you refresh the page.

useNavigate

So far, so good. But you are still on the login page. After the user successfully logs in, it would be nice to redirect them to the home page.

Previously, you used the **Link** component from React Router to change the user's location when they clicked the **Link**. React Router also provides the **useNavigate** hook to perform a similar change programmatically.

Use **useNavigate** to redirect the user to the index path, /.

Listing 17.13 Adding **useNavigate** (Login.js)

```
import { useContext, useState } from 'react';
import { useNavigate } from 'react-router-dom';
import axios from 'axios';
...
function Login() {
  const { setCurrentUser } = useContext(CurrentUserContext);
  const [username, setUsername] = useState('');
  const [password, setPassword] = useState('');

  const navigate = useNavigate();

  const login = async (event) => {
    event.preventDefault();
    try {
      ...
      setCurrentUser(result.data);
      navigate('/');
    } catch (error) {
...
```

This hook returns a function that takes in the new location, using the same format as the to attribute of **Link**. It has options that dictate how to add the new location to the history. By default, it pushes a new browser state, which means the user can click the back button in the browser to go back to the previous page.

Complete the login form and click Log In again. This time, the app redirects you to the home page.

Logout Button

For better security, add a logout button to the header when the user is logged in.

The logout button should

- make a POST request to /api/auth/logout
- use the **setCurrentUser** function from context to update currentUser to an empty object

Listing 17.14 Adding a logout button (UserDetails.js)

```
import axios from 'axios';
import { useContext } from 'react';
...
function UserDetails() {
  const { currentUser } = useContext(CurrentUserContext);
  const { currentUser, setCurrentUser } = useContext(CurrentUserContext);

  const logout = async () => {
    try {
      await axios.post('/api/auth/logout', {});
      setCurrentUser({});
    } catch (error) {
      console.error(error);
    }
  };

  return (
    ...
            <img src={Profile} alt="profile" />
            <p>{currentUser.username}</p>
            <button type="button" onClick={logout}>
              Log Out
            </button>
          </div>
...
```

Why do you have to make the POST request in addition to calling **setCurrentUser({})**? If you only called **setCurrentUser({})**, the app would log the user back in after they refreshed the page, because the server would still remember their session. Making the POST request to the server ensures that the user stays logged out, even after refreshing.

Save your file and test your new logout button in the browser (Figure 17.12).

Figure 17.12 Logging out

Login Error

Your last task for this chapter is to show the login error to the user using the **Alert** component.

The server returns the error in the same place as it does when you submit an order. You can access it from the Axios error object with error?.response?.data?.error.

Listing 17.15 Login error **Alert** (Login.js)

```
import { useContext, useState } from 'react';
import { useNavigate } from 'react-router-dom';
import axios from 'axios';
import Alert from './Alert';
import CurrentUserContext from '../contexts/CurrentUserContext';
import './Login.css';

function Login() {
  const { setCurrentUser } = useContext(CurrentUserContext);
  const [username, setUsername] = useState('');
  const [password, setPassword] = useState('');
  const [apiError, setApiError] = useState('');

  const navigate = useNavigate();

  const login = async (event) => {
    ...
      console.error(error);
      setApiError(error?.response?.data?.error || 'Unknown Error');
    }
  };

  return (
    <div className="login-component">
      <Alert visible={!!apiError} type="error">
        <p>There was an error logging in.</p>
        <p>{ apiError }</p>
        <p>Please try again.</p>
      </Alert>
      <h2>Log In</h2>
...
```

Save your file and try to log in to Code Café with an invalid password.

You will get an error message (Figure 17.13):

Figure 17.13 Login error message

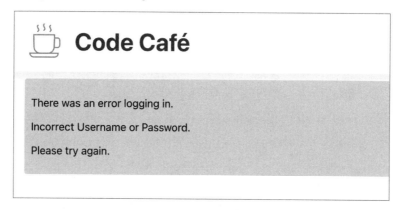

Conclusion

In this chapter, you used context to pass data to multiple components without unneeded prop drilling.

Now users can log in and log out, and Code Café is nearly feature complete! In the next chapter, you will build a page to allow the café's associates to view and complete submitted orders.

For the More Curious: Login Cookie

How does the server remember that you logged in? It uses a cookie.

You can find the login cookie in the DevTools Application tab.

Look under Storage, then Cookies, and then http://localhost:3000. You should see a cookie named coffeeJWT. The JWT at the end of the name indicates that the cookie is a JSON Web Token (Figure 17.14).

Figure 17.14 Login cookie

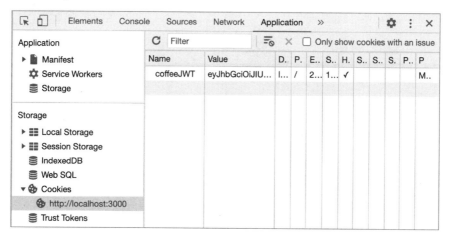

You can edit the cookie value, or you can select it and press the Delete key to delete it. Delete the cookie value, then refresh the page, and you will be logged out.

If you want to learn more about JSON Web Tokens, their website has a nice introduction section: jwt.io/introduction.

Silver Challenge: Items Context

Convert items to a context value so you no longer have to pass it as a prop to the components.

Note: Since the components do not change items, you do not need to put **setItems** in context.

Because this challenge will affect the tests you write later in the book, be sure to work on it in a copy of your code.

18

Fulfilling Orders

In the last chapter, you set up React context so that when a user logs in, you can easily share their information with components at multiple levels throughout the app.

Now that users can log in, you will build on concepts you have already learned to create an orders page that displays existing orders to users with associate access (Figure 18.1).

Figure 18.1 Completed orders page

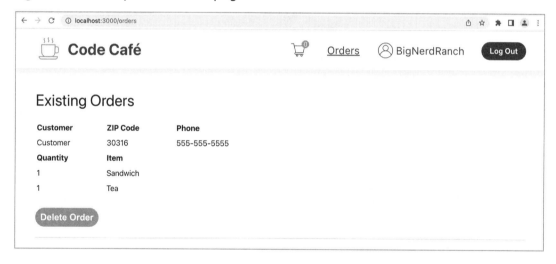

Creating the Orders Component

Start by creating a new **Orders** component to display the orders. For now, keep it simple: Just return a header with the text "Existing Orders." If you have not already done so, copy the Orders.css stylesheet from your downloaded resources file into your components directory. Then import the stylesheet.

Listing 18.1 Creating the **Orders** component (Orders.js)

```
import './Orders.css';

function Orders() {
  return (
    <div className="orders-component">
      <h2>Existing Orders</h2>
    </div>
  );
}

export default Orders;
```

Now add the new component as a new route on **App** for the /orders path. Pass the items array as a prop so you can use it in the **Orders** component.

Listing 18.2 Adding the orders route (App.js)

```
...
import CurrentUserContext from './contexts/CurrentUserContext';
import Login from './components/Login';
import Orders from './components/Orders';

const storageKey = 'cart';

function App() {
  ...
  return (
    ...
            <Route path="/" element={<Home items={items} />} />
            <Route path="/login" element={<Login />} />
            <Route path="/orders" element={<Orders items={items} />} />
            <Route path="*" element={<NotFound />} />
...
```

Save your files and visit http://localhost:3000/orders to see the new page (Figure 18.2).

Figure 18.2 Existing orders

Orders Link

The next step is to add a link to the orders page in the header.

Only associates should see this link. Logged-out users or users without associate-level access should not.

When a user logs in, the server returns a user details object that contains a property called `access`. For associates, this value is `"associate"`. For other users, it is an empty string.

Use a ternary to conditionally render the orders link in the **UserDetails** component.

Listing 18.3 Adding the orders link (`UserDetails.js`)

```
...
function UserDetails() {
  ...
  return (
    <div className="user-details-component">
      { currentUser.username
        ? (
          <div>
            {currentUser.access === 'associate'
              ? <Link to="/orders">Orders</Link>
              : null}
            <img src={Profile} alt="profile" />
...
```

Your ternary returns `null` when the user is not an associate. React skips rendering when the ternary resolves to `false`, `null`, or `undefined`, so users who are not associates will not see the link.

You could also have used `&&` to write this check with less code:

```
{currentUser.access === 'associate' && <Link to="/orders">Orders</Link>}
```

When a statement like this resolves to a Boolean `false`, React does not render anything. In this case, the statement either resolves to `false` (when the user is not an associate) or returns a link (when they are).

Save your file. In the browser, log in with the username *Guest* and the password *pass* to test what happens when a user without associate access logs in. There are no visual changes in the header – the orders link does not render (Figure 18.3).

Figure 18.3 No orders link for a logged-in guest

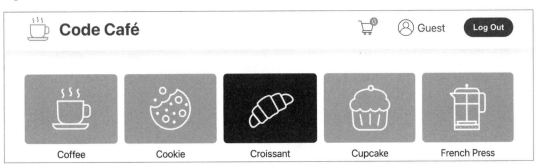

Log out. Code Café's server is configured to treat any username other than *Guest* as an associate. Log in again with any other username and the password *pass*. The orders link appears (Figure 18.4):

Figure 18.4 Orders link for a logged-in associate

Click the link to confirm that it takes you to the orders page.

Fetching and Displaying Orders

Now you need to fetch the orders from the API.

A GET request to /api/orders returns an array of orders, where each order object has the following shape:

```
{
    id: string,
    name: string,
    zipCode: string,
    phone: string,        // optional
    items: [{
        itemId: string,
        quantity: number
    }]
}
```

Recall that the phone number field in the order form is optional. The items array contains item objects with an itemId and a quantity, following the same structure as the cart items.

You passed items to **Orders** as a prop. You will use the itemId to find each order item in the items array so you can display the necessary information.

Add the GET request to **Orders** and store the orders in state. Add the items prop to the component and define it using prop types.

Because you are not using items or orders yet, you will need to disable the ESLint rule about unused variables (or ignore the lint error). You can disable the rule with // eslint-disable-next-line no-unused-vars.

Listing 18.4 Fetching orders from the server (Orders.js)

```
import axios from 'axios';
import { useEffect, useState } from 'react';
import PropTypes from 'prop-types';
import ItemType from '../types/item';
import './Orders.css';

// eslint-disable-next-line no-unused-vars
function Orders() {
function Orders({ items }) {
  // eslint-disable-next-line no-unused-vars
  const [orders, setOrders] = useState([]);

  useEffect(
    () => {
      axios.get('/api/orders')
        .then((result) => setOrders(result.data))
        .catch(console.error);
    },
    [],
  );

  return (
    <div className="orders-component">
      <h2>Existing Orders</h2>
    </div>
  );
}

Orders.propTypes = {
  items: PropTypes.arrayOf(ItemType).isRequired,
};

export default Orders;
```

Save your file. In the browser, navigate to the orders page. Open the DevTools Components tab and look at the hooks section to see the initial state for **Orders**. Then add an item to the cart, place the order, and return to the orders page. Check the DevTools again: Now the state is populated with the order information (Figure 18.5).

Figure 18.5 Order displaying in the DevTools

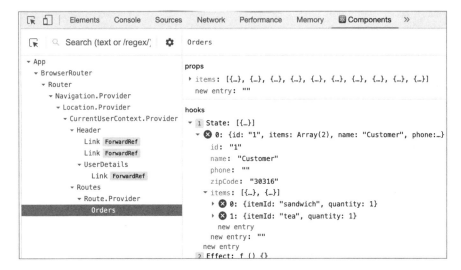

Time to get the orders onscreen. Back in **Orders**, iterate through the orders array and display each order. Use the items array to find each order's items and display their titles. If the orders array is empty, display the text "No Orders."

Listing 18.5 Displaying orders (`Orders.js`)

```
...
import ItemType from '../types/item';
import './Orders.css';

// eslint disable next line no unused vars
function Orders({ items }) {
  // eslint disable next line no unused vars
  const [orders, setOrders] = useState([]);

  useEffect(
    ...
  );

  return (
    <div className="orders-component">
      <h2>Existing Orders</h2>
      {orders.length === 0
        ? <div>No Orders</div>
        : orders.map((order) => (
          <div className="order" key={order.id}>
            <table>
              <thead>
                <tr>
                  <th>Customer</th>
                  <th>ZIP Code</th>
                  {order.phone && <th>Phone</th>}
                </tr>
              </thead>
              <tbody>
                <tr>
                  <td>{order.name}</td>
                  <td>{order.zipCode}</td>
                  {order.phone && <td>{order.phone}</td>}
                </tr>
              </tbody>
              <thead>
                <tr>
                  <th>Quantity</th>
                  <th>Item</th>
                </tr>
              </thead>
              <tbody>
                {order.items.map((item) => (
                  <tr key={item.itemId}>
                    <td>{item.quantity}</td>
                    <td>{items.find((i) => i.itemId === item.itemId)?.title}</td>
                  </tr>
                ))}
              </tbody>
            </table>
          </div>
        ))}
    </div>
...
```

Most of this code probably looks familiar.

You use a table to display the orders so that the columns line up correctly, just like you did with the cart. You conditionally render the phone number, because the field might not exist on the order object. When finding the item with the array **find** method, you use the optional chaining operator (**?.**) to display the title only if the item is found.

Save your file, return to the browser, and place a couple of orders in Code Café. Make sure you are logged in as an associate, then visit the orders page to view the orders (Figure 18.6).

Figure 18.6 Viewing order details

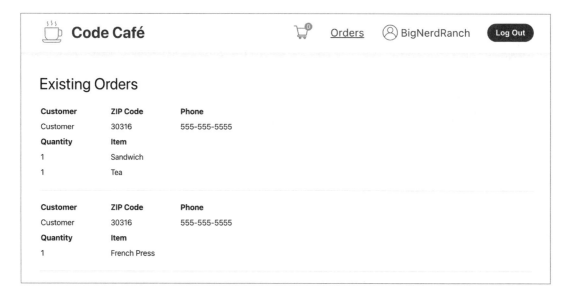

Fulfilling Orders

Now associates can see the orders that customers have placed. But after the associates fulfill an order, they need a way to delete it. You will add a delete button next. Clicking the button will make a DELETE call to /api/orders/:id.

axios.delete makes a call with the DELETE method. You can use a template literal to dynamically create the URL with the order ID at the end.

If the request is successful, the **Order** component should load the orders again. If not, log the error to the console.

Listing 18.6 Deleting an order (Orders.js)

```
...
function Orders({ items }) {
  const [orders, setOrders] = useState([]);

  const loadOrders = () => {
    axios.get('/api/orders')
      .then((result) => setOrders(result.data))
      .catch(console.error);
  };

  useEffect(
    () => {
      axios.get('/api/orders')
        .then((result) => setOrders(result.data))
        .catch(console.error);
      loadOrders();
    },
    [],
  );

  const deleteOrder = async (order) => {
    try {
      await axios.delete(`api/orders/${order.id}`);
      loadOrders();
    } catch (error) {
      console.error(error);
    }
  };

  return (
    ...
              <tbody>
                {order.items.map((item) => (
                  ...
                ))}
              </tbody>
            </table>
            <button
              type="button"
              onClick={() => deleteOrder(order)}
            >
              Delete Order
            </button>
          </div>
...
```

To avoid duplication, we moved the code for loading orders to a separate function. If you did not make this change, refactor your code to continue following along with the book.

Save your file and visit the orders page in your browser to see the new button (Figure 18.7).

Figure 18.7 Delete Order button

Delete one of the orders you placed. It will disappear from the page. If you delete all the orders, the page reports that there are no orders (Figure 18.8).

Figure 18.8 No Orders

Restricting Access with a Custom Hook

Although you already restrict access to the orders link in the header, what if the user logs out while on the orders page, or what if they visit http://localhost:3000/orders directly? The server does not perform any authentication to view the orders, so anyone can see the orders that customers have placed. However, the server does reject order deletions from users who are not associates.

Log out and place an order. Then visit http://localhost:3000/orders.

The orders remain visible on the page (Figure 18.9).

Figure 18.9 Orders are always visible

Now try to delete an order. Nothing happens. However, if you check the Console or Network tabs in the DevTools, you will see that the server rejected the request with the code 401 (unauthorized) (Figure 18.10).

Figure 18.10 Unauthorized order deletion

You will get the same error if you try to delete an order while logged in as a guest.

Custom hooks

Users should not be poking around in data that is meant for café associates, even if they cannot delete that data. You will limit access to the orders page based on the user's access level.

In the previous chapter, you used the **useContext** hook to get at CurrentUserContext. This required multiple imports, because you had to import both the hook and the name of the context. This time, you will create a custom hook that requires only one import and has access to all the information you need.

Custom hooks are JavaScript functions that utilize other hooks. You define the custom hook's arguments and return value as you would for other JavaScript functions. Like other hooks, custom hooks must have a name that begins with use.

In CurrentUserContext.js, add a custom **useCurrentUserContext** hook that returns the value of CurrentUserContext.

Listing 18.7 Adding a custom hook (CurrentUserContext.js)

```
import { createContext } from 'react';
import { createContext, useContext } from 'react';

const CurrentUserContext = createContext();

CurrentUserContext.displayName = 'CurrentUserContext';

export const useCurrentUserContext = () => {
  const context = useContext(CurrentUserContext);
  return context;
};

export default CurrentUserContext;
```

React identifies **useCurrentUserContext** as a hook because its name begins with use. This custom hook uses the **useContext** hook to get the value from CurrentUserContext and then returns it. The returned value is the object containing currentUser and **setCurrentUser**.

Import and use your new hook in **Orders** to get the value of `currentUser`. (Until you use the value, you will have to disable the ESLint rule about unused variables.)

Listing 18.8 Importing a custom hook (`Orders.js`)

```
...
import ItemType from '../types/item';
import './Orders.css';
import { useCurrentUserContext } from '../contexts/CurrentUserContext';

function Orders({ items }) {
  const [orders, setOrders] = useState([]);
  // eslint-disable-next-line no-unused-vars
  const { currentUser } = useCurrentUserContext();

  const loadOrders = () => {
...
```

Instead of importing `CurrentUserContext` and the **useContext** hook, you have one straightforward import that takes no arguments and returns the value you need. You can also use this custom hook in the **Login** and **UserDetails** components. In fact, it will make your code cleaner, so a challenge at the end of this chapter asks you to make this change.

Save your file. In your browser, check the DevTools again to ensure that you are getting the correct values for the current user's username and access level (Figure 18.11).

Figure 18.11 Context in the DevTools

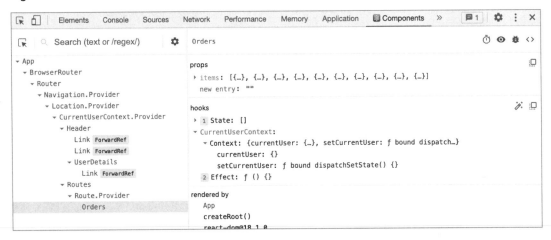

Custom hooks are a handy way to extract logic away from your components, simplifying your code.

Adding to the dependency array

Now that **Orders** knows the currentUser, you can ensure that only associates have access to the orders.

Add a conditional statement to check whether currentUser.access is "associate" before making the request to get orders. Because this side effect depends on currentUser, add currentUser to the dependency array of **useEffect**. This will ensure that the effect executes each time currentUser changes.

Additionally, add a message letting unauthorized users know that they cannot access the orders.

Listing 18.9 Adding the currentUser dependency (Orders.js)

```
...
function Orders({ items }) {
  const [orders, setOrders] = useState([]);
  // eslint-disable-next-line no-unused-vars
  const { currentUser } = useCurrentUserContext();
  ...
  useEffect(
    () => {
      if (currentUser.access === 'associate') {
        loadOrders();
      }
    },
    [],
    [currentUser],
  );
  ...
  return (
    <div className="orders-component">
      <h2>Existing Orders</h2>
      {orders.length === 0
        ? <div>No Orders</div>
        ? (
          <div>
            {currentUser.access === 'associate'
              ? 'No Orders'
              : 'Access Denied'}
          </div>
        )
        : orders.map((order) => (
...
```

Your existing ternary returns the string "No Orders" when orders.length is 0. Here, you add a nested ternary to the code that executes when the first ternary's predicate is truthy. In it, you return the string "Access Denied" instead of "No Orders" when the current user does not have associate access. This provides more specific feedback to the user.

Save your file and try the new functionality in your browser: Log in as an associate and visit the orders page. You see the list of orders as expected. Now log out, using the button in the header. The orders are still visible.

Refresh the page to see the "Access Denied" message (Figure 18.12).

Figure 18.12 Access Denied

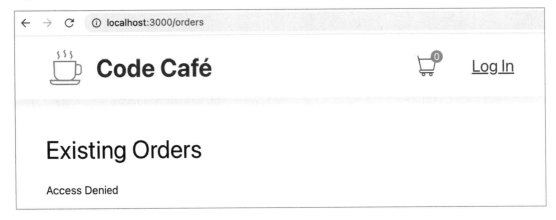

Because you added a check to ensure that the user has access, the app does not make the network request to get orders. This also ensures that users who bypass the Orders link in the header and visit http://localhost:3000/orders directly will see orders only if they have the correct access level.

However, you had to refresh the page before the "Access Denied" message appeared. When you first logged out, the orders remained visible on the page.

How can you ensure that React updates to hide the orders when the user logs out?

Cleaning Up useEffect

React accepts a cleanup function as the return value of **useEffect**. If a dependency for **useEffect** changes, React calls the cleanup function before it runs the main effect again. React also calls the cleanup function when the component is about to be destroyed.

Add a return value to the **useEffect** in **Orders**. This should be a function that sets the state value of orders back to an empty array.

Listing 18.10 Adding a cleanup function (**Orders.js**)

```
...
function Orders({ items }) {
  ...
  useEffect(
    () => {
      if (currentUser.access === 'associate') {
        loadOrders();
        return () => {
          setOrders([]);
        };
      }
      return () => { };
    },
    [currentUser],
    );
  ...
```

React calls your new cleanup function when the user navigates to another page and the `Order` component is destroyed. React will also call the cleanup function when `currentUser` changes, because you added `currentUser` as a dependency to **useEffect** earlier.

Below the `if` block, you add an empty function as the default return value. This is because ESLint expects all branches of **useEffect** to have a consistent return pattern. The conditional `if` is a branch. Because the `if` branch includes a cleanup function, the default branch must also include a cleanup function. There is nothing that needs to happen in this case, so you leave the return function empty.

Save your file and try the experiment again in the browser: Log in as an associate and navigate to the orders page. Now log out.

Ta-da! The "Access Denied" message appears right away. You do not need to refresh the page.

Before we move on from the topic of security, we should mention that Code Café is still not fully secure. Though the front end restricts access to the orders page, the complete source code for your React application – including the **Orders** component – is still publicly available to all users. This means that hackers and malicious users can read through the code to find the order deletion endpoint or hack the context values to make React think they are associates.

In a production app, it is important to double-check access restrictions and form validation *on the server*. (The server we provided does not do this for the endpoint to get the orders, because you needed to be able to list the orders before building authentication.) It is nice to check on the front end as well, so non-malicious users get faster feedback. But the real security is based on the checks you do on the server.

One other reminder about security: Since the complete source code of your application is available to all users, *never* store secret values in the React application. Store those only on the server.

Getting New Orders

The orders page has a problem: It does not update with new orders.

Open the application in two browser tabs. View the orders page in one tab. In the other tab, place an order. The tab with the orders page will not show the new order until you refresh it.

Although you could solve this by polling the server at specified intervals, *websockets* are a better tool. Websockets allow you to subscribe to updates, so the browser does not have to poll and instead gets an update each time an update is there.

Proxying a websocket

Recall that you set up a proxy for the API. It is also possible to proxy a websocket connection. This is not built into the previous proxy configuration, so you will need to manually configure the proxy.

First, you need a new package. In a terminal separate from your app, `cd` into your `code-cafe` directory. Then run `npm install --save http-proxy-middleware@2.0.1` to install the http-proxy-middleware package.

We selected this version because it is the one already bundled in the development server.

Now you can create a custom proxy. Open package.json and delete the previous proxy you set up.

Listing 18.11 Removing the old proxy (package.json)

```
...
  "scripts": {
    ...
  },
  "proxy": "http://localhost:3030",
  "eslintConfig": {
...
```

Now create a new file in the src directory called setupProxy.js. Add the proxy configuration to this file.

Listing 18.12 Setting up the new proxy (setupProxy.js)

```
const { createProxyMiddleware } = require('http-proxy-middleware');

module.exports = (app) => {
  app.use(createProxyMiddleware(
    ['/api', '/ws-cafe'],
    { target: 'http://localhost:3030', changeOrigin: true, ws: true },
  ));
};
```

If you previously needed to change the proxy to 127.0.0.1, you will need to do that here as well. In setupProxy.js, replace

```
    { target: 'http://localhost:3030', changeOrigin: true, ws: true },
```

with

```
    { target: 'http://127.0.0.1:3030', changeOrigin: true, ws: true },
```

The development server inside Create React App uses the Express framework. You use the Express function **app.use** to add a piece of middleware, which, in this case, is a proxy from the http-proxy-middleware package.

The first parameter of **createProxyMiddleware** is the path it should use. The API requests are at /api, and the websocket will be /ws-cafe. You use ['/api', '/ws-cafe'] to match both.

The second parameter has three options:

- target, which is the proxy destination

- changeOrigin, which changes the origin of the host header to the target URL (this is necessary only for name-based virtually hosted sites; however, it is easiest to include it everywhere)

- ws, which tells the proxy to also proxy websocket requests

You can read more about the options in the documentation for the package at github.com/chimurai/http-proxy-middleware.

Once Create React App restarts, it automatically executes in src/setupProxy.js. In the terminal tab currently running Code Café, stop the app with Control-C and restart it using npm start.

Using the websocket

The server already supports websocket connections, so you are ready to create a websocket connection on the orders page.

Listing 18.13 Adding a websocket (`Orders.js`)

```
...
function Orders({ items }) {
  const [orders, setOrders] = useState([]);
  const { currentUser } = useCurrentUserContext();

  const loadOrders = () => {
    axios.get('/api/orders')
      .then((result) => setOrders(result.data))
      .catch(console.error);
  };

  useEffect(
    () => {
      if (currentUser.access === 'associate') {
        loadOrders();
        const ws = new WebSocket(`${(
          window.location.protocol === 'https:' ? 'wss://' : 'ws://'
        )}${window.location.host}/ws-cafe`);
        ws.onopen = () => {
          console.log('connected');
        };
        ws.onerror = (event) => {
          console.error(event);
        };
        ws.onmessage = (message) => {
          const newOrders = JSON.parse(message.data);
          setOrders(newOrders);
        };
        ws.onclose = () => {
          console.log('disconnected');
        };
        return () => {
          ...
  const deleteOrder = async (order) => {
    try {
      await axios.delete(`api/orders/${order.id}`);
      loadOrders();
    } catch (error) {
...
```

You replace the previous code to load orders with code that sets up a websocket and opens a websocket connection.

Once the websocket exists, you tell it what to do for different events:

- **onopen** (when the initial connection opens)
- **onerror** (when there is an error connecting)
- **onmessage** (when it gets a message)
- **onclose** (when it disconnects)

For most of these events, the code logs the event to the console to help with debugging. The exception is **onmessage**.

The server sends a message with the list of orders, via the websocket. This happens right after the websocket connects and also when orders are created, updated, or deleted. The message sends as a JSON-encoded string, so you use **JSON.parse** to get the message. Then you call **setOrders** with the updated orders from the server.

(You can learn more about this process at developer.mozilla.org/en/docs/Web/API/WebSocket.)

The URL to connect to the websocket is a template literal. The first expression in the URL determines the protocol for the websocket request. If the user is on **https:**, the request uses **wss://** for a secure websocket. Otherwise, it uses **ws://**.

The next expression, **window.location.host**, is the hostname and, if the port is non-empty, the port. For Code Café, this will be **localhost:3000**. Finally, **/ws-cafe** is both the path for the websocket proxy you set up and the path for the websocket server on Code Café's back-end server.

You can read more about **window.location.host** at developer.mozilla.org/en-US/docs/Web/API/Location/host.

Save your files and try the experiment again, using two browser tabs to watch for a newly placed order. (Make sure you are logged in, so you can open the websocket and view the orders.) The orders page immediately updates when you place a new order.

Closing the websocket

It is important to close the websocket connection when it is no longer being used, such as when the user navigates away from the page or logs out. A new websocket opens each time the user lands on the orders page, so failing to close the websocket will cause a memory leak.

Close the websocket in the cleanup function of **useEffect**.

Listing 18.14 Closing the websocket (**Orders.js**)

```
...
function Orders({ items }) {
  ...
  useEffect(
    ...
      return () => {
        ws.close();
        setOrders([]);
...
```

As we said earlier, the cleanup function executes when the component will be destroyed or when the **useEffect** hook will run again (such as when **currentUser** changes). So adding the websocket-closing logic to **useEffect**'s cleanup function ensures that the websocket closes when the user navigates away from the orders page or logs out.

Try it out: Make sure you are logged in and viewing the orders page. In the DevTools, open the Console tab. You will see some logs about a failed websocket connection. These logs are the result of React's rerunning the effect in development mode.

The last log message should say connected. Click the button in the header to log out. The orders disappear and, in the console, you see a new log message saying that the websocket has disconnected (Figure 18.13).

Figure 18.13 Websocket disconnected

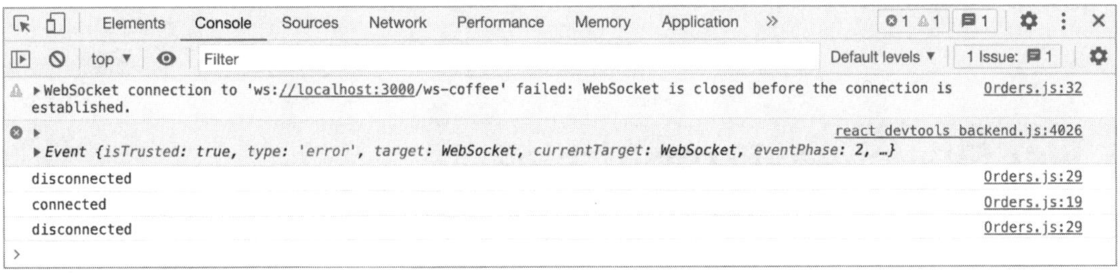

Conclusion

Wow! You did a lot in this chapter. You set up a custom hook and used websockets to get real-time order information so associates can view and fill customer orders.

Now the Code Café application has all its features. In the next chapter, you will learn about tools that React offers to track and optimize the performance of your app. After that, you will use Code Café to learn about testing.

Bronze Challenge: Smarter Redirect

Currently, the app sends all users to the home page after they log in. But associates are usually checking the orders when they log in, not trying to place an order. Edit the **Login** component so that if a user is an associate, it redirects them to the orders page. For a guest user, it should still redirect them to the home page.

This challenge interferes with the expectations for a test in Chapter 22, so make sure to work on it in a copy of your project.

Bronze Challenge: Import a Custom Hook

In this chapter, you made the custom hook **useCurrentUserContext** to get the value of currentUser from context.

You use this context value in two more places. Replace the instances of the **useContext** hook in **Login** and **UserDetails** with your custom hook.

Silver Challenge: Loader

Currently, the user sees "No Orders" while the orders are loading, even if there are actually orders that will load.

Add a new state variable to track loading. It should initially be `true`. When the websocket gets a message with the orders, the variable should update to `false`.

Then, show "Loading…" on the page while the variable is `true`.

If the server returns an empty array, the page should show "No Orders," just like it does now. Otherwise, it should show the orders.

Silver Challenge: Error Display

Most users will not be looking at the Network or Console tabs in the DevTools.

Use the **Alert** component to show an error message if the request to delete an order fails.

19

Introduction to App Performance Optimization

Look how far you have come with Code Café! Your app lets users view and select items for sale, review items in the cart, enter information in a form, and send orders to the café. It also allows associates – but not other users – to review the orders that customers have placed.

As you have developed Code Café, your knowledge of and experience with React have grown. You have built components, added multiple pages with routing, passed data using props and context, and implemented several React hooks. Now you will turn your attention to how your app performs.

In the final two chapters of this book, you will investigate several issues that affect app performance using an app we will provide for you.

In this chapter, you will learn more about the React render cycle using your Code Café code base.

React re-renders an app when its state changes to keep the UI in sync with the data. When you build a component, you describe how you want the app to look in certain scenarios. For example, "If the user is logged in, display the user details. If not, show the login button." Each time the user state changes, React re-renders and recalculates what it should present onscreen.

One reason React is so popular is that it is pretty fast and – most of the time – you can leave it alone to do its job. But you might sometimes find that your app runs slowly or that components seem to re-render more often than they should.

In this chapter, you will use the React Profiler tool to track performance. You will learn about tools that React provides to optimize your components, including the React function **memo**, a new hook called **useCallback**, and the **useMemo** hook you first saw in Chapter 17.

There is a cost associated with adding *any* code to your application, so you normally add optimizations only when an app has a performance issue. Code Café is a small app, and it runs quickly in its current form. If it were a real-world app, you would not add any optimizations to it. However, you will need to use the tools covered in this chapter as you build larger applications, and Code Café is a good project to practice in as you learn how to use them.

To begin, let's take a look at the React Profiler tool and see what happens in the app when a user adds an item to their cart.

React Profiler

In your browser, navigate to the details page for any item and open the React DevTools to the Profiler tab. Using the Profiler, you can record React's render cycle and see how long each component takes to render.

Before you start, you will set the Profiler to record the reason each component renders, in addition to the time it takes to render. Click the settings icon in the Profiler tab (Figure 19.1):

Figure 19.1 Opening the Profiler settings

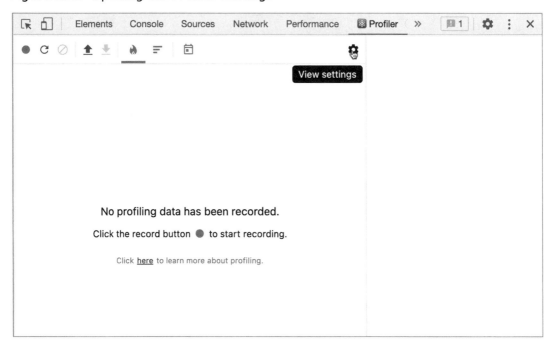

In the settings window, select the Profiler tab, which has an icon depicting a bar graph. Make sure Record why each component rendered while profiling. is selected (Figure 19.2).

Figure 19.2 Choosing to record reasons for rendering

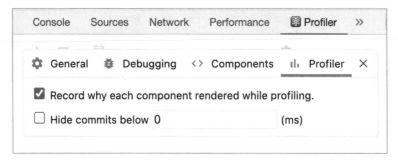

Close the settings. Now click the record button (the circle icon) on the Profiler's menu bar to start profiling (Figure 19.3).

Figure 19.3 Starting profiling

On the item details page, click the Add to Cart button. Then, click the record button on the Profiler tab again to stop recording.

You can view the results of the recording as either a flamegraph or a bar chart. Select the flamegraph chart, which has an icon that looks like a flame (Figure 19.4).

Figure 19.4 Viewing the flamegraph

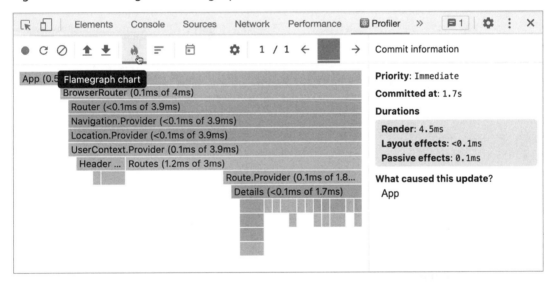

Flamegraphs are visual representations of hierarchical data – in this case, the render times of the components in Code Café. Each bar represents a component, with the different sizes and colors representing the render times of the component and its children. (The details you see will vary, because they depend on your development machine.)

Toward the bottom of the graph, you can see that the **Details** component and its children (the **Thumbnail**s in the sidebar) re-rendered when you clicked Add to Cart.

Click the bar for the **Details** component to see more information (Figure 19.5).

Figure 19.5 **Details** flamegraph

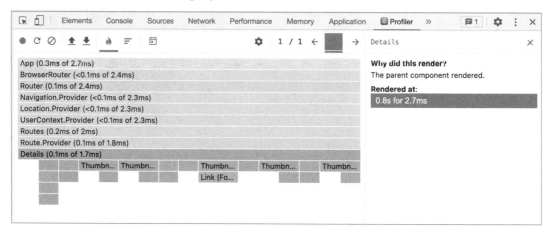

The Profiler tool reports that **Details** re-rendered because its parent re-rendered. Recall that functional components always render when their parent renders. The parent of **Details** is **App**, so this tells you that **App** must have re-rendered. Why?

Click **App** to find out. The Profiler tool reports that Hook 3 changed. Switch to the Components tab in the DevTools and select **App**. In the hooks section, you can see that hook 3 is the cart reducer.

Adding an item to the cart executes the cart reducer, which updates the state of the hook. This causes React to start a render cycle with the component that contains that hook: **App**.

Switch back to the Profiler tab and select **Details** again. In the right-side pane, the Rendered at information supplies a timestamp indicating when the component rendered during the profiling session and how long it took to render. In this case, **Details** rendered in 2.7 milliseconds. (Again, your exact result might not be the same as ours.)

Although that is not very long, when **Details** renders, its children – all the **Thumbnail**s under it – must also render. Because nothing has changed in the **Details** UI, it would be nice if React did not re-render it.

Memo

Recall from Chapter 4 that React supports class components as well as the functional components you have been using. Unlike functional components, class components re-render only if their props, state, or context changes; they do not automatically re-render along with their parent components.

Do you need to make **Details** a class component to stop it from re-rendering when **App** renders? Thankfully, no. There is a way for functional components to mimic the re-rendering behavior of class components. The React helper function **memo** allows functional components to re-render only if their state, props, or context changes.

When **memo** wraps a component, it creates a *memo*. (We say that it *memoizes* the component.) A memo is how React remembers the references of the component's state, props, and context. During render cycles, React compares the current references with the previous ones. If there are no changes, React does not re-render the component.

This comparison is an extra job that React has to perform during the render cycle, so use it only when there are performance concerns. In Code Café, although the **Details** component re-renders often and with the same props, it is fast, so it would not need a memo in a production app. If it were a heavy component, taking a long time to render, it would be a good candidate for memoization in a production app.

(**memo** is not the same as the **useMemo** hook you used when you set up `CurrentUserContext` in Chapter 17. **memo** wraps a component to prevent unnecessary re-renders, while **useMemo** is a hook that prevents unnecessary expensive recalculations.)

To see how memoization works, wrap the **Details** component in the **memo** function.

Listing 19.1 **Details** memoization (Details.js)

```
import { memo } from 'react';
import PropTypes from 'prop-types';
...
function Details({ items }) {
...
}
...
export default Details;
export default memo(Details);
```

You wrap the default export of **Details** with **memo** to memoize the result. Now, when you import **Details** in App.js, the import statement will read the default export and then import the memoized version of **Details**.

Why not write something like const Details = memo(({ addToCart, items }) => { ... });? Though you can, the result would be an anonymous component. Since React's DevTools look for the name of the original component, having an anonymous component complicates debugging.

Save your file and refresh the page in your browser. Then run the experiment again:

1. Click the record button in the Profiler tool.

2. Add an item to the cart.

3. Stop recording.

Check the new results (Figure 19.6):

Figure 19.6 Memoized flamegraph results

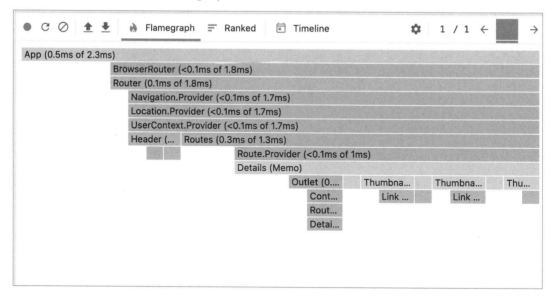

Now the **Details** component and its underlying **Thumbnail**s are gray, indicating that they did not re-render during the recording.

Context Changes

Although the **Thumbnail**s did not re-render, the **Link**s inside each **Thumbnail** did, as the colored highlights indicate. Click one of them to see why: They re-rendered because the context changed (Figure 19.7).

Figure 19.7 Context change

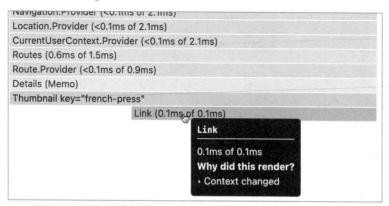

A change in context triggers components to re-render. React context is created inside React Router, and **Link** subscribes to that context. As a result, **Link** re-renders whenever React Router's context changes, regardless of whether its parent component re-renders.

Let's look at another example of this. Select the **DetailItem** component in the flamegraph chart (Figure 19.8):

Figure 19.8 **DetailItem** flamegraph

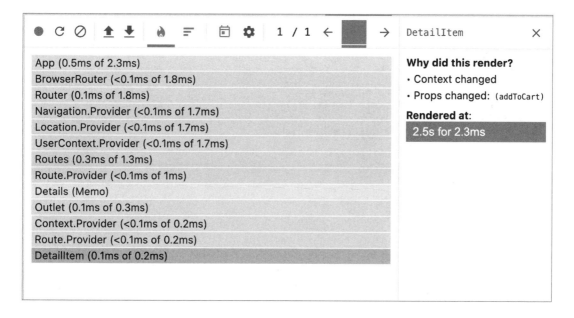

The Profiler reports that the component rendered due to a context change and a props change. First, let's look at the context change.

DetailItem uses the **useParams** hook from React Router to find the id of the item to display. Like the **Link** component, this hook causes the component to re-render because React Router's context has changed.

React Router is a third-party library, so its re-rendering is outside your control. But to prevent **useParams** from causing unnecessary re-renders, you can extract a wrapper component whose sole purpose is to read the id parameter and pass it to **DetailItem**. Then you can wrap **DetailItem** in memo to prevent the wrapper component from triggering **DetailItem**'s re-render.

Try it out.

Listing 19.2 Using a wrapper component (DetailItem.js)

```
import { memo } from 'react';
import { useParams } from 'react-router-dom';
...
function DetailItem({ addToCart, items }) {
function DetailItem({ addToCart, id, items }) {
  const { id } = useParams();
  const detailItem = items.find((item) => item.itemId === id);
  ...
}

DetailItem.propTypes = {
const sharedProps = {
  addToCart: PropTypes.func.isRequired,
  items: PropTypes.arrayOf(ItemType).isRequired,
};

DetailItem.propTypes = {
  ...sharedProps,
  id: PropTypes.string.isRequired,
};

const DetailItemMemo = memo(DetailItem);

function DetailsOuter({ addToCart, items }) {
  const { id } = useParams();
  return (
    <DetailItemMemo
      addToCart={addToCart}
      id={id}
      items={items}
    />
  );
}

DetailsOuter.propTypes = sharedProps;

export default DetailItem;
export default DetailsOuter;
```

Now the **DetailsOuter** component is responsible for getting the id from **useParams** and passing it to **DetailItem**.

Separating **DetailsOuter** from **DetailItem** allows you to address the parts of **DetailItem** that do not depend on React Router. By memoizing **DetailItem**, you stop it from re-rendering unless it has changed.

Save your file and try the experiment again (Figure 19.9).

Figure 19.9 Wrapped **DetailItem**

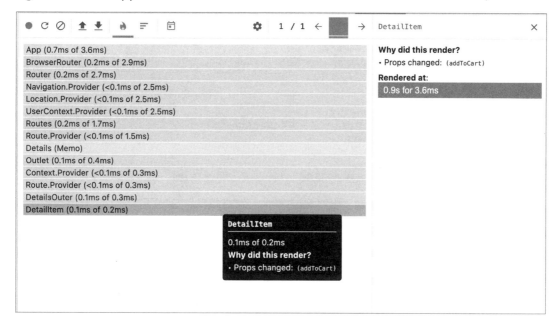

The flamegraph shows that the new **DetailsOuter** component re-renders, as expected, because the React Router context changed. But your memoized **DetailItem** no longer re-renders due to its parent's re-rendering. Instead, it re-renders because of the **addToCart** prop change.

useCallback

Why is the prop **addToCart** causing **DetailItem** to re-render?

To determine whether a component should re-render, React checks the reference equality of props. So when a function such as **addToCart** is in props, React does not look inside the function – it looks at just the reference.

addToCart comes from **App**. When the user adds an item to the cart, the state of the cart reducer changes, causing the **App** component to re-render. The **addToCart** function is re-created each time **App** renders – which means the reference changes, even though the contents of the function are the same.

React sees this reference change as a change in props, so it re-renders **DetailItem**.

To avoid unnecessary renders, React provides a hook called **useCallback** that prevents functions from being re-created. **useCallback** accepts two arguments:

- the callback function that it should return
- a dependency array with the items that should cause the callback to be re-created

In **App**, wrap **addToCart** in **useCallback** to prevent it from being re-created each time **App** re-renders.

Listing 19.3 **useCallback** (App.js)

```
import axios from 'axios';
import {
  useEffect, useMemo, useReducer, useState,
  useCallback, useEffect, useMemo, useReducer, useState,
} from 'react';
...
function App() {
  const [items, setItems] = useState([]);
  const [currentUser, setCurrentUser] = useState({});
  const [cart, dispatch] = useReducer(
    ...
  );
  const addToCart = (itemId) => dispatch({ type: CartTypes.ADD, itemId });
  const addToCart = useCallback(
    (itemId) => dispatch({ type: CartTypes.ADD, itemId }),
    [],
  );

  useEffect(() => {
    localStorage.setItem(storageKey, JSON.stringify(cart));
...
```

Now **useCallback** creates the **addToCart** function.

To prevent stale data, you typically include in the dependency array all the variables in the callback, including other functions. The exceptions are values that React guarantees to remain the same, including **dispatch** and the **useState** setter function. So although **addToCart** uses the **dispatch** function, you do not include it in the dependency array, because it will not change.

Since there are no items in the dependency array, **addToCart** will be created only on the initial render of **App** and will not change in subsequent renders.

Save your file and use the Profiler to record adding an item to the cart one last time (Figure 19.10).

Figure 19.10 **DetailItem** no longer re-renders

Success! **DetailItem** did not re-render.

So does this mean you should wrap all your functions in **useCallback**? Definitely not. There is a cost associated with verifying the dependencies and tracking the original function. Use **useCallback** only when you need to avoid unnecessary re-renders.

Expensive Calculations

Now you have optimized **Details** and **DetailItem** to prevent unnecessary re-renders. But what about expensive calculations that happen during legitimate renders?

In Code Café, add items to your cart and visit the cart page. Recall that in Cart.js, you use taxPercentage and taxRate to calculate the tax rate based on the user's ZIP code. React performs these calculations each time the component re-renders.

Let's see how often that happens. Add a **console.log** statement to check how often the tax calculations run.

Listing 19.4 Adding **console.log** (Cart.js)

```
...
function Cart({ cart, dispatch, items }) {
  ...
  const subTotal = isEmployeeOfTheMonth ? 0 : cart.reduce((acc, item) => {
    ...
  }, 0);

  console.log('compute tax');
  const taxPercentage = parseInt(zipCode.substring(0, 1) || '0', 10) + 1;
...
```

Save your file. Back in the browser, begin recording in the React Profiler to track component re-renders.

Input a name in the checkout form, then stop recording. Take a look at the results (Figure 19.11).

Figure 19.11 **Cart** Profiler results

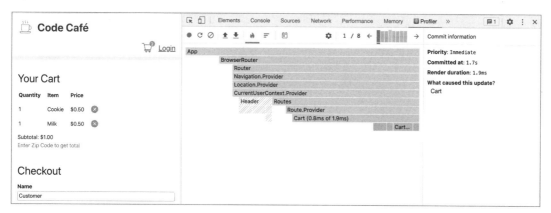

To the right of the settings icon in the Profiler's menu bar, there are two numbers separated by a slash. The second number indicates how many renders occurred during the profiling session (Figure 19.12).

Figure 19.12 Render count

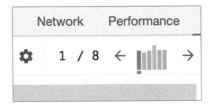

In this example, there were eight renders. This is because the name we used, *Customer*, has eight characters. Each time a character was entered, React updated the UI to ensure that it was in sync with the state.

(You will likely see a different count, depending on the name you entered and whether you pressed Delete and retyped characters.)

Now switch to the console to see the output from the log statement you added. The number of console statements should match the number of renders shown in the Profiler (Figure 19.13).

Figure 19.13 Viewing the `compute tax` logs

Elements	Console	Sources	Network	Performance	Memory » 📵1 ⚙ ⋮ ✕
▶ ⊘ top ▾ ⊙ Filter				All levels ▾ 1 Issue: 📵1 ⚙

```
compute tax                                          Cart.js:26
compute tax                          react_devtools_backend.js:4082
compute tax                                          Cart.js:26
compute tax                          react_devtools_backend.js:4082
compute tax                                          Cart.js:26
compute tax                          react_devtools_backend.js:4082
compute tax                                          Cart.js:26
compute tax                          react_devtools_backend.js:4082
compute tax                                          Cart.js:26
compute tax                          react_devtools_backend.js:4082
compute tax                                          Cart.js:26
compute tax                          react_devtools_backend.js:4082
compute tax                                          Cart.js:26
compute tax                          react_devtools_backend.js:4082
compute tax                                          Cart.js:26
compute tax                          react_devtools_backend.js:4082
>
```

(You likely have duplicate logs printed, as in the example above. This is due to the React.StrictMode tool, which renders each component twice when you are running in development mode. Focus on the logs that come from Cart.js.)

Computing on every render is not problematic if the computations are very fast. But if they are slow, they can slow down rendering – and slow down users trying to type into a form.

Although Code Café's tax calculation is simple and fast, tax calculations in general are complicated and can be slow. You will optimize the tax calculations to rerun only when the ZIP code changes.

In Chapter 17, you used the **useMemo** hook when setting the values for CurrentUserContext. You will use it again here. **useMemo** returns a memoized value and recomputes only when its dependency array changes.

The **useMemo** hook, like **useCallback**, takes two arguments:

- the function to compute the value
- the dependency array

Add **useMemo** to the tax calculations in Cart.js. (You will need to reindent some of the existing code.)

Listing 19.5 Adding **useMemo** (Cart.js)

```
import axios from 'axios';
import PropTypes from 'prop-types';
import { useRef, useState } from 'react';
import { useMemo, useRef, useState } from 'react';
import ItemType from '../types/item';
...
function Cart({ cart, dispatch, items }) {
  ...
  const subTotal = isEmployeeOfTheMonth ? 0 : cart.reduce((acc, item) => {
    ...
  }, 0);

  const taxRate = useMemo(
    () => {
      console.log('compute tax');
      const taxPercentage = parseInt(zipCode.substring(0, 1) || '0', 10) + 1;
      const taxRate = taxPercentage / 100;
      return taxPercentage / 100;
    },
    [zipCode],
  );
  const tax = subTotal * taxRate;
...
```

Here, the function you pass to **useMemo** returns the tax rate, which **useMemo** caches. Because you include zipCode in the dependency array, React recalculates the tax rate only when zipCode changes.

Save your file. In the browser, make sure you are on the cart page. Clear the Console tab with the ⊘ button near the left end of the menu bar, then type a name in the checkout form.

There are no log statements.

Now add a ZIP code. compute tax logs each time the ZIP code changes.

Comparing useCallback, useMemo, and memo

The tools you have used in this chapter have similar names and purposes. Keeping track of when to use each one can be confusing until you build up some experience with them. Let's recap what you have learned.

useCallback and **useMemo** are similar in that they rely on the dependency array to perform their optimizations. However, they serve different purposes and return different values: You use the **useCallback** hook to maintain reference equality by preventing unnecessary re-creation of the function that the hook returns. You use the **useMemo** hook to avoid expensive calculations by preventing unnecessary execution of the function whose *result* the hook returns.

memo is a React function that wraps an entire component to return a memoized version of that component. **memo** prevents the default behavior of re-rendering a functional component when its parent re-renders. A memoized component re-renders only if its props, state, or context changes.

Cleaning Up

Before moving on, remove the **console.log** statement from the **Cart** component. Though log statements are often helpful while you are optimizing components, they can clutter the console if you do not clean them up.

Listing 19.6 Removing **console.log** (Cart.js)

```
...
function Cart({ cart, dispatch, items }) {
  ...
  const taxRate = useMemo(
    () => {
      console.log('compute tax');
      const taxPercentage = parseInt(zipCode.substring(0, 1) || '0', 10) + 1;
...
```

Conclusion

In this chapter, you saw how to optimize components using **memo**, **useCallback**, and **useMemo**. You also took the React Profiler for a spin.

The components in Code Café are not actually complicated enough to warrant this much effort for optimization. But you will often see developers use these tools in large applications, so it is important to understand how and why you might use them.

In the next three chapters, you will dive into testing, using various techniques to test Code Café. Then, in the final two chapters of the book, you will explore other issues that can affect app performance and see more ways you can optimize your apps to give your users the best possible experience.

Silver Challenge: Memoized UserDetails

Use the React Profiler to examine **Header** while you add an item to the cart. **Header** re-renders, and so does **UserDetails**.

Use **memo** to prevent **UserDetails** from re-rendering when you add items to the cart.

Note: As you saw with the **Details** component, the **Link** component inside **UserDetails** will still re-render.

20
Testing Overview

You will finish your work on Code Café by adding tests to check that things are working properly.

Normally, we recommend developing tests while you are developing an app's features. In this case, we saved it until the end so you could focus on learning one thing at a time. Now that you have learned the basics of React code, including how to use hooks and integrate with an API, you are ready to learn how to test your app.

This chapter introduces four types of testing and discusses the trade-offs between them. When testing a React application, you will probably use more than one kind of test at any given time – and different sets of tests at different times.

You will not do any coding as you read this chapter. In the next two chapters, you will implement two types of tests from this chapter: unit tests, using Jest and the React Testing Library, and end-to-end tests, using Cypress and the Cypress Testing Library.

Deciding What Tests to Use

To decide what type of testing to use, you can ask yourself a few questions to help identify your needs at this particular point in the project's lifecycle.

Why are you testing?

Ideally, you are implementing testing to create dependable code from the beginning of a project.

But we do not always live in an ideal world. While the beginning of the project is the best time to introduce testing, the second best time is *now*!

One reason to introduce tests to a previously untested project might be that you are about to refactor the project, and you want to be sure the application works the same after refactoring as it did before.

Another reason might be to increase confidence in either existing code or new features you are developing.

With any of these motivations, your first instinct might be to write tests that generate high code coverage (meaning they check lots of things) using automated code inspections. However, high code coverage does not guarantee that your tests will actually catch bugs.

Which leads us to another question.

What do you want to know?

What you want to know from your tests affects how many of them you write and at what level of the application you write them. Some things you might want to know are that

- the basic happy paths (flows that should execute without throwing exceptions) work

- every happy path and every unhappy path (which should result in an error) produces the expected outcome

- the parts of the app work in isolation

- the parts work together

- the design looks right

Bear in mind that trying to test every possible path through an application is rarely possible, due to *path explosion* – the number of available paths increasing as the app grows more complex.

Imagine an application similar to Code Café but with two ways to add an item to the cart. Once on the cart page, this app's user can edit or not edit the cart. Then, the user can check out with Visa or PayPal, and the transaction can be approved or declined. This is already 16 possible paths ($2 \times 2 \times 2 \times 2$, or 2^4).

Sixteen paths might be testable. But these paths do not include the user searching for items or needing to go back in the checkout flow – or lots of other possible scenarios. It quickly becomes impossible to test everything, even in a fairly simple app.

Having a good idea about what you want to gain from your tests can help determine which paths to focus on.

Which brings us to our last question.

What does the future look like?

Are you planning to start a refactor? Are you in a discovery phase, so you need to be ready to pivot the app in a new direction? Or are you just adding incremental functionality to your app, or maybe fixing bugs?

Jumping into testing without considering the future can lead to extra work, such as needing to rewrite your tests because you refactored the feature they were testing.

(This is not to say you will never refactor tests. There are cases where, even though you know you will need to refactor the tests later, you implement granular testing – detailed testing of very specific items. When granular tests fail, they give you a very specific point of failure, which can be valuable depending on your needs.)

Types of Testing

Each type of test has pros and cons, and there is no single best type.

Once you have an idea of why you are testing, what you want to know, and what the future looks like, you can weigh the different types of testing to find the best fit for your needs at the time. You will also need to consider variables such as cost and speed.

Static Testing

Static tests analyze code without requiring the application to run. They are the simplest type of test and the first line of defense, and you use them primarily during the development process.

In Code Café, you implemented static testing with ESLint. Linting, as you have seen, checks your code for common errors and pitfalls.

Another type of static testing is type checking. In React applications, you will frequently see developers use TypeScript, which adds stronger type checking to JavaScript.

Advantages

- Static tests are fast. They flag potential errors before the code even runs.

- Static tests give you an exact line of failure. You saw this in Code Café when ESLint highlighted errors in Visual Studio Code with red squiggles or displayed errors in the browser.

- Once you set up a tool such as ESLint, it runs continuously during development.

- Tools such as TypeScript have built-in type checking and do not need additional setup.

Disadvantages

- Static tests are limited to the available code, so they can result in false positives or negatives.

- Linting, such as with ESLint, mixes code style and code quality checks, and it can be hard to tell which is which.

Static tests are generally useful at any point in the development process. They keep code consistent across teams and provide quick feedback when they find potential errors.

Unit and Integration Testing

Unit and integration tests both test code in a controlled environment instead of using a real browser with the live server. Unit tests focus on small pieces of code in isolation, such as a function. Integration tests focus on pieces of code that interact with other code.

When testing components, it can be hard to decide if the component is truly isolated or if multiple elements are interacting. As a result, there is often a gray area between these two terms. We will call all tests of components "integration tests," since there are typically at least two components involved.

You need a test runner to perform unit and integration tests. There are many options available. The tests you write for Code Café will use Jest, a JavaScript testing framework that comes bundled with Create React App. There are quite a few tests that the Jest testing system can run, including tests that target individual functions or components as well as tests for the full app.

Unit testing for functions

When you give a function certain parameters, you expect it to return a certain value. You can write a unit test to validate that the function returns the correct value.

For example, the `setFormattedPhone` function in Code Café accepts a string of digits, and you expect it to return a formatted phone number. You can test that result with a unit test.

But suppose that Code Café later expands internationally and you localize `setFormattedPhone` to format the phone number based on the user's region. Even if the resulting formatted phone number stays the same in most cases, you would need to refactor your tests to include the location information to get the expected output values.

Advantages

- Function tests are fast and isolated to a single function.

- They make it easy to find the source of any failure.

Disadvantage

- If you later refactor the function you are testing, you might have to refactor the tests as well.

You can add unit tests to existing code – for example, before a refactor – or you can add them incrementally as you add new features.

Integration testing for components

Testing a component validates that what renders onscreen (and how the user can interact with a component) matches expectations.

This is the standard mode of testing that the React Testing Library provides. The library works with Jest to render a component and all its children into HTML nodes – not in the browser, but to a fake DOM, using a library called jsdom.

Although testing a component can involve isolating it entirely, most often it involves some integration with other components.

Advantages

- Integration tests are fast and somewhat isolated, depending on how many child components the tested component has. You can test a small component with no children more quickly than a high-level component, such as **Details**, that contains many children.

- When you extract code to a subcomponent, you likely do not need to change your tests. As long as the rendered output does not change, tests for components do not care about implementation details.

Disadvantages

- You cannot easily test the data passed between parent and child components.

- You need some knowledge of the component tree to find the source of failures.

- Using a fake DOM means that jest does not actually draw the page on a screen. Instead, the integration test uses the HTML output to determine what elements exist. This means that in the fake DOM, elements are still clickable and readable even if other elements obscure them or if they are hidden with CSS.

- If the component or its child components make network requests, you might need to create mock APIs to support a test.

Do not be afraid of the longer list of disadvantages for this type of test. Testing components is usually fast, and you can implement these tests at any point in the development process. They are great for testing multiple states of a component, such as a success state and an error state. And they compensate for their disadvantages by making it less likely that refactoring will force you to rewrite tests.

Testing the full app

You can also test the full application using the React Testing Library, Jest, and jsdom. Rather than rendering an individual component, these tests render the entire application – including the router, which allows Jest to "navigate" around the application.

Although jsdom cannot actually change pages, React Router uses the History API to show different URLs in the address bar. This means that tests can use React Router to "navigate" between components in jsdom, just like users can in the browser. So these tests allow you to test complete paths through your application.

When testing components, you might be able to avoid mocking some APIs by providing data through props or context. But when testing the whole application, you must mock out the API, which makes test setup more complicated. However, these tests are much faster than end-to-end tests, which have to start a real browser.

Advantages

- The React Testing Library can navigate with React Router.

- All the advantages of integration tests for components, listed above, also apply.

Disadvantages

- You need to know the full component tree to find the source of a failure.

- You need to mock APIs to support the test.

- All the disadvantages of integration tests for components, listed above, also apply.

Although full-app integration tests can do *almost* everything that end-to-end tests can, they do it in a fake DOM instead of a real browser.

You can implement these tests at any point in the development process and use them to test happy or unhappy paths through your application.

Snapshot testing

Snapshot tests detect changes in the application UI. With snapshot testing, you avoid writing the conditions for truth and instead store the rendered HTML as the source of truth. Then you use Jest to render the UI and compare it with the previously stored snapshot.

This type of test relies on the assumption that the DOM was correct when you stored the first snapshot. Also, it is important to understand that a snapshot is not a picture – it is the HTML output. So although a CSS change can significantly alter how the page *looks*, as long as the HTML remains the same, the snapshot does not change and the test passes.

Advantages

- Snapshot tests are easy to write. You need only one line of code to assert that the current code matches the stored snapshot.

- When you request code reviews from other developers, you can include snapshot changes to show what changes you have made (and, in fact, you must include them if you are using snapshot tests).

Disadvantages

- Any HTML change requires a change in the snapshot.

- Snapshot changes can be large, making it hard to differentiate intentional changes from unintentional ones. It can be easy to miss mistakes when reviewing large code changes to verify a snapshot.

Because of these disadvantages, we recommend limiting the use of snapshot tests. They can be valuable when, for example, you want to verify the HTML output after a code refactor. If you use snapshot tests, consider pairing them with other types of tests to minimize the potential for missing unintentional changes.

End-to-End Testing

End-to-end tests validate user workflows. They work by running the application in a real browser and interacting with the application just like a user would. Popular tools for end-to-end testing include Cypress, Selenium WebDriver, Puppeteer, and CodeceptJS. You will use Cypress in Chapter 22.

In general, end-to-end tests come with the following advantages and disadvantages:

Advantages

- You should not need to change your tests when you refactor your front-end code.

- End-to-end tests can test navigation between pages, since the application runs in a browser.

- They let you test full workflows across multiple pages.

- They use a real browser, so the test environment is the closest to the real user experience.

- They catch issues with obscured buttons that the fake DOM cannot catch.

Disadvantages

- Launching real browsers is slow.

- End-to-end tests require you to run a web server for the browser to load the page.

- They are significantly slower than unit tests.

- It is easy to write *flaky* end-to-end tests, which sometimes pass and sometimes fail, despite there being no code changes to the test or project.

End-to-end testing with a live back end

Since end-to-end tests run in a browser, you can allow them to interact with the real back-end code.

Advantages

- In this setup, there is no extra mocked back end to maintain.

- This kind of testing ensures that the contract between the front end and the back end works.

Disadvantages

- The live back end might be slow, leading to slow end-to-end tests.

- You must set up test data and isolate the tests in the live back end.

- It can be difficult to know where an error is coming from, since the back end is live and the front end is fully rendered.

End-to-end testing with a mocked back end

Another option is to use mock data to run your application. Some tools, including Cypress, allow you to mock out requests as a part of your tests. Other tools require you to write a separate, fake back end to accomplish this goal.

Advantage

- Mocked back ends are usually fast.

Disadvantages

- You have to maintain the mock back end.

- The mock back end and the live back end might not have the same API contract, so even though the test passes, you might have failures in production.

Which to use?

When your team owns both the front-end and back-end code, end-to-end testing with the live back end doubles as end-to-end testing for the back end itself. This can save the team work because you do not have to write separate end-to-end tests for the back end.

If your team owns only the front-end application, it can be useful to mock the back end so that you are not blocked if the back end stops working because of a bug or outage. Mocking the back end also lets you work ahead of the back-end team, as long as you mock according to the API contract that the teams have agreed on. If you choose to work ahead, make sure to test that the front end truly integrates with the live back end before going to production.

Visual or Screenshot Testing

A final type of testing is visual or screenshot testing. Visual tests take screenshots of the page and compare the images for style changes. You can write one of these tests by adding a line to match a screenshot in an end-to-end test. As a result, visual tests come with all the same advantages and disadvantages of end-to-end tests, and you can run them with a mocked or live back end.

They also have a few advantages and disadvantages of their own:

Advantages

- These tests prevent design regressions.

- They catch side effects from shared CSS.

- They catch slightly obscured elements that might pass end-to-end tests.

Disadvantages

- Anti-aliasing (which helps text and other objects onscreen look smooth around the edges) can render differently on different runs, and different operating systems and browser versions can cause objects to shift by a pixel or two onscreen. Because of this, a direct pixel-by-pixel comparison can easily fail a test that should pass.

- To combat pixel shifts, you can allow a tolerance level – a percentage of difference that is OK. But with too much tolerance, certain changes, such as a change in border color, might not trigger a desired test failure.

- The smartest comparison tools use machine learning. Unfortunately, they are primarily available through paid software-as-a-service offerings that can be expensive, and companies that require on-site solutions might prohibit them.

Conclusion

There are multiple approaches to app testing. When you think about what testing approach you will take, consider your motivation for testing, what you want to gain from your tests, and what the future holds for the application you are adding tests to.

In the next two chapters, you will write various tests for Code Café. Although you will not write every test that an application like yours might need, you will get your feet wet and see a couple of different approaches to testing.

21

Testing with Jest and the React Testing Library

In the next two chapters, you will implement some tests in Code Café. Though all the details of testing a React app could fill a book of their own, these chapters will give you some initial experience to build on.

In this chapter, you will use libraries included with Create React App to write unit and integration tests.

Create React App automatically includes four libraries for testing your application. The first is *Jest*, a JavaScript testing framework that includes all the features you need to write and run tests, including a test runner, a mocking library, and an assertion library. Jest creates a fake DOM (called jsdom) to simulate the browser environment without rendering HTML to an actual screen.

The second library, the *React Testing Library*, is a small package for testing React components. It is one of several frameworks available from the @testing-library suite that are designed to test applications in a way similar to how a user would interact with them. The React Testing Library is not a test runner; it works with Jest to create robust tests.

When testing components, the React Testing Library uses only fully mounted components, so all child components render to the fake DOM.

Although you can test the implementation details of your components with the React Testing Library, such as by mocking functions, looking for element IDs, or looking for class names, that is not what the library is intended for. Instead, the library encourages you to test how a user interacts with your application, such as by reading text or clicking elements. This approach helps catch bugs that directly affect the user experience.

The third library is the *user-event* library, also available from @testing-library. This library coordinates with other @testing-library packages to simulate browser interactions, such as typing or mouse clicking, in the fake DOM.

Finally, the *jest-dom* library provides access to additional matchers to improve the readability of your tests.

Housekeeping

There are two pieces of housekeeping to take care of before you begin writing tests.

First, at the time of this writing, the version of @testing-library/user-event that `create-react-app` installs is outdated and does not interact properly with React Router and React 18.

Check the version of @testing-library/user-event in the list of dependencies in `package.json`. It looks like this:

```
"dependencies": {
...
"@testing-library/user-event": "^13.5.0",
...
}
```

If the version listed is 14.2.0 or higher, you do not need to reinstall.

If the version listed is lower than 14.2.0, run the following command to update it:

```
npm install --save @testing-library/user-event@14.2.0
```

Next, Create React App includes one test for you: `src/App.test.js`. However, the tests in it will fail at this point. When you trigger the React Testing Library, it runs all tests, so for the moment this guaranteed-to-fail test will be an annoyance. Delete it for now, either by using your file explorer or by right-clicking the file in Visual Studio Code and choosing Delete, then confirming your intentions in the pop-up.

You will re-create this test later.

Before you start testing, a note about file names and locations: Jest identifies test files by their name or their location. When running tests, Jest includes files that end with `.test.js` or `.spec.js`, such as the `src/App.test.js` file you just deleted. Jest also includes tests with the `.js` extension when they are in a _tests_ folder (at any level under `src`).

You will follow the Create React App pattern and create test files ending in `.test.js`, located at the same level as the code they test. Keeping the test files close to the code they target helps you find them quickly, even in larger projects, and it makes importing needed components easier.

Unit Testing

It is time to write your first test: a unit test for the **cartReducer** function.

This test will not render any components. Instead, it will test the output of the **cartReducer** function when you give it certain parameters. Unit testing of functions is best for functions that perform complex operations; it helps you check whether their output matches your expectations.

Add a new file called `cartReducer.test.js` to `src/reducers`, the directory that `cartReducer.js` is in.

In `cartReducer.test.js`, write your first test, as shown below.

Listing 21.1 Adding a unit test (`cartReducer.test.js`)

```
import { cartReducer, CartTypes } from './cartReducer';

describe('cartReducer', () => {
  it('adds a new item', () => {
    const initialCartState = [];
    const itemId = 1;

    const cartReducerOutput = cartReducer(
      initialCartState,
      { type: CartTypes.ADD, itemId },
    );

    const finalCartState = [{
      itemId,
      quantity: 1,
    }];

    expect(cartReducerOutput).toEqual(finalCartState);
  });
});
```

The `describe` block groups related tests. (Right now, you have only one test.) Each test within this block will test **cartReducer**.

The `it` block is the actual test that will run. The strings in the `describe` block and the `it` block should form a statement that describes the outcome of the test. In this case, you are testing **cartReducer**'s ADD action, so the outcome statement is `cartReducer adds a new item`.

You list several variables within the test. The **cartReducer** function executes with the `initialCartState`, the action type, and the `itemId` to add a new item. You save the result of the function to the `cartReducerOutput` variable. And the `finalCartState` is the expected outcome of the function.

The expect statement then uses a Jest *matcher*, `toEqual`, to assert that the actual output of the function (`cartReducerOutput`) equals the expected output (`finalCartState`).

So, in English, this test asserts that when you give the **cartReducer** function an empty array as an initial state, the ADD action, and an `itemId` of 1, it returns a cart that holds a single instance of the item whose `itemId` is 1.

You are ready to run your test. Make sure you are in the code-cafe directory in your terminal, and run npm test. You should see something like this:

```
PASS  src/reducers/cartReducer.test.js
  cartReducer
    ✓ adds a new item (2 ms)

Test Suites: 1 passed, 1 total
Tests:       1 passed, 1 total
Snapshots:   0 total
Time:        0.264 s, estimated 1 s
Ran all test suites.

Watch Usage
 › Press f to run only failed tests.
 › Press o to only run tests related to changed files.
 › Press q to quit watch mode.
 › Press p to filter by a filename regex pattern.
 › Press t to filter by a test name regex pattern.
 › Press Enter to trigger a test run.
```

The test passed.

The terminal also indicates that your tests entered *watch usage* mode by default. Each time you save a file while in watch usage mode, Jest will intelligently rerun some or all of your tests. The terminal output also lists some handy keyboard shortcuts for watch usage mode. One shortcut it does not include: You can type a to run all the tests.

For the rest of this chapter, leave the terminal open and in watch usage mode so you can check that your new tests pass. If you need to take a break, you can exit watch usage mode with Control-C and restart it later with npm test.

Next, add a test in another `it` block to check that **cartReducer** updates the quantity of an item added to the cart.

As you did for your first test, create a variable called `initialCartState`. Since this test also adds an item to the cart, you can reuse the `cartReducerOutput` variable from your previous test. But this time, the `initialCartState` array will not be empty; it will contain a cart item (with a `quantity` and an `itemId`).

As before, pass the **cartReducer** function the `initialCartState` and the action type to add an item to the cart. Finally, compare the value of `cartReducerOutput` with `finalCartState`, which should show an increase of 1 in the quantity of the item from `initialCartState`.

Listing 21.2 Testing updates to the item quantity (`cartReducer.test.js`)

```
...
describe('cartReducer', () => {
  ...
    expect(cartReducerOutput).toEqual(finalCartState);
  });

  it('updates item quantity when adding existing item', () => {
    const itemId = 1;
    const initialCartState = [{
      itemId,
      quantity: 1,
    }];

    const cartReducerOutput = cartReducer(
      initialCartState,
      { type: CartTypes.ADD, itemId },
    );

    const finalCartState = [{
      itemId,
      quantity: 2,
    }];

    expect(cartReducerOutput).toEqual(finalCartState);
  });

});
```

Now add tests in new `it` blocks to cover **cartReducer**'s other behaviors: emptying the cart and removing a single item. In both new tests, provide **cartReducer** with arguments that match the behavior you are testing, and then compare the actual output with the expected output.

Listing 21.3 More **cartReducer** tests (cartReducer.test.js)

```
...
describe('cartReducer', () => {
  ...
    expect(cartReducerOutput).toEqual(finalCartState);
  });

  it('empties cart', () => {
    const initialCartState = [{
      itemId: 1,
      quantity: 1,
    }];

    const cartReducerOutput = cartReducer(
      initialCartState,
      { type: CartTypes.EMPTY },
    );

    const finalCartState = [];

    expect(cartReducerOutput).toEqual(finalCartState);
  });

  it('removes item', () => {
    const itemId = 1;
    const initialCartState = [{
      itemId,
      quantity: 1,
    }];

    const cartReducerOutput = cartReducer(
      initialCartState,
      { type: CartTypes.REMOVE, itemId },
    );

    const finalCartState = [];

    expect(cartReducerOutput).toEqual(finalCartState);
  });
});
```

Like your first two tests, these tests store the output of **cartReducer** as cartReducerOutput and compare that value with the expected finalCartState.

Save your file and check out your terminal.

Watch usage mode runs your tests as soon as you save your file, so you do not need to run them yourself. You should see the four strings describing your tests and that all four tests passed:

```
PASS  src/reducers/cartReducer.test.js
  cartReducer
    ✓ adds a new item (3 ms)
    ✓ updates item quantity when adding existing item
    ✓ empties cart
    ✓ removes item (1 ms)

Test Suites: 1 passed, 1 total
Tests:       4 passed, 4 total
...
```

You could add more tests to this function, such as checking if an error is thrown for an unknown action type or if removing an item from a cart with multiple items works as expected. But the goal of this exercise is not to be exhaustive, only to expose you to multiple types of testing. Check out the challenges at the end of this chapter for more practice writing tests.

Integration Testing

Next you will write integration tests for two of your components, **Thumbnail** and **Home**. The test for **Thumbnail** is very focused, and you could consider it a unit test. But as we mentioned in the last chapter, we will call all tests of components integration tests. The test will check whether the **Thumbnail** component displays the item's title and image.

Testing Thumbnail

Put the test in a new Thumbnail.test.js file that lives alongside Thumbnail.js in the components directory.

You will not test navigation for this test; you will test that later in this chapter, also using the React Testing Library.

Write your test as shown below:

Listing 21.4 Adding a **Thumbnail** test (Thumbnail.test.js)

```
import { render, screen } from '@testing-library/react';
import { MemoryRouter as Router } from 'react-router-dom';
import Thumbnail from './Thumbnail';
import { itemImages } from '../items';

describe('Thumbnail', () => {
  it('displays item title and image', () => {
    render(
      <Router>
        <Thumbnail itemId="coffee" title="Coffee" image={itemImages.coffee} />
      </Router>,
    );
    screen.getByText(/Coffee/i);
    screen.getByAltText(/Coffee/i);
  });
});
```

Why do you need to import **MemoryRouter**? The **Thumbnail** component uses **Link**, which React Router provides. Like other React Router components, **Link** must be a descendant of a **Router**.

MemoryRouter (which you rename **Router**, as you did in Chapter 9) provides a fake browser History API, since jsdom does not provide one. Wrapping **Thumbnail** with **MemoryRouter** allows **Link** to render with no errors.

screen is the fake DOM that the **render** function populates. screen gives you access to six query methods, including the **getBy** query method you use here.

getBy tells the React Testing Library that exactly one item should match the given criteria. The **getBy** method throws an exception if no items match or if multiple items match.

There are several options you can pair with the query methods to find elements. You will see many of them in this chapter. Here, you use text and altText to find elements on the screen.

getByText and **getByAltText** tell the test to look for exactly one element with the text or alt text passed to them. If either query fails, the test throws an exception.

getBy, like other query methods, searches for matches using strings, regular expressions, or functions.

/Coffee/i is a regular expression (often called a *regex*). You use regular expressions in your tests to match text without needing to worry about capitalization or whitespace.

Because an exception will make the test fail, you do not need to add an expect clause to a query method that throws an exception. Some developers choose to include an expect clause anyway, to make the expectation explicit. It would look like this:

```
expect(screen.getByText(/Coffee/i)).toBeInTheDocument();
expect(screen.getByAltText(/Coffee/i)).toBeInTheDocument();
```

This is a style choice; you can include expect clauses like this or not, as you prefer.

Putting it all together, this test renders a **Thumbnail** component with an itemId of "coffee" and a title of "Coffee". It then uses the query method **getBy** to verify that the correct title and image appear in the HTML. (Remember, these tests use a fake DOM that does not apply styling, so the image might not actually be visible to the user.)

Save your file and check your terminal. Now you have two test suites, because you have two files that Jest identified as test files (src/reducers/cartReducer.test.js and src/components/Thumbnail.test.js). You should see that all the tests have passed.

Testing Home

Now let's test the **Home** component. You have already tested that the individual **Thumbnail** renders correctly, so the goal of this test is to check whether **Home** displays **Thumbnail**s for all the items you give it. This test will render **Home** and its child components, including **Thumbnail** and each **Link** in the **Thumbnail**s.

As with your **Thumbnail** test, you will not test any navigation here; you will test only the **Home** component.

To find out how many **Thumbnail**s the **Home** component renders, you need a way to identify them. At the moment, there is no easy way to reference the **Thumbnail**s without resorting to an element selector. But the React Testing Library discourages the use of selectors such as IDs or CSS class names, since they are not usually available to the end user. Also, you might change or remove IDs and CSS classes for styling or other reasons.

If a test needs to access an element using a selector, the library provides a way to get elements by *test ID*. A test ID is a data attribute, meaning it attaches arbitrary data to a DOM node. The attribute's name, data-testid, indicates to future developers that it is related to tests in the source code.

Add the test ID attribute to the **Link** that the **Thumbnail** component returns:

Listing 21.5 Adding data-testid to **Thumbnail** (Thumbnail.js)

```
...
function Thumbnail({ itemId, image, title }) {
  return (
    <Link
      className="thumbnail-component"
      data-testid="thumbnail-component"
      to={`/details/${itemId}`}
...
```

With the test ID in place, you can write a test to render the **Home** component and count how many items render with the test ID. Do this in a new components/Home.test.js file.

Listing 21.6 Adding a **Home** test (Home.test.js)

```
import { render, screen } from '@testing-library/react';
import { MemoryRouter as Router } from 'react-router-dom';
import Home from './Home';
import { items } from '../items';

describe('Home', () => {
  it('displays items', () => {
    render(
      <Router>
        <Home items={items} />
      </Router>,
    );
    const thumbnails = screen.queryAllByTestId('thumbnail-component');
    expect(thumbnails).toHaveLength(items.length);
  });
});
```

Since **Home** renders **Thumbnail**, which renders **Link**, you need to wrap **Home** in a **Router** just like you wrapped **Thumbnail** earlier.

This time, you use the query method **queryAllBy**, which can return any number of matching elements, including none. You pair the **queryAllBy** method with the option **TestId** to find elements whose data-testid attribute matches the given string.

Unlike **getBy**, **queryAllBy** does not throw an exception if no elements match the selector; it returns an empty array instead. Because it does not throw an exception, you must include an expect clause. The expect clause checks that the number of items found matches the number of items originally passed to **Home**.

You could have written this statement many ways:

```
expect(thumbnails.length === items.length).toBeTruthy();
expect(thumbnails.length).toBe(items.length);
expect(thumbnails).toHaveLength(items.length);
```

Your test uses the more specific matcher toHaveLength. This lets Jest print more helpful messages if the expectation fails.

For example, if the expectation fails because only 9 items render when 10 items are given, toBeTruthy prints this message:

```
expected false to be true
```

But toHaveLength prints this message:

```
Expected length: 9
Received length: 10
Received array:
  [
    <a class="thumbnail-component" data-testid="thumbnail-component"
        href="/details/bubble-tea">
      <div><img alt="Tea" src="bubble-tea.svg" /></div>
      <span>Tea</span>
    </a>,
    ... // Array contents truncated for brevity
  ]
```

Having the actual array contents is helpful for debugging, and you get them automatically when you use matchers such as toHaveLength and toContain.

You can read more about the Jest matchers at jestjs.io/docs/en/expect.

To recap, this test gives the array of items to the **Home** component, then uses the **queryAllBy** method to find the rendered **Thumbnail**s by their data-testid attribute. It asserts that all items render correctly by expecting that the number of rendered **Thumbnail**s matches the length of the items array.

Save your file and check your terminal again to confirm that the test passes.

Mocking the Server

Next, you will add integration tests for the full application. First, you will confirm that the username displays when a user is logged in.

Since this test targets the full application as rendered by **App**, it should, as much as possible, mimic how the application works in the browser.

So far, your tests have checked whether the targeted component and its children render correctly when you provide particular props. Although **App** does not have props, it does make network requests. To test the username display functionality, you will need to mock the API request for /api/auth/current-user.

There are a number of options for mocking API calls. For example, you can use Jest mock functions to mock **axios.get**. There are also npm packages specifically to help mock Axios.

You will use the same approach that the examples in the React Testing Library use: a package called MSW (Mock Service Worker). This package mocks out all the API calls with a mock server. One benefit of MSW is that if you are developing the client app and the server is not available, you can use the same mocks in the browser.

Install MSW with `npm install --save msw@0.47.4`.

(To run this command, you can open a separate terminal tab or stop your tests. If you stop your tests, restart them with `npm test` after installing MSW.)

Add a new directory called `src/mocks`. In it, create a file called `handlers.js` and add your mock server handlers, as shown below:

Listing 21.7 MSW handlers (`handlers.js`)

```
import { rest } from 'msw';
import { items } from '../items';

const handlers = [
  rest.get('/api/items', (req, res, ctx) => res(ctx.json(items))),
  rest.get('/api/auth/current-user', (req, res, ctx) => (
    res(ctx.json({ access: 'associate', username: 'Tester' }))
  )),
];

export default handlers;
```

MSW provides a **rest** method that allows you to mock GET, POST, PUT, and DELETE calls. The `handlers` array is an array of requests that return the mock response you specify. MSW also provides context (here named `ctx`) that contains a variety of helper functions for things such as responding with JSON.

You mock two GET requests – the call for items and the call for the current user – because the main **App** file makes both requests.

The request for `/api/auth/current-user` returns an object with the username `Tester`. You will reference this username in your tests.

Now create a `server.js` file for your mock server in the `mocks` directory. Separating your handlers and server lets you use the handlers to mock the calls in the browser, if you want to.

Listing 21.8 MSW server (`server.js`)

```
import { setupServer } from 'msw/node';
import handlers from './handlers';

// Set up requests interception using the given handlers
export default setupServer(...handlers);
```

You set up the server using **setupServer** from the node folder of MSW. Then you import the handlers you created and pass them to **setupServer**.

Finally, you need to modify the `src/setupTests.js` file that Create React App created. This file houses any additional configuration you need when running your tests. It already imports the @testing-library/jest-dom package, which gives you access to custom matchers.

In `setupTests.js`, import your server and tell Jest how to interact with it.

Listing 21.9 Modifying the setup file (`setupTests.js`)

```
// jest-dom adds custom jest matchers for asserting on DOM nodes.
// allows you to do things like:
// expect(element).toHaveTextContent(/react/i)
// learn more: https://github.com/testing-library/jest-dom
import '@testing-library/jest-dom';
import server from './mocks/server';

beforeAll(() => server.listen({ onUnhandledRequest: 'error' }));
afterAll(() => server.close());
afterEach(() => server.resetHandlers());
```

Jest needs to start the mock server before it runs tests, stop it at the end of the tests, and reset it between each test. You express this with the `beforeAll`, `afterAll`, and `afterEach` blocks, respectively.

You can read more about MSW at mswjs.io/docs.

Testing the Logged-In User's Username

Now the mock server is set up to intercept all network requests. You are ready to test that the logged-in user's username appears in the header.

Create a new `src/App.test.js` file and add a test that renders **App** and looks for an element with the username `Tester`.

Listing 21.10 Adding a username test to **App** (`App.test.js`)

```
import { screen, render } from '@testing-library/react';
import App from './App';

describe('App', () => {
  it('displays the logged in user\'s username', async () => {
    render(<App />);
    await screen.findByText(/Tester/i);
  });
});
```

App already contains a router, so you can render it directly without needing to wrap it with **MemoryRouter**.

Although you have mocked the API, **App** still loads user details asynchronously. This means that the username `Tester` will not be present in the first render. The **getBy** and **queryAllBy** methods you used in other tests expect the element to be present immediately, so they would cause failures here.

Instead, you use the query method **findBy**. Like **getBy**, **findBy** looks for exactly one matching element. But **findBy** returns a promise that is fulfilled when one element matches the selector.

findBy waits for the element to be present, so the test must await its resolution before moving on. The promise will be rejected if **findBy** finds multiple matching elements or if it finds no elements within the set timeout period, which is 1000 milliseconds by default.

Because you use **findBy**'s promise, you mark the function in the it block as async. Jest notices when an it block contains an async function; the test automatically waits for the promise to complete and fails if the promise fails.

As you get more experience writing tests, knowing which query method to use will become more intuitive. The table below summarizes the available query methods.

Query	Resolves immediately?	Success criteria	Failure behavior
getBy	Yes	Matches exactly one element	Throws exception
getAllBy	Yes	Matches one or more elements	Throws exception
queryBy	Yes	Matches zero or one element (returns null for zero elements)	Throws exception
queryAllBy	Yes	Matches any number of elements (returns empty array for zero elements)	None (no failure state)
findBy	No; returns a promise	Matches exactly one element	Rejects promise
findAllBy	No; returns a promise	Matches one or more elements	Rejects promise

Save your file and check your terminal to confirm that App.test.js passes.

Testing Navigation

Next you will build a test that checks the user's full path through Code Café. Your test will check that

1. **Home** displays correctly.
2. Clicking a **Thumbnail** navigates to the details page.
3. Clicking Add to Cart adds an item to the cart.
4. Clicking the cart link navigates to the cart page.
5. The Order Now button is disabled until the required fields are filled.
6. Clicking Order Now results in a successful checkout.
7. Orders are stored correctly on the server.

Although this test includes navigation, it still runs with Jest, the same framework you used for the tests you wrote earlier.

Add a test to `App.test.js` that describes this user flow, starting with the home page check to see if the items load correctly. Since this test will include multiple parts that check different aspects of the user flow, use a descriptive comment to make your code easy to read and follow.

Listing 21.11 Testing the user's starting point (`App.test.js`)

```
import { screen, render } from '@testing-library/react';
import { screen, render, waitFor } from '@testing-library/react';
import App from './App';
import { items } from './items';

describe('App', () => {
  it('displays the logged in user\'s username', async () => {
    render(<App />);
    await screen.findByText(/Tester/i);
  });

  it('allows the user to build a cart and place an order', async () => {
    render(<App />);

    // Home displays correctly
    await waitFor(() => {
      const thumbnails = screen.queryAllByTestId('thumbnail-component');
      expect(thumbnails).toHaveLength(items.length);
    });
  });
});
```

This test renders **App**, then checks whether the **Thumbnail**s load on the home page. Like the username in your previous test, items loads asynchronously, so no **Thumbnail**s render until the request completes.

You put the expectation in the **waitFor** method from the React Testing Library so that the test will wait until there are exactly items.length **Thumbnail**s. Like the **findBy** methods, **waitFor** will reject the promise if the expectation is not met within the set timeout period, which is 1000 milliseconds by default. Unlike using the **findBy** query (which checks for exactly one element) or **findAllBy** (which checks for at least one element), using expect inside **waitFor** allows you to check for a specific number of elements.

Save your file and check the terminal to make sure your new test passes.

Now that you know the **Thumbnail**s have loaded correctly, use the user-event library to simulate clicking a **Thumbnail** and navigating to the details page.

When testing navigation, you need a way to verify that the test has arrived at the correct page. You do this by looking for something that appears only on that page. What is present on the details page and no other page in your app? The Add to Cart button. Look for it in your test.

Listing 21.12 Testing navigation to the item details (App.test.js)

```
import { screen, render, waitFor } from '@testing-library/react';
import userEvent from '@testing-library/user-event';
import App from './App';
import { items } from './items';

describe('App', () => {
  ...
  it('allows the user to build a cart and place an order', async () => {
    render(<App />);

    // Home displays correctly
    await waitFor(() => {
      const thumbnails = screen.queryAllByTestId('thumbnail-component');
      expect(thumbnails).toHaveLength(items.length);
    });

    // Clicking a Thumbnail navigates to the details page
    await userEvent.click(screen.getByRole('link', { name: /Tea/i }));
    await screen.findByRole('button', { name: /Add to Cart/i });
  });
});
```

userEvent, which you import from the user-event library, lets you simulate a user action, such as clicking an element. You pass the target element as an argument to the event function.

Here, you use the query method **getBy** to locate the **Link** element as the target element. You get the element by its role, link – specifically, a link containing the text Tea.

The browser uses the role to determine the element's accessibility features. Some elements, including links, buttons, and headings, have a default role that the browser sets. You can also assign roles to elements yourself. For example, in Chapter 16, you set the role of the **Alert** component to alert so that screen readers can read it correctly.

The React Testing Library recommends finding elements by their role when possible. Following this pattern in your tests can help you make sure your components have roles to support accessibility.

After finding the correct element, the test waits for routing to occur by testing that the Add to Cart button (which is visible only on the details page) has rendered.

Once again, save your file and confirm that all your tests are passing.

Testing the Add to Cart button

Next you want to check that when the user clicks Add to Cart, the cart quantity updates. To do that, you will need a data-testid so that you can grab the cart quantity element. Add that to the cart badge in Header.js.

Listing 21.13 Adding a test ID for the cart quantity (Header.js)

```
...
function Header({ cart }) {
  const cartQuantity = cart.reduce((acc, item) => acc + item.quantity, 0);
  return (
    ...
      <Link to="/cart">
        <img src={CartIcon} alt="Cart" />
        <div className="badge">{cartQuantity}</div>
        <div
          className="badge"
          data-testid="cart-quantity"
        >
          {cartQuantity}
        </div>
      </Link>
...
```

With the data-testid in place, add to your test in App.test.js. Add two teas to the cart, using userEvent to model clicks on the Add to Cart button, then confirm that the cart contains the expected items.

Listing 21.14 Adding items to the cart (App.test.js)

```
...
describe('App', () => {
  ...
  it('allows the user to build a cart and place an order', async () => {
    ...
    // Clicking a Thumbnail navigates to the details page
    await userEvent.click(screen.getByRole('link', { name: /Tea/i }));
    await screen.findByRole('button', { name: /Add to Cart/i });

    // Items are successfully added to the cart
    await userEvent.click(screen.getByRole('button', { name: /Add to Cart/i }));
    await waitFor(() => {
      expect(screen.getByTestId('cart-quantity')).toHaveTextContent('1');
    });
    await userEvent.click(screen.getByRole('button', { name: /Add to Cart/i }));
    await waitFor(() => {
      expect(screen.getByTestId('cart-quantity')).toHaveTextContent('2');
    });
  });
});
```

Think about what happens in your code when an item is added to the cart: The **dispatch** method fires to update the state of the cart reducer, causing the affected components to re-render. Though all of this happens pretty quickly, it is not instantaneous. You use the **waitFor** method to wait until the components have updated and the expected text is visible.

toHaveTextContent is a matcher you have not used yet. It comes from jest-dom, one of the Create React App libraries imported in src/setupTests.js. Once the test locates the cart badge, this matcher asserts what the text content of the badge node should be.

Matchers from jest-dom assert what should be on the screen at a given time, helping you keep your tests declarative and easy to read. You can read about toHaveTextContent and other jest-dom matchers at github.com/testing-library/jest-dom#custom-matchers.

Save your file and check the terminal to make sure all your tests pass before moving on.

Testing checkout

After adding items to the cart, the user navigates to the cart page and checks out. Your next task is to test that clicking the cart link takes the user to the cart page, that the Order Now button is disabled until required fields in the order form are filled, and that clicking Order Now displays the successful order message and empties the cart.

To do this, you will need to mock the POST request to /api/orders in the MSW handlers. Add this change to handlers.js.

Listing 21.15 Adding a mock orders request (handlers.js)

```
...
const handlers = [
  rest.get('/api/items', (req, res, ctx) => res(ctx.json(items))),
  rest.get('/api/auth/current-user', (req, res, ctx) => (
    res(ctx.json({ access: 'associate', username: 'Tester' }))
  )),
  rest.post('/api/orders', (req, res, ctx) => res(ctx.status(201))),
];

export default handlers;
```

This new request does not do any validation. It just responds with 201 (created).

Like the other mocked requests, this request is inside the handlers array, which you are already exporting. You do not need any additional code to be able to use this request.

In your test, navigate to the cart page and verify the navigation by looking for something that appears on that page and nowhere else, such as the Name label in the checkout form. Then fill in the checkout form with a name and ZIP code (the required fields), and submit an order. Add checks to confirm that the Order Now button is correctly disabled and enabled based on whether the required fields are present.

Listing 21.16 Testing order submission (`App.test.js`)

```
...
describe('App', () => {
  ...
    // Items are successfully added to the cart
    ...
    await waitFor(() => {
      expect(screen.getByTestId('cart-quantity')).toHaveTextContent('2');
    });

    // Clicking the cart link navigates to the cart
    await userEvent.click(screen.getByRole('link', { name: /Cart/i }));
    await screen.findByLabelText(/Name/i);

    // The Order Now button is disabled until the required fields are present
    expect(screen.getByRole('button', { name: /Order Now/i })).toBeDisabled();
    await userEvent.type(screen.getByLabelText(/Name/i), 'Big Nerd Ranch');
    await userEvent.type(screen.getByLabelText(/ZIP Code/i), '30316');
    expect(screen.getByRole('button', { name: /Order Now/i })).toBeEnabled();

    // Clicking the Order Now button results in a successful checkout
    await userEvent.click(screen.getByRole('button', { name: /Order Now/i }));
    await waitFor(() => {
      expect(screen.getByText(/Thank you for your order/i)).toBeVisible();
    });
    await waitFor(() => {
      expect(screen.getByTestId('cart-quantity')).toHaveTextContent('0');
    });
  });
});
```

There is a lot going on here. Though each step uses code that you have seen before, let's break it down line by line:

- The test gets the cart link by its role and text, then clicks it (just like a user would click the cart link).

- To check that it has navigated to the cart page, the test finds the name input by its label text.

- The test finds the Order Now button by its role and text, then checks that the button is initially disabled.

- The test fills out the name and ZIP code in the checkout form, using input labels to get the target elements.

- Now that the required fields are present, the test checks that the Order Now button is enabled.

- The test clicks the Order Now button to place the order.

- The test waits until the thank-you message in the **Alert** component is visible.

  (Because the **Alert** component is always present on the screen, the additional matcher toBeVisible checks the status of the hidden attribute. Like toHaveTextContent, this matcher comes from jest-dom.)

- To check that the cart has reset, the test waits until no items are showing in the cart.

Save your file and check your terminal. All your tests should still be passing.

Verifying order submission

The last part of the order submission flow that you will test is confirming that the order made it to the server. Ideally, the test would visit the orders page and check that the order shows up there. But mocking websockets requires other testing libraries and is uncommon enough to be outside the scope of this book. (However, you will test the orders page in the end-to-end tests you write in the next chapter.)

Instead, you will add a data layer to the mock API.

Add a new file in the src/mocks directory called data.js. Create mock order data, as shown below:

Listing 21.17 Adding mock order data (data.js)

```
let orders = [];

export const reset = () => {
  orders = [];
};

export const getOrders = () => orders;

export const addOrder = (newOrder) => {
  orders.push({ ...newOrder });
};
```

You set up the variable orders to store the current test orders. The **reset** function resets the value of orders to an empty array. **getOrders** returns the current value of orders. Finally, **addOrder** pushes a new value to the orders array.

Although this method of storing data is not persistent, it is sufficient for testing.

Now update your handlers to use the data layer.

Listing 21.18 Using the data layer in the handlers (`handlers.js`)

```
import { rest } from 'msw';
import { items } from '../items';
import { addOrder } from './data';

const handlers = [
  rest.get('/api/items', (req, res, ctx) => res(ctx.json(items))),
  rest.get('/api/auth/current-user', (req, res, ctx) => (
    res(ctx.json({ access: 'associate', username: 'Tester' }))
  )),
  rest.post('/api/orders', (req, res, ctx) => res(ctx.status(201))),
  rest.post('/api/orders', async (req, res, ctx) => {
    addOrder(await req.json());
    return res(ctx.status(201));
  }),
];

export default handlers;
```

You update the POST request to /api/orders, getting the order details from the request using await req.json() and passing the result to the new **addOrder** function. This will store the order in the orders variable, similar to how you would store it in a database.

Finally, update your test setup file to reset the data layer after each test.

Listing 21.19 Resetting the data layer (`setupTests.js`)

```
...
import '@testing-library/jest-dom';
import * as data from './mocks/data';
import server from './mocks/server';

beforeAll(() => server.listen({ onUnhandledRequest: 'error' }));
afterAll(() => server.close());
afterEach(() => server.resetHandlers());
afterEach(() => {
  data.reset();
  server.resetHandlers();
});
```

You use the **reset** function in the afterEach block to reset the data layer, in addition to the server handlers, after each test. This keeps your tests clean and isolated so that if one test places an order, it will not interfere with any other tests.

With the data layer set up, add one final check to the checkout test to confirm that the server has an order.

Listing 21.20 Checking the number of orders (`App.test.js`)

```
...
import { items } from './items';
import { getOrders } from './mocks/data';

describe('App', () => {
  ...
    // Clicking the Order Now button results in a successful checkout
    ...
    await waitFor(() => {
      expect(screen.getByTestId('cart-quantity')).toHaveTextContent('0');
    });

    // Orders are stored correctly
    expect(getOrders()).toHaveLength(1);
  });
});
```

You import the **getOrders** function from the data layer to read the current value of orders, and you check that its length is 1.

Save your file and check your tests in the terminal. Everything passes! You have completed a full happy path test for the user.

Checkout Error

But you are not done, because you do not want to test only the happy paths. Your last test for this chapter will check that the error alert shows up if something goes wrong during the checkout flow.

Does this mean you need to test the entire add-to-cart flow again? No way! To test the checkout error, you only need to render **Cart**. Focusing on this one component allows you to skip some flows that you already tested, such as starting on the home page and adding items to the cart. Instead, you can mock the cart with an array and pass it as a prop to the component.

You will still use the mock server to mock placing an order.

Create a new `components/Cart.test.js` file and set up your test as shown:

Listing 21.21 Testing the checkout error (`Cart.test.js`)

```
import { screen, render, waitFor } from '@testing-library/react';
import userEvent from '@testing-library/user-event';
import { rest } from 'msw';
import Cart from './Cart';
import { items } from '../items';
import server from '../mocks/server';

describe('Cart Errors', () => {
  it('shows checkout failure error', async () => {
    const testErrorMessage = 'Code Café is Closed';
    server.use(
      rest.post('/api/orders', async (req, res, ctx) => (
        res(ctx.status(500), ctx.json({ error: testErrorMessage }))
      )),
    );
    const cart = [{ itemId: items[0].itemId, quantity: 1 }];
    const dispatch = jest.fn(() => {});
    render(
      <Cart cart={cart} dispatch={dispatch} items={items} />,
    );
    expect(screen.getByRole('button', { name: /Order Now/i })).toBeDisabled();
    await userEvent.type(screen.getByLabelText(/Name/i), 'Big Nerd Ranch');
    await userEvent.type(screen.getByLabelText(/ZIP Code/i), '30316');
    expect(screen.getByRole('button', { name: /Order Now/i })).toBeEnabled();
    await userEvent.click(screen.getByRole('button', { name: /Order Now/i }));
    await waitFor(() => {
      expect(screen.getByText(testErrorMessage)).toBeVisible();
    });
    expect(dispatch).not.toHaveBeenCalled();
  });
});
```

The MSW library allows you to temporarily override a server endpoint. This means that the order endpoint can fail with an error message without having to make the happy path worker run any validations. In this test, any requests made to the order endpoint will fail with a status of 500 and the error message `Code Café is Closed`.

After setting up the mock failed request, you add some mock prop variables, including the `cart` prop as an array with one item. You also mock the **dispatch** function with a Jest function wrapper, which allows you to test whether **dispatch** was called. Although you can provide a real implementation for **dispatch**, you do not expect it to be called, so you provide a blank function.

After rendering the cart, the test fills out the checkout form, as before. But when the test submits the form, the request to `/api/orders` fails because of the override you created. The test expects the **Alert** component to be visible with the error message. Then, the test expects the **dispatch** function *not* to have been called, since an error should not clear the cart.

Save your file and check your terminal for the updated test output.

Mocking console.error

When the test runs, it dumps a giant error log to the console, above the message that the tests passed. Although this is helpful when an error is unexpected, when the error *is* expected, like now, it just clutters up the console.

Mock the console in the test suite so you can clean up the output while ensuring that unexpected errors will still log.

Listing 21.22 Mocking the console (`Cart.test.js`)

```
...
describe('Cart Errors', () => {
  beforeEach(() => {
    jest.spyOn(console, 'error').mockImplementation(() => {});
  });

  afterEach(() => {
    console.error.mockRestore();
  });

  it('shows checkout failure error', async () => {
    ...
    await waitFor(() => {
      expect(screen.getByText(testErrorMessage)).toBeVisible();
    });
    expect(dispatch).not.toHaveBeenCalled();
    expect(console.error).toHaveBeenCalledTimes(1);
  });
});
```

Now your test suite sets up actions that run before and after the checkout error test. Before the test runs, you provide a mock implementation for **console.error** using the Jest **spyOn** method. In this case, your mock implementation simply removes the console output. After the test runs, you restore **console.error** to its default implementation so that errors encountered anywhere outside the checkout error test will still print as usual.

There are a couple of other ways you could have done this.

You could have added **spyOn** and **mockRestore** at the top and bottom of the it block. However, if you put **mockRestore** at the bottom of the it block and the test fails, **console.error** will not be restored, which can cause you to miss legitimate errors in other tests. You could then have used try/catch/finally syntax in the it block to ensure that the method would be restored. But it is easier to let Jest handle things by using beforeEach and afterEach.

Finally, you add an expect statement that asserts that there should be exactly one console error as a result of this test.

Save your file and check the test in your terminal. It passes, displaying the normal Jest output and no error log.

Conclusion

Now you have a unit test and some integration tests that run with Jest and the React Testing Library.

Stop the test watcher with Control-C. Then run all your tests as they would run in a continuous integration (CI) pipeline with `CI=true npm test`. Using `CI=true` stops Jest from entering watch usage mode, so it will exit after running all the tests.

```
> code-cafe@0.1.0 test
> react-scripts test

PASS src/reducers/cartReducer.test.js
PASS src/components/Thumbnail.test.js
PASS src/components/Home.test.js
PASS src/components/Cart.test.js
PASS src/App.test.js

Test Suites: 5 passed, 5 total
Tests:       9 passed, 9 total
Snapshots:   0 total
Time:        3.41 s
Ran all test suites.
```

Though the time might vary slightly on your machine, at just a few seconds long, these tests are quite fast.

If you were developing new features or refactoring your app, these tests would give you confidence that your code changes have not broken Code Café.

In the next chapter, you will add end-to-end tests to Code Café using Cypress.

For the More Curious: File Structure for Test Files

So far, you have created test files in the same directory as the file they are testing. Another common pattern is to put the test files in a separate folder named _tests_ (for example, `src/reducers/_tests_/cartReducer.test.js`).

Most developers use one of these two approaches. As we mentioned earlier, this book follows the same pattern as Create React App: The example test, `src/App.test.js`, lives alongside `App.js`. In your own apps, you might prefer to use another structure.

For the More Curious: React Testing Library Queries

In its documentation, the React Testing Library offers valuable recommendations for how to use its query methods most effectively, at testing-library.com/docs/queries/about/#overview.

Bronze Challenge: Testing Removing an Item from the Cart

Test that the button to remove an item from the cart works as expected.

Silver Challenge: Additional cartReducer Tests

Add tests to `cartReducer.test.js` to test that

- removing an item from a cart with multiple items works as expected
- an error is thrown if the action type is unknown

Jest provides the matcher `toThrow` to test that an error occurs as expected. When using `toThrow`, you must wrap the code in a function to catch the error, like so: `expect(() => cartReducer(...)).toThrow();`.

Silver Challenge: Testing Phone Number Formatting

Test that the checkout form adds dashes to the text in the phone number field as expected.

For example, entering 5555555555 should result in a value of 555-555-5555, and entering 555-5555555 should also result in a value of 555-555-5555.

There are a few jest-dom matchers you can use to assert the value of the input fields, including `toHaveValue` and `toHaveDisplayValue`.

Silver Challenge: Testing Tax Details

Test that the tax details adjust properly on the cart page when the ZIP code changes.

Gold Challenge: Additional Login Tests

So far, you have tested your app's login by returning a logged-in user from the current user endpoint.

Now add tests for the login page.

The happy path test for logging in as an associate should do the following:

- Override the POST `/api/auth/login` endpoint to return `{"access":"associate","username":"test"}`. (For an added challenge, return the username from the request body.)

- Override the current user endpoint so it returns an empty object, signifying that no user is logged in.

- Visit the login page.

- Fill in a username and password, then click the Log In button.

- Verify that the user is logged in and can see the Orders link. (The displayed username will be the one that the mocked endpoint returns, which might not match the one you provide for the username field.)

The happy path test for logging in as a guest should do the following:

- Override the POST /api/auth/login endpoint to return {"access":"guest","username":"test"}.

- Override the current user endpoint so it returns an empty object, signifying that no user is logged in.

- Visit the login page.

- Fill in a username and password, then click the Log In button.

- Verify that the user is logged in but cannot see the Orders link.

The unhappy path should do the following:

- Override the POST /api/auth/login endpoint to return a 401 status code and {"error":"Incorrect Username or Password."}.

- Override the current user endpoint so it returns an empty object, signifying that no user is logged in.

- Visit the login page.

- Fill in a username and password, then click the Log In button.

- Verify that the alert message shows up and displays the correct error message.

22

End-to-End Testing

Now that you have seen how unit and integration testing work, you are ready to move on to end-to-end testing, which validates user workflows using an actual browser.

There are many end-to-end testing solutions. One of the most popular tools for testing front-end applications is Cypress. In this chapter, you will use Cypress and the Cypress Testing Library to write end-to-end tests.

Like Jest and the React Testing Library do for unit testing, Cypress and the Cypress Testing Library work together to allow you to write and run end-to-end tests. Cypress runs tests in a browser window, replicating real user interactions. The Cypress Testing Library is part of the same family of frameworks as the React Testing Library, so you can reuse testing patterns when writing unit and end-to-cnd tests.

Installing and Configuring Cypress

First, install Cypress and the Cypress Testing Library. You will also need the Cypress ESLint plugin for linting. Install all three packages with

```
npm install --save cypress@10.8.0 eslint-plugin-cypress@2.12.1
    @testing-library/cypress@8.0.3
```

Cypress takes a few minutes to install, so do not worry if the install command looks stuck.

Configuring scripts

The command to start Cypress from your terminal requires you to target the full path, like this:

```
./node_modules/.bin/cypress open
```

Instead of typing out the target path every time you want to run Cypress, it is easier to use a script that you can run in your application's root directory. You might recall that you added a script to run ESLint in Code Café back in Chapter 5.

In the `scripts` block in `package.json` (the same place you added your previous script), add the two scripts you need to run Cypress.

Listing 22.1 Adding Cypress scripts (`package.json`)

```
{
  "name": "code-cafe",
  "version": "0.1.0",
  ...
  },
  "scripts": {
    "cypress:open": "cypress open",
    "cypress:run": "cypress run",
    "start": "react-scripts start",
...
```

The first script, `cypress:open`, opens Cypress and allows you to run tests one at a time.

The second script, `cypress:run`, runs all the tests in headless mode. (This mode is mostly meant for continuous integration, or CI.)

In your terminal, try out your new script:

```
npm run cypress:open
```

Cypress takes a few seconds to open, then displays the Cypress welcome window (Figure 22.1). (If it crashes with an error telling you that Cypress verification timed out, try the command again.)

Figure 22.1 Cypress welcome window

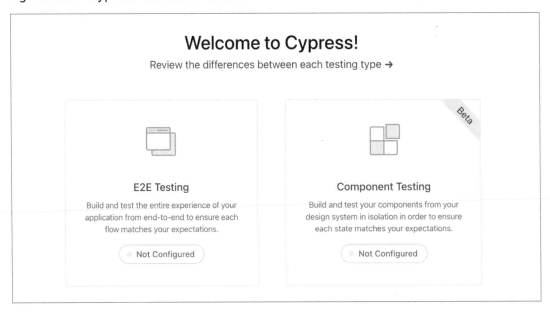

The welcome window presents you with two choices: **E2E Testing** and **Component Testing**. "E2E" is short for "end-to-end," which is what you want, so click the **E2E Testing** box.

The next screen shows a list of files that Cypress has added to your project (Figure 22.2).

Figure 22.2 Cypress configuration files

You can open the dropdowns to learn more about each file that Cypress created.

Click Continue. On the next screen, you can choose the browser you want to use to run your tests (Figure 22.3).

Figure 22.3 Choosing a browser

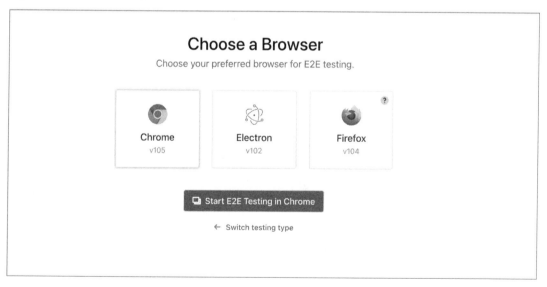

(Your list of available browsers will likely be different.) Select Chrome, then click Start E2E Testing in Chrome.

The final setup screen gives you options to begin creating test files, or *specs* (Figure 22.4).

Figure 22.4 Cypress spec window

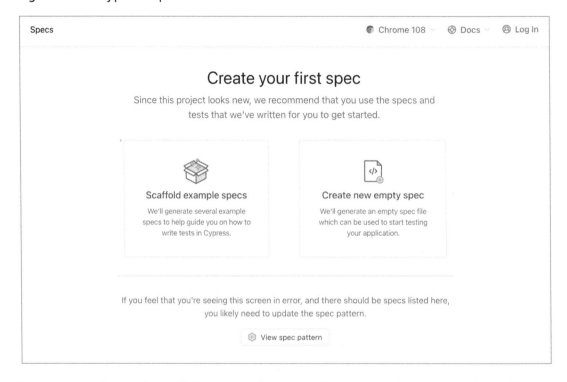

Later, tests you have written will show up in this window. For now, you do not have to do anything here.

Close the Cypress window by clicking the X in its top-left corner.

Setting up ESLint for Cypress

Next, you need to set up ESLint to check that the new files Cypress created – and the new tests you will write – conform to Code Café's lint rules.

In Visual Studio Code's explorer, locate the directory called `cypress` and the `cypress.config.js` configuration file that Cypress created for you. They are in your project's top-level directory, along with the `src` directory and the `package.json` file.

Open `cypress.config.js`. ESLint identifies several lint errors (Figure 22.5):

Figure 22.5 Lint errors in `cypress.config.js`

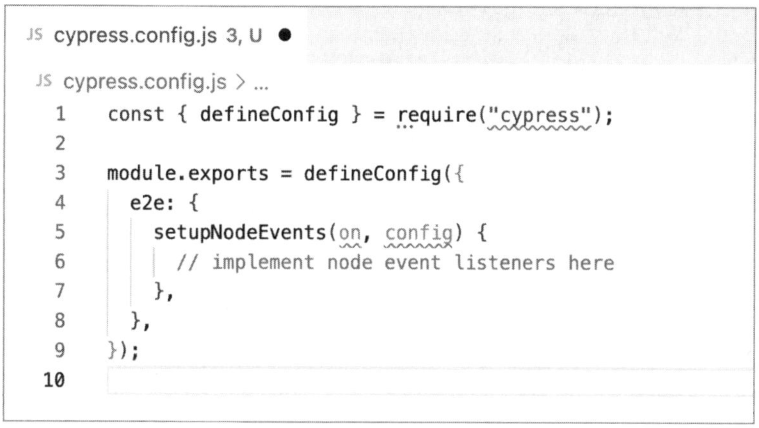

```
JS cypress.config.js 3, U  ●

JS cypress.config.js > ...
  1    const { defineConfig } = require("cypress");
  2
  3    module.exports = defineConfig({
  4      e2e: {
  5        setupNodeEvents(on, config) {
  6          // implement node event listeners here
  7        },
  8      },
  9    });
 10
```

Now, in a new terminal tab, run `npm run lint` in the Code Café directory. The linting script reports no errors. Why the discrepancy?

Although the ESLint extension you added to Visual Studio Code checks all the files in the project, the linting script you set up when you started working on Code Café checks only files in the `src` directory. The `cypress` directory and the `cypress.config.js` file are outside of `src`, so the command does not check them.

You will add the end-to-end tests you write to the `cypress` directory, so it is important to have ESLint enforce code rules there. Update ESLint's configuration in `package.json` so that it lints the `cypress.config.js` file and `cypress` directory files as well.

Listing 22.2 Updating the ESLint configuration (`package.json`)

```
...
  "scripts": {
    ...
    "test": "react-scripts test",
    "lint": "eslint src --max-warnings=0",
    "lint": "eslint cypress.config.js cypress src --max-warnings=0",
    "eject": "react-scripts eject"
...
```

Run npm run lint again in your terminal. Now the output reports several errors:

```
> eslint cypress.config.js cypress src --max-warnings=0

/.../code-cafe/cypress.config.js
  1:34  error  Strings must use singlequote        quotes
  5:21  error  'on' is defined but never used      no-unused-vars
  5:25  error  'config' is defined but never used  no-unused-vars

/.../code-cafe/cypress/support/commands.js
  25:78  error  Newline required at end of file but not found  eol-last

/.../code-cafe/cypress/support/e2e.js
  17:20  error  Missing semicolon                              semi
  20:25  error  Newline required at end of file but not found  eol-last

✖ 6 problems (6 errors, 0 warnings)
  4 errors and 0 warnings potentially fixable with the `--fix` option.
```

There are six problems in all. Four are auto-fixable errors related to three ESLint rules:

- Strings must use single quotes.
- Files must end with a newline character.
- Lines must end with a semicolon.

These errors are related to code style. Fixing them will not affect your app's behavior, so they are OK to auto-fix. Now run the command to auto-fix the errors: npm run lint -- --fix.

Rerun npm run lint. The remaining two errors highlight unused variables in cypress.config.js:

```
> eslint cypress.config.js cypress src --max-warnings=0 --fix

/../code-cafe/cypress.config.js
  5:21  error  'on' is defined but never used      no-unused-vars
  5:25  error  'config' is defined but never used  no-unused-vars

✖ 2 problems (2 errors, 0 warnings)
```

You cannot auto-fix the no-unused-vars rule – you have to manually update the file to use the variables, delete the code that creates them, or ignore the lint rule. Although you are not using these variables now, you might need them as you add custom configurations to your Cypress setup, so your best option is to exempt them from the lint rule.

Open cypress.config.js and disable the no-unused-vars rule with the comment line you have used before.

Listing 22.3 Ignoring a lint rule in the Cypress configuration file (cypress.config.js)

```js
const { defineConfig } = require('cypress');

module.exports = defineConfig({
  e2e: {
    // eslint-disable-next-line no-unused-vars
    setupNodeEvents(on, config) {
      // implement node event listeners here
    },
  },
});
```

Now you have resolved the current linting errors. Next, you need to set up ESLint to make use of the Cypress plugin.

In the `cypress` directory, create a file called `.eslintrc.js`. (Do not forget the dot at the beginning of the filename. The dot identifies it as a configuration file. By default, files beginning with a dot are hidden.)

Add the Cypress plugin to the new file, as shown below.

Listing 22.4 Adding the Cypress plugin (`.eslintrc.js`)

```
module.exports = {
  extends: ['plugin:cypress/recommended'],
};
```

ESLint allows you to override and extend your configurations by directory. Here, you add Cypress-specific rules from the Cypress ESLint plugin that will apply only within the `cypress` directory. These rules will enforce best practices recommended for writing Cypress tests.

Now you can continue your work without any complaints from ESLint.

Importing commands

The commands that Cypress provides are like statements that describe the interaction happening during a particular test. The Cypress Testing Library provides additional commands, such as **findBy**, that are similar to the query methods you used in the last chapter. To use the commands from the Cypress Testing Library, add an import statement to `cypress/support/commands.js`.

Listing 22.5 Importing Cypress commands (`commands.js`)

```
...
// -- This will overwrite an existing command --
// Cypress.Commands.overwrite('visit', (originalFn, url, options) => { ... })
import '@testing-library/cypress/add-commands';
```

Setting the base URL

There is one final piece of configuration you need before writing your first test: setting the app's base URL. Do this in `cypress.config.js`.

Listing 22.6 Setting the base URL (`cypress.config.js`)

```
const { defineConfig } = require('cypress');

module.exports = defineConfig({
  e2e: {
    baseUrl: 'http://localhost:3000',
    // eslint-disable-next-line no-unused-vars
    setupNodeEvents(on, config) {
...
```

Setting the baseUrl makes it easy to change the expected URL of the application. It also saves you some time when you write your tests. Instead of writing out the URL each time, like this:

```
cy.visit('http://localhost:3000/details/coffee')
```

you can omit the base URL and write just this:

```
cy.visit('/details/coffee')
```

Testing the Login Flow

By default, Cypress looks for test files that match the following pattern:

```
cypress/e2e/**/*.cy.{js,jsx,ts,tsx}
```

Create a subdirectory in cypress called e2e to house your end-to-end test files. In the cypress/e2e directory, add a test file called login.cy.js.

Your first Cypress test will validate the user's login flow. Add a test that starts at the home page and tests that a user can log in successfully, as shown below.

Listing 22.7 Adding a login test (login.cy.js)

```
describe('login', () => {
  it('shows logged-in user\'s username', () => {
    cy.visit('/');
    cy.findByRole('link', { name: /Log In/i }).click();
    cy.findByLabelText(/Username/i).type('Tester');
    cy.findByLabelText(/Password/i).type('pass');
    cy.findByRole('button', { name: /Log In/i }).click();
    cy.findByRole('link', { name: /Log In/i }).should('not.exist');
    cy.findByText(/Tester/i);
  });
});
```

Cypress uses the same structure for test files as Jest does, with describe and it blocks, so this code looks similar to the tests you wrote in the previous chapter. Using the Cypress Testing Library also allows you to use the familiar **findBy** and **findAllBy** methods to query for elements.

Cypress requires all commands to be retryable, so it can rerun them in the event of a failure. **findBy** and **findAllBy** each return a promise that is fulfilled if the element is found and rejected if it is not. This allows Cypress to execute code after the promise is fulfilled.

getBy and **getAllBy** throw exceptions if the criteria are not met, so these methods are not retryable, and Cypress does not support them.

What about **queryBy** and **queryAllBy**? To get the same results with Cypress, you use a modified *chainer*, like this:

```
cy.findByText(...).should('not.exist')
```

A chainer creates an assertion, similar to expect in Jest.

Using Cypress to interact with the page is a bit different from using Jest. With Cypress, you identify the target element, then chain the Cypress user event methods. The chainer **click** simulates clicking on an element, while **type** simulates typing, with the value to type passed in as the argument.

Reading from top to bottom, this test

- starts by visiting the home page at / (taking advantage of the base URL you set)
- finds and clicks the Log In link
- types the username *Tester*
- types the password *pass*
- finds and clicks the Log In button
- tests that the Log In link is no longer visible in the header
- tests that the username *Tester* displays in the header

Save all your files, and let's run your first test.

Make sure your Code Café front end and back end are running in separate terminal windows or tabs. In your browser, visit Code Café at http://localhost:3000 if it is not already open.

In a third terminal window, run `npm run cypress:open`. The Cypress window opens to the initial welcome screen. Select E2E Testing and then Start E2E Testing in Chrome, as you did before. The Chrome window that launches will display a list of test files – currently, a list of one (Figure 22.6).

Figure 22.6 Cypress test file

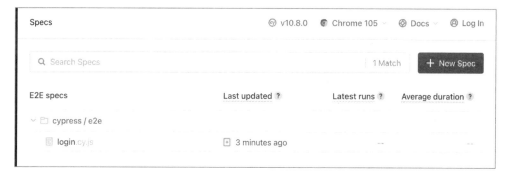

Click login.cy.js to run the test in the browser (Figure 22.7).

Figure 22.7 Cypress successful run

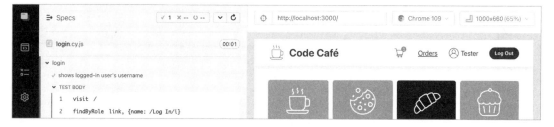

(Cypress uses a dark theme by default. For the screenshots in this book, we used the tool available at www.npmjs.com/package/cypress-light-theme to run Cypress in a light theme.)

Cypress uses green for passing tests and red for failing tests, so the green bar alongside your test code indicates that it has passed.

Testing the Checkout Flow

Next, test the checkout flow in a new cypress/e2e/checkout.cy.js file.

In the previous chapter, you wrote an integration test for the checkout process using a mocked server. Take a look at your code in src/App.test.js. Copy the relevant portion of it into your new file and see if you can update it to work with Cypress.

For your testing flow, start at the home page, add two of an item to the cart, fill out the checkout form with a name and ZIP code, submit the order, and confirm that the correct alert displays and the cart empties. Also, check that the Order Now button is disabled and enabled correctly. Do not worry about testing that the server received the order.

Listing 22.8 Checkout test (checkout.cy.js)

```
describe('checkout', () => {
  it('user can build a cart and place an order', () => {
    cy.visit('/');
    cy.findAllByTestId('thumbnail-component').should('have.length', 10);
    cy.findByRole('link', { name: /Tea/i }).click();
    cy.findByRole('button', { name: /Add to Cart/i }).click();
    cy.findByTestId('cart-quantity').should('contain', '1');
    cy.findByRole('button', { name: /Add to Cart/i }).click();
    cy.findByTestId('cart-quantity').should('contain', '2');
    cy.findByRole('link', { name: /Cart/i }).click();
    cy.findByLabelText(/Name/i);
    cy.findByRole('button', { name: /Order Now/i }).should('be.disabled');
    cy.findByLabelText(/Name/i).type('Big Nerd Ranch');
    cy.findByLabelText(/ZIP Code/i).type('30316');
    cy.findByRole('button', { name: /Order Now/i }).should('be.enabled');
    cy.findByRole('button', { name: /Order Now/i }).click();
    cy.findByText(/Thank you for your order/i).should('be.visible');
    cy.findByTestId('cart-quantity').should('contain', '0');
  });
});
```

Most of this code looks just like the test from the React Testing Library. To make the code retryable, you replace **getBy** with **findBy**. You also use **click** and **type** chainers for user interactions and **should** chainers in place of assertions.

Let's look at each step. This test

- starts by visiting the home page at /
- asserts that there are 10 **Thumbnail** components
- finds and clicks the **Thumbnail** for Tea
- on the details page, finds and clicks the Add to Cart button
- asserts that the cart icon displays 1
- finds and clicks the Add to Cart button again
- asserts that the cart icon updates to display 2
- finds and clicks the cart link
- verifies that it is on the cart page by finding the name input
- verifies that the Order Now button is disabled
- inputs a name and ZIP code using the **type** chainer
- verifies that the Order Now button is enabled

- clicks the Order Now button to submit the order
- verifies that the **Alert** component with the thank-you message is visible
- verifies that the cart is empty by asserting that the cart icon displays 0

Save your file and go back to the Chrome test window.

Click Specs at the top of the window to view the available test files (Figure 22.8).

Figure 22.8 Expanding the specs

Now your new checkout test file is available (Figure 22.9).

Figure 22.9 Available specs

Click checkout.cy.js to run the new test (Figure 22.10).

Figure 22.10 Checkout test success

Success!

In your test, you check for the name field using `cy.findByLabelText(/Name/i)`. Although Cypress has an assertion for `.should('exist')`, **findBy** throws an error by default if the item does not exist, so these two lines are equivalent:

```
cy.findByLabelText(/Name/i);
cy.findByLabelText(/Name/i).should('exist');
```

Feel free to try out both versions. You will notice a slight difference in output, because the second version will show an `assert` (Figure 22.11).

Figure 22.11 `assert` in the test results

```
16    findByLabelText  /Name/i

17     - assert  expected  <input#name> to exist in the DOM
```

If you change the search text to make the command fail, you will get the same error message either way (except that the second version will show an assertion, as above). If you find it more readable to include `.should('exist')` on find commands to make the assertion explicit, feel free to do so.

Cypress supports many assertions from Chai, Sinon, and jQuery. You can read about them here: docs.cypress.io/guides/references/assertions.html.

Interacting with the server

The end-to-end tests in this chapter use the real server to test the integration between the server and the client.

This Cypress checkout test, like the one you wrote with Jest, checks the number of items the café offers. Your Jest test got the number from the mock data (`items.length`), so it knew exactly how many items to expect. In your Cypress test, the items load from the real server instead. Though the server does currently return 10 items, you might add more items to Code Café in the future.

The most useful tests are not those you write and run once, but rather those that continually check your code base for issues throughout development. It is better not to assert a specific number of items in this test, so that you do not have to update it when you add or remove items from the server.

Update the test so that it is more flexible.

Listing 22.9 Removing the specific number of items (`checkout.cy.js`)

```
describe('checkout', () => {
  it('user can build a cart and place an order', () => {
    cy.visit('/');
    cy.findAllByTestId('thumbnail-component').should('have.length', 10);
    cy.findByRole('link', { name: /Tea/i }).click();
...
```

Cypress also supports mocking the server, in which case it would be safe to assert a specific number without risking a test failure if the server changes. But the trade-off is that you would no longer be testing server-client integration.

Testing errors in the checkout flow

Now that you've tested the checkout happy path, create a test for checkout errors in a new it block in `checkout.cy.js`.

Unfortunately, Cypress cannot start with a mock cart, so your new test will have to build the cart out again. However, you can reuse your earlier code to start at the home page, add a tea to the cart, navigate to the cart page, enter a name, and click the Order Now button.

This time, enter the ZIP code 99999 to trigger an error from the server, and then check for the correct alert message.

Listing 22.10 Cart error test (`checkout.cy.js`)

```
describe('checkout', () => {
  it('user can build a cart and place an order', () => {
    ...
  });

  it('shows an error when the order fails', () => {
    cy.visit('/');
    cy.findByRole('link', { name: /Tea/i }).click();
    cy.findByRole('button', { name: /Add to Cart/i }).click();
    cy.findByRole('link', { name: /Cart/i }).click();
    cy.findByLabelText(/Name/i).type('Big Nerd Ranch');
    cy.findByLabelText(/ZIP Code/i).type('99999');
    cy.findByRole('button', { name: /Order Now/i }).click();
    cy.findByText(/There was an error/i);
    cy.findByText(/We don't ship to 99999/i);
  });
});
```

This test uses simpler code to put an item in the cart, since the happy path test already checks that the cart badge updates with the correct quantity for multiple items.

Save your file and run the updated `checkout.cy.js` test in Cypress. It passes.

Although Cypress does not show the console error by default, it would still be nice to assert that the error logged. Like Jest, Cypress can spy on the console.

Listing 22.11 Testing **console.error** (checkout.cy.js)

```
describe('checkout', () => {
  it('user can build a cart and place an order', () => {
    ...
  });

  it('shows an error when the order fails', () => {
    cy.visit('/');
    cy.visit('/', {
      onBeforeLoad(win) {
        cy.stub(win.console, 'error').as('consoleError');
      },
    });
    cy.findByRole('link', { name: /Tea/i }).click();
    ...
    cy.findByText(/There was an error/i);
    cy.findByText(/We don't ship to 99999/i);
    cy.get('@consoleError').should('be.calledOnce');
  });
});
```

Each **cy.visit** call creates a *window*. **onBeforeLoad** gives you access to the moment just before Cypress loads the window. In this case, you stub **console.error** (which replaces the console error function with a blank one) and save a reference to it as consoleError. (**cy.stub** and **jest.mock** provide essentially the same functionality; they just have different names and slightly different APIs.) After the test workflow, cy.get('@consoleError') returns the stub reference, and the test expects the stub to have been called once.

Save your file and run your test again to confirm that it still passes (Figure 22.12).

Figure 22.12 Passing checkout tests

Testing the Flow to View and Delete Orders

Because you use the live back end and do not mock the API, you can add a test to view the orders page and check the workflow to complete and delete an order.

Add a new file in your e2e directory called orders.cy.js to test the flow for viewing and deleting an order. Since only associates can view and delete orders, you will need to begin by logging in an authorized user. For now, duplicate the login flow from your login test. Then add a tea to the cart and check out. You can also duplicate most of the checkout flow from previous tests. (Later, you will factor out both duplicate flows.)

(This test will fail if you run it. You will fix it in the next step.)

Listing 22.12 Adding a view-and-delete orders test (orders.cy.js)

```
describe('orders', () => {
  it('user can view and delete orders', () => {
    cy.visit('/');
    cy.findByRole('link', { name: /Log In/i }).click();
    cy.findByLabelText(/Username/i).type('Tester');
    cy.findByLabelText(/Password/i).type('pass');
    cy.findByRole('button', { name: /Log In/i }).click();
    cy.findByRole('link', { name: /Tea/i }).click();
    cy.findByRole('button', { name: /Add to Cart/i }).click();
    cy.findByRole('link', { name: /Cart/i }).click();
    cy.findByLabelText(/Name/i).type('Big Nerd Ranch');
    cy.findByLabelText(/ZIP Code/i).type('30316');
    cy.findByRole('button', { name: /Order Now/i }).click();
    cy.findByRole('link', { name: /Orders/i }).click();
    cy.findByRole('button', { name: /Delete Order/i }).click();
    cy.findByText(/No Orders/i);
  });
});
```

After logging in and placing an order, the test clicks the Orders link to go to the orders page. From the orders page, the test clicks the button to delete the order. Since the test placed only one order, it asserts that the text "No Orders" exists on the page.

From the Cypress window, run your `orders.cy.js` file. The test fails (Figure 22.13).

Figure 22.13 Delete Order failure

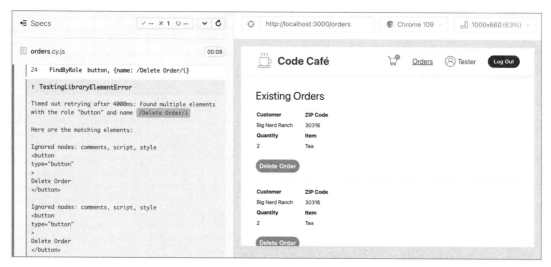

Why did it fail? Scroll up in the Cypress output to find the beginning of the red text. The error says the test failed because it found multiple elements with the role `"button"` and the name `Delete Order`. **findBy** expects to find exactly one matching element; if there is more than one, it throws an error.

Although this test places only one order, you can see in the browser window on the right that there are several existing orders, each with a **Delete Order** button. Why? Because the server is not cleared between test runs, it sees the orders from all previous test runs.

You might think that a quick fix for this issue would be to restart the server before each test run. Although this would clear existing orders from previous runs, a single run can contain multiple tests that place orders.

It is important to isolate the conditions needed for a test to run so that it does not interfere with other tests. Before this particular test starts, you need to clear the orders to ensure that no previous orders are hanging around.

(As your application grows, you might want to run tests in parallel to save time and resources. This would involve splitting up your test suites and running them separately but simultaneously. You would need to take additional steps to ensure that no new orders are placed while you test the orders workflow. But for this book you will continue to run your tests in sequence, so you do not need to worry about this.)

Clearing the orders

The API includes an endpoint for deleting all orders. Cypress can send network requests, so make a DELETE request to /api/orders to erase all the orders at the beginning of the orders test workflow.

Listing 22.13 Clearing all orders (`orders.cy.js`)

```
describe('orders', () => {
  before(() => {
    cy.request('DELETE', '/api/orders');
  });
  it('user can view and delete orders', () => {
...
```

In Cypress, the hook that runs once before all the tests is named `before`, not `beforeAll` as it is in Jest. (Cypress also has a `beforeEach`, which behaves like `beforeEach` in Jest.)

`cy.request` sends requests to the server. The endpoint at /api/orders will delete all the orders.

Save your file and run your `orders.cy.js` test again. This time, it passes.

Factoring Out Custom Commands

In writing your three end-to-end tests, you have used some of the same workflows over and over. Duplicating code is tedious and makes your testing code (or any code) harder to read and maintain. To avoid repeating common bits of code, Cypress allows you to create custom commands.

Open the file `cypress/support/commands.js`, where you imported the command set from the Cypress Testing Library. This file includes examples to follow when writing new commands or overwriting existing commands.

Parent commands start a new command chain. *Child commands*, such as the **click** chainer, chain off a parent or off another child command. *Dual commands*, such as the **contains** chainer, combine elements of both parent and child commands; you will rarely use them.

At the bottom of the file, add a command for logging in to Code Café, using the workflow duplicated in the login and orders tests. Since this will be a new command chain, follow the sample code for creating a parent command.

Listing 22.14 Adding the **login** command (`commands.js`)

```
...
// -- This will overwrite an existing command --
// Cypress.Commands.overwrite('visit', (originalFn, url, options) => { ... })
import '@testing-library/cypress/add-commands';

Cypress.Commands.add('login', (username = 'Tester', password = 'pass') => {
  cy.findByRole('link', { name: /Log In/i }).click();
  cy.findByLabelText(/Username/i).type(username);
  cy.findByLabelText(/Password/i).type(password);
  cy.findByRole('button', { name: /Log In/i }).click();
});
```

The custom **login** command is a JavaScript function, where the first argument is the name of the command, and the second argument is a callback function. You can also pass arguments to the callback function. You need different usernames for your tests, so you allow the caller to specify the username and password, and you provide default values if the caller does not specify them.

Now replace the workflow in the login test with your new command, using the default values for the username and password.

Listing 22.15 Replacing the login workflow with a command (`login.cy.js`)

```
describe('login', () => {
  it('shows logged-in user\'s username', () => {
    cy.visit('/');
    cy.findByRole('link', { name: /Log In/i }).click();
    cy.findByLabelText(/Username/i).type('Tester');
    cy.findByLabelText(/Password/i).type('pass');
    cy.findByRole('button', { name: /Log In/i }).click();
    cy.login();
    cy.findByRole('link', { name: /Log In/i }).should('not.exist');
...
```

(You will replace the workflow in the orders test in a moment.)

Save your files. In the Cypress window, run the login spec again to confirm that it still passes.

You also have a shortened checkout workflow that you duplicate in the checkout error test and the orders test.

Add a new custom command for checking out. Allow the caller to specify the ZIP code. (This is not intended to replace the happy path workflow for checking out, which is more in depth.)

Listing 22.16 Adding the **checkout** command (`commands.js`)

```
...
// -- This will overwrite an existing command --
// Cypress.Commands.overwrite('visit', (originalFn, url, options) => { ... })
import '@testing-library/cypress/add-commands';

Cypress.Commands.add('login', (username = 'Tester', password = 'pass') => {
  ...
});

Cypress.Commands.add('checkout', (name = 'Customer', zipCode = '30316') => {
  cy.findByRole('link', { name: /Tea/i }).click();
  cy.findByRole('button', { name: /Add to Cart/i }).click();
  cy.findByRole('link', { name: /Cart/i }).click();
  cy.findByLabelText(/Name/i).type(name);
  cy.findByLabelText(/Zip Code/i).type(zipCode);
  cy.findByRole('button', { name: /Order Now/i }).click();
});
```

Now replace the workflow in the checkout test with the new command.

Listing 22.17 Replacing the checkout workflow with a command (checkout.cy.js)

```
describe('checkout', () => {
  ...
  it('shows an error when the order fails', () => {
    ...
    });
    cy.findByRole('link', { name: /Tea/i }).click();
    cy.findByRole('button', { name: /Add to Cart/i }).click();
    cy.findByRole('link', { name: /Cart/i }).click();
    cy.findByLabelText(/Name/i).type('Big Nerd Ranch');
    cy.findByLabelText(/ZIP Code/i).type('99999');
    cy.findByRole('button', { name: /Order Now/i }).click();
    cy.checkout('Big Nerd Ranch', '99999');
    cy.findByText(/There was an error/i);
  ...
```

You pass the username *Big Nerd Ranch* and the ZIP code 99999 to the command as arguments to overwrite the default values.

Save your files and run the checkout test again to confirm that it passes.

Next, refactor the orders test to use both of your custom commands.

Listing 22.18 Refactoring the orders test (orders.cy.js)

```
describe('orders', () => {
  ...
  it('user can view and delete orders', () => {
    cy.visit('/');
    cy.findByRole('link', { name: /Log In/i }).click();
    cy.findByLabelText(/Username/i).type('Tester');
    cy.findByLabelText(/Password/i).type('pass');
    cy.findByRole('button', { name: /Log In/i }).click();
    cy.findByRole('link', { name: /Tea/i }).click();
    cy.findByRole('button', { name: /Add to Cart/i }).click();
    cy.findByRole('link', { name: /Cart/i }).click();
    cy.findByLabelText(/Name/i).type('Big Nerd Ranch');
    cy.findByLabelText(/ZIP Code/i).type('30316');
    cy.findByRole('button', { name: /Order Now/i }).click();
    cy.login();
    cy.checkout();
    cy.findByRole('link', { name: /Orders/i }).click();
  ...
```

You can replace a lot of code with these two commands. Custom commands save you typing and allow you to focus on the unique workflows in each test.

Save your files and confirm that all your tests still pass.

Invisible Elements

One of the main benefits of running end-to-end tests in a browser is that the browser actually draws the elements on the page. This means that CSS applies.

Let's make a couple of edits to prove this. First, hide the checkout inputs with CSS:

Listing 22.19 Hiding elements with CSS (`Cart.css`)

```
...
.cart-component label {
  ...
}

.cart-component input {
  display: none;
  border-radius: 5px;
...
```

Save your file and, in a new terminal tab, run your Jest component tests (npm run test). They still pass: Even though the inputs would not be visible to the user, the tests run through all the workflows.

Now run checkout.cy.js in the Cypress window. This test fails, and Cypress displays a helpful error message about why it could not type in the input field (Figure 22.14):

Figure 22.14 Cypress test failure

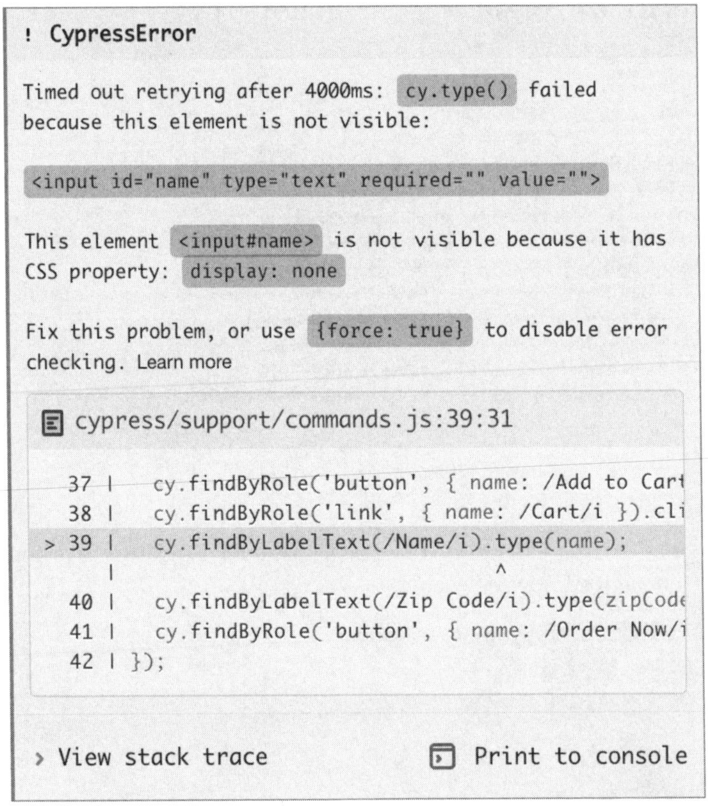

```
!  CypressError

Timed out retrying after 4000ms:  cy.type()  failed
because this element is not visible:

<input id="name" type="text" required="" value="">

This element  <input#name>  is not visible because it has
CSS property:  display: none

Fix this problem, or use  {force: true}  to disable error
checking.  Learn more

 ▤ cypress/support/commands.js:39:31

   37 |    cy.findByRole('button', { name: /Add to Cart
   38 |    cy.findByRole('link', { name: /Cart/i }).cli
 > 39 |    cy.findByLabelText(/Name/i).type(name);
      |                               ^
   40 |    cy.findByLabelText(/Zip Code/i).type(zipCode
   41 |    cy.findByRole('button', { name: /Order Now/i
   42 | });

 › View stack trace              ▣ Print to console
```

Because the `orders.cy.js` test also uses the checkout form, it will fail as well. Run it to verify this.

Cypress allows you to disable error checking for hidden elements with `{ force: true }`. But generally, you do not want to disable it, so you can catch bugs such as this one.

Revert your change to the CSS file.

Listing 22.20 Reverting the CSS change (`Cart.css`)

```
...
.cart-component label {
  ...
}

.cart-component input {
  display: none;
  border-radius: 5px;
...
```

Rerun `checkout.cy.js` to confirm that it passes, as before.

Avoiding Flaky Tests

As we said in Chapter 20, flaky tests sometimes pass and sometimes fail, even if there are no code changes to the test or project. This often happens because the browser page takes longer than usual to load, and an element is not present on the screen when expected.

Cypress protects against flaky tests by making each command retryable. Still, to avoid flaky tests that fail if the timing is slightly off, your assertions should not target elements that rely on timing, such as animations or loaders. Generally, this means not making assertions about loading or animation while it is in progress. Instead, make assertions only about the page's final content by waiting for the loader to be gone (when the loading is complete) or the animation to be done.

Conclusion

Stop your testing by pressing Control-C in the terminal tab running Cypress. Now run all your tests as they would run during CI with the command `npm run cypress:run` (Figure 22.15).

Figure 22.15 Cypress CI run

```
================================================================================

  (Run Finished)


       Spec                                   Tests  Passing  Failing  Pending  Skipped
  ┌────────────────────────────────────────────────────────────────────────────┐
  │ ✓ checkout.spec.js          00:03        2        2        -        -        - │
  ├────────────────────────────────────────────────────────────────────────────┤
  │ ✓ login.spec.js             00:01        1        1        -        -        - │
  ├────────────────────────────────────────────────────────────────────────────┤
  │ ✓ orders.spec.js            00:02        1        1        -        -        - │
  └────────────────────────────────────────────────────────────────────────────┘
    ✓ All specs passed!         00:07        4        4        -        -        -
```

Although the three tests do not take very long to run, they are noticeably slower than the unit and integration tests from the last chapter. For a larger application, the extra time would be much more noticeable.

One reason for this is that your end-to-end tests have to execute most of the checkout flow to set up for other workflow tests. In the integration tests, you pass in a mock cart prop, which is faster.

Another reason is that the end-to-end tests have to start a real browser for each test, and that takes far more time than using jsdom.

So, why use end-to-end tests at all? Because these tests use the real server, they help test the integration between the server and your React application. Even if the tests mock the server, they help you check that elements are actually visible, which is possible only when the browser actually draws the page. Cypress can also test in multiple browsers, in case they differ in how they they draw the page or other behaviors.

In many cases, you can write most of the tests you need as integration or unit tests, which are faster than end-to-end tests. Then you can write just a few end-to-end tests for testing the integration with the server and focusing on important workflows to catch covered elements.

In the next chapter, you will wrap up your work on Code Café by building the app for production use.

For the More Curious: Cypress Media Files

When Cypress runs in headless mode, it saves screenshots and videos. You should not commit these files when using version control.

Create React App created a file for you called .gitignore, which lists files that Git should not commit to version control. In this file, you can list directories or specific files or patterns to ignore. You can also include .gitignore files in subdirectories to extend the rules. Adding the following lines to the .gitignore file will ensure that Git does not commit the Cypress media directories:

```
# cypress
/cypress/screenshots
/cypress/videos
```

For more reading on .gitignore, see git-scm.com/book/en/v2/Git-Basics-Recording-Changes-to-the-Repository#_ignoring.

For the More Curious: Cypress Network Requests

Cypress can do many things with network requests.

It can send requests to set up test data, as you saw in this chapter when you used a DELETE request to clear the cart. It can also wait for requests to complete, so you can verify that a network request is done before looking at the browser for updates. This is particularly helpful for slower requests that might otherwise time out.

Cypress can also make assertions with network requests, so your test that places an order could have made a GET request to /api/orders to check that the order made it to the server.

And, if needed, Cypress can stub requests so it does not make actual server calls at all.

To learn more about using network requests in Cypress tests, see docs.cypress.io/guides/guides/network-requests.html.

Silver Challenge: Testing Phone Number Formatting

Test with Cypress that the checkout form adds dashes to the text in the phone number field as expected.

For example, entering 5555555555 should result in a value of 555-555-5555, and entering 555-5555555 should also result in a value of 555-555-5555.

When you are done, compare your code with the Jest version you wrote for a similar challenge in the previous chapter.

Silver Challenge: Testing Cart Details

Test with Cypress that the tax details adjust properly when the ZIP code changes.

Also, check that adding different items and multiples of the same item both work as expected.

When you are done, compare your code with the Jest version you wrote for a similar challenge in the previous chapter.

Silver Challenge: Testing Removing an Item from the Cart

Test with Cypress that the button to remove an item from the cart works as expected.

When you are done, compare your code with the Jest version you wrote for a similar challenge in the previous chapter.

Gold Challenge: Additional Tests

Implement any other tests that you can come up with, using either Cypress or Jest.

23

Building Your Application

Now that Code Café is fully coded and (for the purposes of this book) fully tested, you are ready to build it for production use.

So far, you have done all your work in development mode, using npm start to run the server built into Create React App. By the end of this chapter, you will have a folder of files ready for you to deploy onto a production server.

Manifest

First, you need to update the application's public/manifest.json file. This file contains information that the browser will consume. Locate and open the file in Visual Studio Code.

Update manifest.json to reflect the app's title and color scheme.

Listing 23.1 Updating the manifest (manifest.json)

```
{
  "short_name": "React App",
  "short_name": "Café",
  "name": "Create React App Sample",
  "name": "Code Café",
  "icons": [
    ...
  "start_url": ".",
  "display": "standalone",
  "theme_color": "#000000",
  "theme_color": "#B9A28D",
  "background_color": "#ffffff"
}
```

The short_name field is used if there is not enough space to display the full name – for example, on the home screen of a phone.

An app's name should not exceed 45 characters, and the short name should not exceed 12 characters. You use Code Café as the app name and Café as the short name. You could also have used a verbose app name such as Big Nerd Ranch Presents: Code Café and then used Code Café as the short name.

The OS sometimes uses the theme_color to adjust the display. For example, Chrome on Android uses it to color certain browser UI elements, such as the address bar. You update the theme_color to match the base color you use throughout Code Café.

If the user loads the app from a bookmark, the `background_color` will show before the app loads the stylesheet. Since the background for Code Café is white, no changes are needed.

The manifest is particularly important if you are making a progressive web application, or PWA (which is outside the scope of this book). You can read more about the manifest at developer.mozilla.org/en-US/docs/Web/Manifest.

Building the Application

In a terminal separate from the one running your app, `cd` into your `code-cafe` directory.

Then build your application with the following command:

```
npm run build
```

It will take about a minute to complete.

When the build completes, you will see `Compiled successfully.` followed by information about file sizes and details about deployment options:

```
Compiled successfully.

File sizes after gzip:

  63.16 kB  build/static/js/main.e09ba5e9.js
  1.93 kB   build/static/css/main.e5132e68.css
  1.79 kB   build/static/js/787.4539c236.chunk.js

The project was built assuming it is hosted at /.
You can control this with the homepage field in your package.json.

The build folder is ready to be deployed.
You may serve it with a static server:

  npm install -g serve
  serve -s build

Find out more about deployment here:

  https://cra.link/deployment
```

(The file sizes you see might differ from the ones listed above.)

Look back in Visual Studio Code. Now there is a `build` directory, which contains all the files you need to deploy your website to production.

Expand the `build` directory to see its contents. Next, expand the `static` subdirectory and the `css`, `js`, and `media` directories under it.

Every file in these directories has a hash in its name. This hash stays constant as long as the file does not change, and it updates if the file does change. This means that the files under the `static` directory are safe for users and content-delivery networks, or CDNs, to cache for long periods of time.

What do these files actually contain? The `main.*.css` file (where `*` takes the place of the hash in the filename) has the combined and minified result of all the CSS files you imported. The `main.*.js` file has the combined and minified version of the JavaScript your application needs. In `787.*.js` (which might begin with a different number), you will find web-vitals, a package that Create React App imports in `src/reportWebVitals.js`.

How does the webpack build process decide what JavaScript your application needs? Starting with `src/index.js`, it traverses all the imported files and dependencies and places them in `main.*.js`. This means that if you install a dependency and never use it, it will not end up in the file. It also means that your test files (such as `App.test.js`), test dependencies (such as @testing-library/react), and build dependencies (such as ESLint) do not end up in `main.*.js`, because nothing under `src/index.js` imports them.

You can learn more about the production build at create-react-app.dev/docs/production-build.

Deploying Your Application

There are various ways to deploy your site, each with its own unique configuration. In general, you need to place the files from the `build` folder onto a web server.

To deploy Code Café, you would need some additional code on the server to support client-side routing. You would also need to deploy the back-end server and proxy the API and websocket requests.

It is outside the scope of this book to cover all the steps you need to deploy Code Café online. To learn more about options for deployment, follow the link in your terminal output from after you built the app: cra.link/deployment.

Conclusion

You did it! Code Café is complete.

Code Café includes prop types to help future developers understand the application and ESLint to enforce code style. You used **useReducer** to handle complex state for the cart. You used React Router and conditional rendering to create your application with multiple pages that respond to changes in that cart state. And you used additional hooks such as **useState**, **useEffect**, and **useRef** to interact with the server, respond to user events, and collect input with forms.

You also added advanced features to your application by sharing state with context and composing components to make alerts for the cart. And you optimized your application with **memo**, **useMemo**, and **useCallback**.

In the next two chapters, you will leave Code Café behind and learn more about performance tuning in React – with the help of some playful penguins.

24

Data Loading

In the last two chapters of this book, you will investigate several issues that affect app performance and learn about more ways to optimize your apps. You will not build your own app in this section of the book; instead, you will work with an app we provide for you in your downloaded resources file.

In this chapter, you will examine the amount of data coming across the network and its effect on performance. You will also see two ways you can improve the performance of apps: keeping an eye on the size of image files and using lazy loading for large files that you do not need throughout the app.

Begin by setting up the Performance Penguins application. In your downloaded resources file, locate the `performance` folder. Copy it into your `react-book` directory.

In your terminal, navigate to `react-book/performance` and run `npm install`. Once the install finishes, run `npm start` to make sure the app runs.

If you run into any issues with this app, check the forum for this book for help.

Once the app starts, you will see the home page of the Performance Penguins website in your browser (Figure 24.1):

Figure 24.1 Welcome!

Production Build

What you have running is the development server from Create React App. To analyze the app's performance, you need to look at the production version. Although the production build does not live reload as you edit files, it gives you details on how things will load for your users.

Exit the current server by pressing Control-C in the terminal window. Run npm run serve to serve a production build, and visit http://localhost:3001 in your browser.

(npm run serve is not a standard React command; it is a command we created for this project.)

You will see the same home page as before.

Analysis

You are ready to analyze the application. Because you are running it locally, you can load a lot of data very quickly.

Let's see how the website loads for a user on a 3G network connection.

Open the DevTools to the Network tab. Change the throttling setting to Fast 3G and check the box for Disable cache (Figure 24.2).

Figure 24.2 Setting network throttling

Now refresh the page. It spends a long time on a blank white screen while it loads the content.

Look at the bottom of the Network tab for some statistics about the load time (Figure 24.3):

Figure 24.3 Network statistics

| 7 requests | 2.5 MB transferred | 2.5 MB resources | Finish: 15.73 s | DOMContentLoaded: 8.90 s | Load: 8.90 s |

To load the home page for your application, the browser has to load 2.5MB over seven requests. It takes 8.90 seconds to initially load the DOM and 15.73 seconds before it finishes. (As usual, your results might be different.)

Look at the individual requests to get a better idea of what the browser is loading (Figure 24.4). (You might need to set the filter to All to see the requests.)

Figure 24.4 Network requests

Name	Status	Type	Initiator	Size	Time
localhost	200	document	Other	962 B	581 ms
main.eaef045e.js	200	script	(index)	1.4 MB	8.26 s
main.e6c13ad2.css	200	stylesheet	(index)	645 B	589 ms
penguinFull.05b05cff0369c3a3c104.j...	200	jpeg	react-dom.produc...	1.0 MB	6.80 s
favicon.png	200	png	Other	13.0 kB	730 ms
manifest.json	200	manifest	Other	808 B	579 ms
logo192.png	200	png	Other	78.7 kB	1.44 s

The table below describes each file. (As in Chapter 23, the * in each filename takes the place of the generated hash.)

File	Description
localhost	The index.html file, which provides the base HTML.
main.*.js	The compiled JavaScript for the React application.
main.*.css	The compiled CSS for the website.
penguinFull.*.jpg	The image in the header.
favicon.png	The site's favicon.
manifest.json	The site's manifest.
logo192.png	The site's 192 × 192 px logo.
react_devtools_backend.js	You might not see this file, which is injected by the React DevTools if they are enabled. You can safely ignore it.

Looking at the file sizes, the biggest files are the penguin image at 1.0MB and main.*.js at 1.4MB.

Large Images

The first thing to address is the large size of the penguin image. Click the network request for the image to get more details. Switch to the preview pane and check out the dimensions of the image in the footer (Figure 24.5).

Figure 24.5 Penguin image dimensions

This image loads at 1840 × 2760 px.

Now let's look at where it renders in the header. Right-click the penguin image in the header and select Inspect. Then select the computed pane in the DevTools (Figure 24.6).

Figure 24.6 Image element dimensions

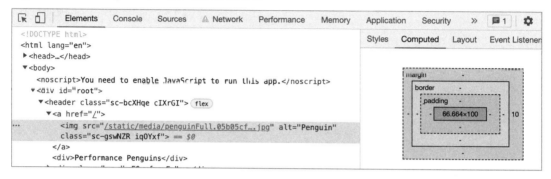

The image displayed on the page is only 66 × 100 px.

To get high-quality images on displays with greater pixel density (such as retina screens), you might want the source image to be larger than 66 × 100 px. But the current image is much bigger than that, so the file size is much larger than necessary.

Open Performance Penguins in Visual Studio Code. The project already includes a smaller penguin image file. In Header.js, swap the large image for the smaller logo.

Listing 24.1 Using a smaller penguin image file (Header.js)

```
import styled from 'styled-components';
import { Link, NavLink } from 'react-router-dom';
import Penguin from '../images/penguinFull.jpg';
import Penguin from '../images/penguinLogo.jpg';

function Header() {
...
```

After making this edit, you will need to exit the existing server with Control-C and rerun npm run serve to rebuild the production site.

Next, navigate back to the Network tab and refresh the page (Figure 24.7).

Figure 24.7 Network requests with a smaller image

Name	Status	Type	Initiator	Size	Time
localhost	200	document	Other	962 B	591 ms
main.27aaee8c.js	200	script	(index)	1.4 MB	8.34 s
main.e6c13ad2.css	200	stylesheet	(index)	645 B	583 ms
penguinLogo.12f49ee446578f21fa63...	200	jpeg	react-dom.produc...	25.0 kB	805 ms
favicon.png	200	png	Other	13.0 kB	726 ms
manifest.json	200	manifest	Other	808 B	582 ms
logo192.png	200	png	Other	78.7 kB	1.01 s

| 7 requests | 1.5 MB transferred | 1.5 MB resources | Finish: 10.60 s | DOMContentLoaded: 8.99 s | Load: 8.99 s |

Now the Network tab shows penguinLogo.*.jpg, which is only 25KB. And with just that change, you have reduced the finish time by 5 seconds; now it is 10.6 seconds.

If you are working with an image-heavy website, there are other improvements you can make, such as using CSS and other rules to load images of the correct size based on the pixel density of the viewer's screen.

There are also some build plugins that can automate resizing for you. If your project does not use one of these tools, it is important for you as a developer to pay attention to the file size and dimensions of the images provided to you. If you get images that are too large, work with your team and designers to get smaller images.

If you are working with *scalable vector graphics*, or SVGs, there are a couple of things to consider. First, SVGs do not have a fixed size; instead, their contents specify a path to draw with a certain precision based on decimal points. Design tools often generate SVGs with a larger number of decimal points than necessary for displaying the image on a website. You can use an SVG optimizer to reduce the number of decimal points without otherwise harming the image.

Also, it is worth looking at the source of SVGs you receive for a project. Occasionally, a generated SVG contains only a JPG or PNG in hexadecimal. This means the file is larger than necessary, because it is no longer in binary – and it is not actually a vector graphic.

Analyzing JavaScript Files

The next thing to look at in Performance Penguins is why the main.*.js file is 1.4MB.

Since the build prepared this file for production, opening it and reading the source is unlikely to be useful. However, there are other ways to analyze a file.

Your production build created a .js.map file, and your downloaded project has source-map-explorer, an npm package that helps analyze .js.map files.

In your terminal, stop the app with Control-C, then run npm run analyze.

Your browser will open to a page that looks like Figure 24.8:

Figure 24.8 JavaScript file analysis

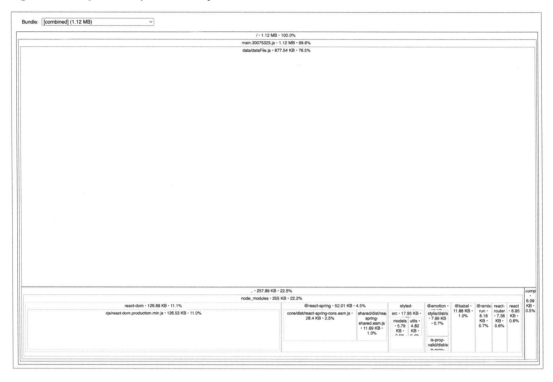

This page maps items by their size and nesting hierarchy, so the sizes of the blocks you see correspond to the amount of space each item uses.

This kind of mapping is not always easy to interpret. Focus on the largest blocks, especially the ones without children. The biggest one is data/dataFile.js (Figure 24.9).

Figure 24.9 Analysis of the largest block

/ • 1.12 MB • 100.0%
main.30075325.js • 1.12 MB • 99.6%
data/dataFile.js • 877.54 KB • 76.5%

What is this? src/components/Data.js, which is the component for the Penguin Data page, imports src/data/dataFile.js, which is the data that the browser will process and display on the page.

Next, look at blocks with only a few children. These children are often npm packages (Figure 24.10).

Figure 24.10 Analysis of packages

react-dom, in the lower-left corner, is the largest of these. It is an essential package that powers React.

The third-largest piece is @react-spring, which shows to the right of react-dom. react-spring is the package that powers the animation in the Penguin Game page. `src/components/Game.js` imports this package.

The code after that is all small. Sometimes, a lot of small pieces can add up to a very large file. But in this case, the remaining parts total less than 60KB.

The home page does not need the data file for the Penguin Data page or the animations for the Penguin Game page. How can you change the code so the home page loads faster – even on a slow connection?

Lazy Loading

The solution is *lazy loading*, a technique that allows your application to load components only when it needs them. This is also known as *code splitting*. You will implement lazy loading in Performance Penguins so that the data file and animations will load not with the home page, but only when the app needs them.

You will also use special import syntax to tell webpack that you want to load an import asynchronously. This is called a *dynamic* import. Dynamic imports invoke `import` as a function. When you invoke `import`, it returns a promise that resolves when it receives the file.

To add lazy loading, you will use two new React features, **lazy** and **Suspense**. **lazy** is a function for rendering a dynamic import as a component. It accepts an arrow function, which it invokes when a caller wants to render the component onscreen.

Consider this example:

```
const Thing = lazy(() => import('./components/Thing'));
```

When <Thing /> first renders, React invokes the dynamic import to load the code for the **Thing** component. Once the code loads, <Thing /> will render onscreen.

So what happens while <Thing /> is loading? This is where the React component **Suspense** comes in: **Suspense** provides fallback code for the lazy-loaded component.

You place **Suspense** higher in the component tree than the lazy-loaded component. During loading, React navigates up the component tree from the lazy-loaded component to find the closest **Suspense** component. Then it replaces all of the **Suspense** component's descendants with the fallback code. Once loading is complete, the descendants and the newly loaded component display onscreen.

In Performance Penguins, update App.js to use lazy loading. (You will need to reindent the code nested in **Suspense**.)

Listing 24.2 Adding lazy loading (App.js)

```
import {
  ...
} from 'react-router-dom';
import { lazy, Suspense } from 'react';
import Header from './components/Header';
import NotFound from './components/NotFound';
import Home from './components/Home';
import Data from './components/Data';
import Game from './components/Game';

const Data = lazy(() => import('./components/Data'));
const Game = lazy(() => import('./components/Game'));

function App() {
  return (
    <Router>
      <Header />
      <Suspense fallback={<div>Loading...</div>}>
        <Routes>
          ...
        </Routes>
      </Suspense>
    </Router>
...
```

Now you are lazy loading two components, **Data** and **Game**. Let's see what this change does to the site's loading time.

Restart your server with npm run serve. Refresh the home page and check the Network tab (Figure 24.11).

Figure 24.11 Network requests with lazy loading

Name	Status	Type	Initiator	Size	Time
▤ localhost	200	document	Other	962 B	594 ms
◎ main.d5b14a2c.js	200	script	(index)	207 kB	1.92 s
☑ main.e6c13ad2.css	200	stylesheet	(index)	645 B	593 ms
▮ penguinLogo.12f49ee446578f21fa63...	200	jpeg	react-dom.produc...	25.0 kB	789 ms
☐ favicon.png	200	png	Other	13.0 kB	719 ms
☐ manifest.json	200	manifest	Other	808 B	592 ms
☐ logo192.png	200	png	Other	78.7 kB	1.09 s

| 7 requests | 326 kB transferred | 324 kB resources | Finish: 4.24 s | DOMContentLoaded: 2.53 s | Load: 2.53 s |

Now the page loads in 2.53 seconds and finishes in 4.24 seconds on fast 3G, a reduction of 6 seconds from the previous build.

Leave the Network tab open and click the Penguin Game link in the website's header. You will see Loading... on the page while it fetches the content, then the Penguin Game will appear.

Look back in the Network tab: Two new .chunk.js files have loaded (Figure 24.12).

Figure 24.12 New .chunk.js files

Name	Status	Type	Initiator	Size	Time
localhost	200	document	Other	962 B	594 ms
main.d5b14a2c.js	200	script	(index)	207 kB	1.92 s
main.e6c13ad2.css	200	stylesheet	(index)	645 B	593 ms
penguinLogo.12f49ee446578f21fa63.jpg	200	jpeg	react-dom.producti...	25.0 kB	789 ms
favicon.png	200	png	Other	13.0 kB	719 ms
manifest.json	200	manifest	Other	808 B	592 ms
logo192.png	200	png	Other	78.7 kB	1.09 s
139.a49ea08c.chunk.js	200	script	load script:41	64.7 kB	1.00 s
711.38582877.chunk.js	200	script	load script:41	2.2 kB	599 ms
penguinLogo.12f49ee446578f21fa63.jpg	200	jpeg	react-dom.producti...	25.0 kB	711 ms

This is lazy loading in action.

Before you added lazy loading, clicking the link would have instantly loaded the game, because all the files loaded with the home page. Now, these two files wait and load only when the game page loads.

So lazy loading involves a trade-off: Although the home page loads more quickly, now other pages take longer to load. However, React keeps each page in memory after it loads, so now you can quickly navigate between the home page and the Penguin Game without waiting for files to load again.

(What is a *chunk*? Chunks are specific to webpack; it uses them internally to manage the bundling process. Bundles are composed of chunks, and typically – though not always – chunks correspond directly to output bundles.)

Incidentally, you might have noticed that the penguinLogo image reloaded when you navigated to the game page. This happened because you disabled caching; it would not happen to normal users.

Naming the bundles

The names of the bundles and resulting .chunk.js files are currently just hashed values. For development and analysis purposes, it can be nice to know what is inside each chunk. You can use special comment syntax to tell webpack what to name the chunks. The comment looks like this:

```
/* webpackChunkName: "modulename" */
```

You can also assign the same name to two imports, and webpack will group them into a single chunk.

Update `App.js` to give the chunks names.

Listing 24.3 Adding chunk names (`App.js`)

```
...
import NotFound from './components/NotFound';
import Home from './components/Home';

const Data = lazy(() => import('./components/Data'));
const Data = lazy(() => import(
  /* webpackChunkName: "data" */
  './components/Data'
));
const Game = lazy(() => import('./components/Game'));
const Game = lazy(() => import(
  /* webpackChunkName: "game" */
  './components/Game'
));

function App() {
...
```

Stop and restart your server. In the browser, return to the home page, then click the link in the header to reopen the Penguin Game.

Check out the Network tab. As before, two chunk files load. Now one of them uses the name you set: `game.*.chunk.js`. Why does the other chunk file still have a generic name (Figure 24.13)?

Figure 24.13 Network chunk names

Name	Status	Type	Initiator	Size	Time
139.a49ea08c.chunk.js	200	script	load script:41	64.7 kB	4 ms
game.187dc9ce.chunk.js	200	script	load script:41	2.2 kB	4 ms
penguinLogo.12f49ee446578f21fa63.jpg	200	jpeg	react-dom.production....	25.0 kB	4 ms

Webpack separates the JavaScript that comes from dependencies (`node_modules`) from the JavaScript in your `src` folder for the game. You can name vendor chunks only by directly editing the webpack configuration, which is not recommended when using Create React App. Therefore, these files' names will always begin with a number. We can tell you this file contains @react-spring.

Other Considerations

You have looked at the effect of large file sizes on app performance. Two other considerations related to data loading are file compression and latency.

Most packages that list their size will also include the compression format. The most common compression format is currently gzip. However, Brotli is smaller, and most browsers support it.

Although the files whose sizes you see in source-map-explorer are uncompressed, files with a lot of repeated names, such as your data file, compress very well. Here is the size comparison:

File	Compression	Size
data.*.chunk.js	none	881KB
data.*.chunk.js.gz	gzip	130KB
data.*.chunk.js.br	Brotli	93KB

Though Performance Penguins' minimal server does not include compression, many web server programs automatically compress files before sending them to the client.

It can be confusing for a library that advertises itself as less than 25KB, minified and gzipped, to show up in your analysis as over 50KB. What you see includes minification but not compression.

Assuming your server uses compression, the compressed size is what will actually make it to your user. Therefore, that size is most important when trying to meet a benchmark loading speed.

When building an app that supports cellular users, it is also important to consider latency, which is normally higher on cellular connections. Each request to the server has lag as a result of latency. To address this, you can combine several pages into one bundle by using the same webpackChunkName in the pages' import statements. All files imported with the same webpackChunkName will end up in the same bundle.

It often makes sense to combine all the components of a single flow, such as checkout, into a single bundle, rather than using a bundle for each component.

Conclusion

Now Performance Penguins' pages load only the data necessary to display them, and the header image is much smaller.

Before you wrap up your work in this chapter, go back into the Network tab, uncheck the box for Disable Cache, and change the throttling setting from Fast 3G back to No Throttling.

In the next chapter, you will improve the application's rendering performance.

Gold Challenge: Lazy Loading

Make a copy of your Code Café project, analyze its files, and split it into multiple bundles.

You will need to install source-map-explorer and add the analyze script to package.json:

```
"analyze": "source-map-explorer 'build/static/js/*.js'",
```

Also, you will need to run npm run build after each adjustment to get the most up-to-date analysis. (For Performance Penguins, npm run serve also builds the app, so you do not have to run the builds separately.)

25

Component Speed

In the last chapter, you looked at how loading data affects your app's performance. In this final chapter, you will look at another aspect of performance: the speed at which components display on the screen, both when they initially render and when they update. To do this, you will use the React DevTools Profiler tool that you first saw in Chapter 19.

Throughout this chapter, the exact render times will vary between your machine and what this book shows. That is OK. Focus on the relative scale between fast and slow, and pay attention to the improvements in the times as you optimize the application.

Inspecting Performance

The React Profiler requires a development or profiling build of your application to work. If you are still running the production build of Performance Penguins with `npm run serve` in your terminal, exit it by pressing Control-C. Then start the app in development mode by running `npm start`. If it does not open automatically, open the Performance Penguins home page at http://localhost:3000/.

Next, in the DevTools, make sure you have disabled network throttling in the Network tab. If not, change Fast 3G back to No Throttling. Also, make sure the box for Disable Cache is unchecked.

Now open the Profiler tab. Click the blue record button. In the website's header, click the Penguin Data link, wait for the page to load, then click the record button again to stop profiling.

If this is your first time opening Penguin Data, the numbers toward the right side of the Profiler tab's menu bar will indicate two commits. A commit occurs each time React writes the virtual DOM to the real DOM. Generally speaking, it does this each time state changes and components re-render.

The first commit's flamegraph looks like Figure 25.1:

Figure 25.1 First commit's flamegraph

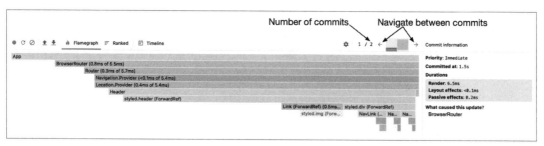

In the header, the colored bars between the commit navigation arrows make up a bar chart depicting the relative amount of time each commit required. The selected commit is blue. Here, it is much shorter than the other commit, because it took less time.

This commit includes the tasks for loading the screen while the dynamic import resolves. (If you previously visited the Penguin Data page, you will not see this commit, which is fine.)

View the flamegraph for the second commit by clicking the right arrow in the menu bar. It looks like Figure 25.2:

Figure 25.2 Second commit's flamegraph

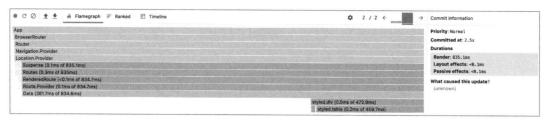

The right pane shows that the duration for this render was 835ms. The previous commit rendered in 6ms.

This flamegraph shows that the **Data** component, highlighted in yellow, takes up most of the time spent rendering. Though your specific results will be different, for our test, **Data** took 361ms to render, over a third of the 835ms for the page as a whole.

Now take a moment to familiarize yourself with the Penguin Data page by playing with the filters and sorting options. Be patient! The data table loads slowly, and it can look like the app freezes because the radio buttons and dropdowns do not show the new values for a couple of seconds.

Refresh the page to reset the filters.

Let's record the results of changing a filter. In the Profiler tab, click the blue record button. Next, on the Penguin Data page, click the radio button to filter the data for female penguins only. Wait for the table to update, then click the record button in the Profiler tab to stop recording.

The result looks like Figure 25.3:

Figure 25.3 Profiling the filter change

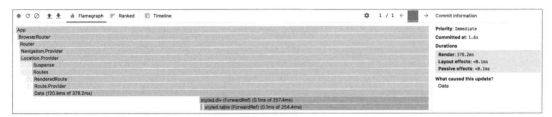

Though **Data** still takes up most of the rendering time, now it loads much more quickly – in only 120ms.

The flamegraph shows details about how long each component took to render. The timeline view shows a broader view of both the time it took to render components and the time it took to write the changes out to the browser.

Switch to the Profiler's timeline tool by clicking its calendar icon in the menu bar. Mouse over the different bars to see information about them (Figure 25.4).

Figure 25.4 Timeline view

The first blue bar shows the time spent rendering, which you saw broken down in the flamegraph. The purple bar to its right shows how long it took to commit the change to the DOM. The next line shows a breakdown of how long certain parts of the render took. The **Data** component took 120ms to render. (The first blue bar, which shows the full rendering time, includes this time.)

You will continue referring to the timeline view as you work on the rendering performance as a whole.

Transitions

Though users of Performance Penguins want access to its important penguin data, having the data controls lock up while the data loads is a bad user experience. It would be better if the radio buttons, for example, updated quickly to make the app feel more responsive.

React *transitions* allow your code to yield to important updates. React assigns a lower priority to changes that happen within a transition than to other updates. You will tell React that the filtered penguin data is low priority by updating it in a transition. As a result, React will prioritize the updates to the form fields, which are not in a transition, and keep the form responsive.

React uses state updates to track what is important versus what is a transition, so the first step in using a transition is to store the filtered data in state.

Update components/Data.js to store data in state. (You will need to reindent the newly nested code.)

Listing 25.1 Saving data in state (Data.js)

```
import { useState } from 'react';
import { useState, useEffect } from 'react';
import styled from 'styled-components';
...
function Data() {
  ...
  const [sort, setSort] = useState('age');
  const [renderedData, setRenderedData] = useState([]);
  const [totalRows, setTotalRows] = useState(DataFile.length);
  const updateSex = (e) => setSexFilter(e.target.value);
  const setExactAge = (age) => {
    setMinAge(age);
    setMaxAge(age);
  };

  useEffect(() => {
    let filteredData = [...DataFile];
    ...
    filteredData = filteredData.filter(({ age }) => age >= minAge);
    filteredData = filteredData.filter(({ age }) => age <= maxAge);

    const totalRows = filteredData.length;
    filteredData.sort((a, b) => a[sort] - b[sort]);
    setTotalRows(filteredData.length);
    setRenderedData(filteredData);
  }, [sexFilter, minAge, maxAge, sort]);

  return (
    ...
      <Table>
        <thead>
          ...
        </thead>
        <tbody>
          {filteredData.map(({
          {renderedData.map(({
            id, sex, height, weight, age,
...
```

You move the computation of the filtered data into a **useEffect** hook so that the computation reruns only when the filters or sorting change.

A side effect of this change is that the update to the filter and the update to the data are in separate render cycles. This already makes the radio buttons more responsive.

Because of the amount of data on this page, live reload does not always work. Save your file and refresh the page manually, then play with the filters to see the changes.

Unfortunately, now it is not obvious that an update is happening, since the table shows old data for a bit after the radio button updates. Also, the Matching Rows count does not update until the table updates. This is where a transition comes in.

useTransition from React will help fix both of these issues. It returns an array with two values: The first is a boolean called isPending that indicates whether a transition is waiting to be applied. The second is a function to start a new transition.

Add a transition in components/Data.js:

Listing 25.2 Starting a transition (Data.js)

```
import { useState, useEffect } from 'react';
import { useState, useEffect, useTransition } from 'react';
import styled from 'styled-components';
...
function Data() {
  ...
  const [renderedData, setRenderedData] = useState([]);
  const [totalRows, setTotalRows] = useState(DataFile.length);
  const [isPending, startTransition] = useTransition();
  const updateSex = (e) => setSexFilter(e.target.value);
  ...
  useEffect(() => {
    ...
    filteredData.sort((a, b) => a[sort] - b[sort]);
    setTotalRows(filteredData.length);
    setRenderedData(filteredData);
    startTransition(() => setRenderedData(filteredData));
  }, [sexFilter, minAge, maxAge, sort]);

  return (
    ...
      <Matches>
        ...
      </Matches>
      <Table>
      <Table style={{ opacity: isPending ? 0.5 : 1 }}>
        <thead>
...
```

You leave **setTotalRows** outside of the new transition. This flags it as an important update, so it will happen quickly.

On the other hand, you include **setRenderedData** inside the transition. This means React will defer its execution while other, more significant updates take place.

Finally, you take advantage of isPending to reduce the opacity of the table, graying it out while updates are pending. This will help cue the user that an update is taking place.

Refresh the page and play with the filters again to see the results.

Now let's use the Profiler to quantify the results of adding a transition. Refresh the page to reset the filters, and wait for the table to finish loading. Then click the Profiler's blue record button. On the website, click the radio button to filter the data for female penguins only. Wait for the table to finish updating, then click the record button again to stop profiling.

The flamegraph shows three commits. The first is the update to the filter state, the second is the update to the total rows, and the third is the transition update to the data.

Comparing three commits with the previous one commit is difficult in the flamegraph. Switch to the timeline view, where you can see data from all three commits at once (Figure 25.5).

Figure 25.5 Timeline with a transition

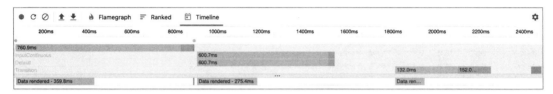

Take a look at the labels in gray. They are organized by the priority levels of the updates they represent.

The first row (whose label is hidden behind the blue bar) is Sync. It represents the highest-priority updates: the ones based on the state change that clicking the Female radio button causes.

InputContinuous and Default, shown next, process simultaneously. InputContinuous represents processing done before the transition starts. Default represents the update to the total rows in state.

Finally, Transition is the lowest-priority update. It updates renderedData.

Though the purple commit bars after the first two sets of updates are very short, React then spends 152ms committing the transition data.

The bottom of the timeline shows that **Data** renders three times, once for each of the updates. The first render changes the selection of the radio button, and the second changes the number next to Matching Rows. Though the amount of time decreases, **Data** spends about 750ms rendering in total. Why does it take so long to render those small changes?

Storing Rendered Content

Recall from Chapter 4 that React maintains a virtual DOM, which it computes when rendering components.

In this case, React re-renders all 20,000 rows of data in the virtual DOM with every change. The commit to the *real* DOM is fast, because React can tell that it has to update only one small thing. But React does a lot of work computing the virtual DOM.

How can you stop the virtual DOM from re-rendering all the data every time something changes? You can use a memo to save the work.

Edit `components/Data.js` to move the table rows into a memo with **useMemo**:

Listing 25.3 Caching table rows (`Data.js`)

```
import { useState, useEffect, useTransition } from 'react';
import {
  useState, useEffect, useTransition, useMemo,
} from 'react';
import styled from 'styled-components';
...
function Data() {
  ...
  useEffect(() => {
    ...
    startTransition(() => setRenderedData(filteredData));
  }, [sexFilter, minAge, maxAge, sort]);

  const rows = useMemo(() => renderedData.map(
    ({
      id, sex, height, weight, age,
    }) => (
      <tr key={id}>
        <td>{sex}</td>
        <td>{height}</td>
        <td>{weight}</td>
        <td>{age}</td>
      </tr>
    ),
  ), [renderedData]);

  return (
    ...
      <Table style={{ opacity: isPending ? 0.5 : 1 }}>
        ...
        <tbody>
          {renderedData.map(({
            id, sex, height, weight, age,
          }) => (
            <tr key={id}>
              <td>{sex}</td>
              <td>{height}</td>
              <td>{weight}</td>
              <td>{age}</td>
            </tr>
          ))}
          {rows}
        </tbody>
...
```

Now, iterating over all the data takes place inside **useMemo**. React will recompute this only when `renderedData` changes, since it is a dependency of **useMemo**.

In this case, you could have placed **useMemo** inline instead of creating the `rows` variable. But it is often easier and more understandable to put your hooks before the return statement rather than inside the returned JSX.

Play with the filters on the site a bit. They respond faster than before.

To see a new timeline, repeat your steps from before:

- Refresh the page to reset the filters.
- Wait for the table to load.
- In the Profiler tab, click the blue record button.
- On the site, click the radio button to filter the data for female penguins only.
- When the table finishes updating, click the record button again to stop profiling.

Look at the change to the beginning of the timeline (Figure 25.6). (Hover your mouse over the blue bars to see the times.)

Figure 25.6 Timeline with **useMemo**

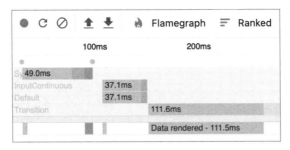

The first few times **Data** renders, it uses the memo, so the first blue bars at the bottom are tiny. And now the total times for Sync (the top bar), InputContinuous, and Default are all much shorter. Although the Transition phase takes about the same amount of time as before, now the other phases are much faster, so the page feels more responsive.

Storing a Rendered Component

Switch to the flamegraph to see what else you might be able to improve.

In the first and second commits, the bottom row shows a yellow component. Hover your mouse over it to find out what it is (Figure 25.7).

Figure 25.7 Flamegraph showing the **Stats** component

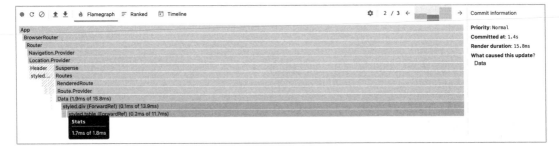

It is the **Stats** component, which renders at the top of the data page. Open components/Stats.js in Visual Studio Code to see what the component does.

This component computes the average age, height, and weight of the penguins in the data set. The data set has 20,000 rows, so this is a fair amount of work.

Recall from Chapter 19 that a functional React component always re-renders when its parent re-renders. Currently, none of the results are cached, so the component recomputes the average for every render.

On a fast computer, this takes only a couple of milliseconds. But this is long enough that when a filter updates, the Profiler flags it in yellow as a slow part of the render. On a phone or slower computer, it could take much longer.

There are several ways to fix this. You can call **useMemo** on the averages to cache them. Though the component will still re-render, the cached values will speed it up. You can also use **useEffect** or **useState** to store the values. Or, working with your project's back-end team, you could have the server precompute the averages, so the client never has to do it.

Another option is to cache the entire component with **memo**. This will make the component behave like a class-based React component, re-rendering only if props, state, or context changes.

Since nothing about this component will change (unless the data were to change), the last option is the best one. Add a **memo** to components/Stats.js:

Listing 25.4 Caching the **Stats** component (Stats.js)

```
import PropTypes from 'prop-types';
import { memo } from 'react';
import StyledH3 from '../styles/StyledH3';

function Stats({ data, setExactAge }) {
  ...
Stats.propTypes = {
  ...
};

const StatsMemo = memo(Stats);

export default Stats;
export default StatsMemo;
```

Repeat the experiment from above to get a new flamegraph so you can see whether **Stats** still re-renders: Refresh the page and wait for the data to load. Then start profiling, filter the data to show only female penguins, and stop profiling once the table finishes updating (Figure 25.8).

Figure 25.8 The **Stats** component still re-renders

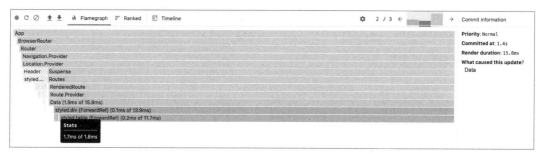

The flamegraph looks the same; **Stats** still re-renders. Why?

Recall that **memo** re-renders if context, props, or state changes. Though **Stats** does not use context or state, you can see in Data.js that it does have props:

```
return (
  <DataDiv>
    <Stats data={DataFile} setExactAge={setExactAge} />
    ...
```

Two props are passed in: data and setExactAge.

The value for data is DataFile, which is a static import of penguin data. Therefore, this value cannot change.

Now look at setExactAge. Its value is the **setExactAge** function, which is defined earlier in the file, and its contents do not change. However, because the function is created within the **Data** component, it is re-created each time **Data** renders.

This changes the identity of the function. React compares props by identity, so it thinks the function has changed each time its identity changes.

As you have seen before, the **useCallback** hook memoizes a function so that it is not re-created and its identity does not change. Memoize **setExactAge** with **useCallback**:

Listing 25.5 Memoizing **setExactAge** (Data.js)

```
import {
  useState, useEffect, useTransition, useMemo,
  useState, useEffect, useTransition, useMemo, useCallback,
} from 'react';
...
function Data() {
  ...
  const [isPending, startTransition] = useTransition();
  const updateSex = (e) => setSexFilter(e.target.value);
  const setExactAge = (age) => {
  const setExactAge = useCallback((age) => {
    setMinAge(age);
    setMaxAge(age);
  }
  }, []);

  useEffect(() => {
...
```

Recall that React guarantees the setter functions that **useState** returns will always have the same identities, so you do not need to include them as dependencies.

Repeat your profiling experiment once again to get a new flamegraph. The **Stats** component no longer renders (Figure 25.9).

Figure 25.9 The **Stats** component does not render

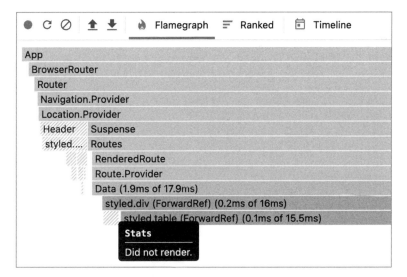

Because of other processes on your computer and because you have taken only one sample for each state, it is possible that **Data** might now show a longer rendering time than it did previously. That is OK. The important part is that **Stats** no longer re-renders unnecessarily.

Conclusion

Take a few minutes to play with the filters. Notice how much more responsive they are.

You might be wondering whether a better solution for the Penguin Data page would have been to implement pagination in the data table so that only 50 rows would render at a time. The answer is yes – in this case, pagination would make the commit phase much faster, and you might not even need to use **startTransition**.

But in some cases, rendering 20,000 rows or 20,000 data points on a graph is necessary. This is where **startTransition** comes in handy. It is also useful for more computationally heavy rendering, such as highlighting all instances of a word or computing values for a complex graph.

For a production app, it would be ideal to run these tests on multiple devices, such as a slower computer and a smartphone, and to take the average of multiple samples.

In this section, you learned about analyzing and optimizing the amount of data your React application needs, which is especially important for clients loading your app over slower connections. You learned about a new hook, **useTransition**, which you can use to set a lower priority for certain updates, and you used **useMemo** and **memo** to fix an especially slow component. You also used **useCallback** again to preserve the identity of a function.

Gold Challenge: Caching the Filtered Data

Users of the Penguin Data page are sorting data much more often than they are filtering it. Split the current **useEffect** hook into two effects. The first effect should handle data filtering, and the second effect should handle data sorting.

Your goal is to lessen the performance impact for users sorting the data by separating the sorting logic from the filtering logic.

Note: This is a hard one. If you are having trouble, chat with us on the forums.

26
Afterword

Congratulations! You are at the end of this book. Not everyone has the discipline to do what you have done and learn what you have learned. Take a quick moment to give yourself a pat on the back.

Your hard work has paid off: You are now a React developer.

The Final Challenge

We have one last challenge for you: Become a *good* React developer. Good developers are good in their own ways, so you must find your own path from here on out.

Where might you start? Here are some ideas:

Write code.

Right away. You will quickly forget what you have learned here if you do not apply your knowledge. Contribute to a project or write a simple application of your own. Whatever you do, waste no time: Write code.

Learn.

You have learned a little bit about a lot of things in this book. Did any of them spark your imagination? Write some code to play around with your favorite thing. Find and read more documentation about it – or an entire book, if there is one. If you need suggestions, check out the React Community Resource list at reactjs.org/community/support.html.

Meet people.

Local meetups are good places to meet like-minded developers. Lots of top-notch React developers are active on Twitter, such as Sophie Alpert (@sophiebits) and Dan Abramov (@dan_abramov). And you can attend conferences to meet other developers. (Maybe even us!)

Explore the open-source community.

Explore public repositories on www.github.com. When you find a cool library, check out other projects from its contributors. Share your own code too – you never know who will find it useful or interesting. The React newsletter can also clue you in to some cool things. Check it out at reactjsnewsletter.com.

Shameless Plugs

You can find us on Twitter: @bignerdranch.

If you enjoyed this book, check out the other Big Nerd Ranch Guides at www.bignerdranch.com/ books. We also have a broad selection of weeklong courses for developers where we make it easy to learn a book's worth of stuff in only a week. And of course, if you just need someone to write great code, we do contract programming too. For more info, go to www.bignerdranch.com.

Thank You

Without readers like you, our work would not exist. Thank you for reading our book!

Index

Symbols

!! (double NOT) operator (JavaScript), 166, 170
&& (logical AND) operator (JavaScript), 165
... (spread) syntax (JavaScript), 175
: (in JavaScript ternaries), 160
<> ... </> (fragment) syntax, 163
? (in JavaScript ternaries), 160
?? (nullish coalescing) operator (JavaScript), 169
` ... ` (template literal) syntax, 152
{/* */} (comment) syntax, 143
|| (logical OR) operator (JavaScript), 167

A

accessibility
    about, 240
    aria-label, 240
    component roles and, 256
    form input focus and, 240
    form input labels and, 205
action creators, 181
afterAll blocks (Jest testing library), 342
afterEach blocks (Jest testing library), 342
App.js file
    about, 11
    responsibilities, 107
application state (see state)
applications
    (see also React applications)
    building, 382
    deploying, 383
    favicons, 13
    performance (see performance)
    security, 299
    testing (see testing)
    titles, 13
Array.filter (JavaScript), 196
Array.find (JavaScript), 66, 157
Array.map (JavaScript), 48
Array.reduce (JavaScript), 178
as keyword, 138
async construct (JavaScript)
    about, 246
    async/await vs then/catch, 248
asynchronous events, 132, 246

await (React Testing Library), 343
await construct (JavaScript)
    about, 246
    async/await vs then/catch, 248
Axios library
    DELETE requests, 134
    GET requests, 128, 134
    installing, 127
    POST requests, 134, 244, 281
    promises, 132-133, 246-249
    PUT requests, 134

B

beforeAll blocks (Jest testing library), 342
beforeEach blocks (Jest testing library), 353
BrowserRouter component (React Router library), 138, 141
buttons, 16, 57, 208

C

catch construct (JavaScript)
    about, 132
    then/catch vs async/await, 248
children prop
    about, 254
    passing child elements inline vs, 258
Chrome Developer Tools
    Application tab, 228, 283
    Components tab (React Developer Tools), 40
    Console tab, 48
    device toolbar, 119
    Elements tab, 22
    HTTP requests and, 129
    inspecting website elements, 388
    modeling network conditions, 249
    Network tab, 129
    opening, 21
    Profiler tab (React Developer Tools), 306
        (see also React Profiler)
    React Developer Tools, 39
    viewing server responses, 131
chunks, webpack, 393
clearTimeout (JavaScript), 237
code splitting, 391
command line, xviii-xxiv
commits, React render cycle, 397
components

411